THE POLITICS OF HISPANIC EDUCATION

SUNY Series, United States Hispanic Studies

Gary D. Keller, Editor

THE POLITICS OF HISPANIC EDUCATION

UN PASO PA'LANTE Y DOS PA'TRAS

Kenneth J. Meier
Joseph Stewart, Jr.

State University of New York Press

Production by Dana Foote
Marketing by Theresa A. Swierzowski

Published by
State University of New York Press, Albany

For information, address State University of New York
Press, State University Plaza, Albany, N.Y., 12246

Library of Congress Cataloging-in-Publication Data

Meier, Kenneth J., 1950-
    The Politics of Hispanic education: un paso pa' lante y dos
pa'tras/Kenneth J. Meier and Joseph Stewart, Jr.
        p. cm.—(SUNY Series, United States Hispanic Studies)
    Includes bibliographical references.
    ISBN 0–7914–0507–9 (alk. paper).—ISBN 0–7914–0508–7 (pbk.:
alk. paper)
    1. Hispanic Americans—Education. 2. Discrimination in education-
-United States. 3. Educational equalization—United States.
    4. Education and state—United States. I. Stewart, Joseph, 1951-
. II. Title.
LC2670.M45 1991
370'.8968073—dc20   90-33101
                                                                         CIP

    10 9 8 7 6 5 4 3 2

To Felix Tijerina and José Angel Gutiérrez,
two men who understand the politics of education.

Contents

Tables and Figures

Acknowledgments

This book is the culmination of several years work on the topic of educational discrimination. Much of our research examined second-generation discrimination against black students. Our recent book *Race, Class and Education: The Politics of Second Generation Discrimination* (Madison, WI: University of Wisconsin Press, 1989) summarizes that research.

Our intellectual debts to our colleagues are many. Rodney Hero, Genie Stowers, Franklin Gilliam, Jerry Polinard, and Bob Wrinkle shared preliminary research with us on questions that were crucial to our own work. We received helpful comments and suggestions at various stages of our work from Charles S. Bullock, III, Genie Stowers, Karl Taeuber, Theodore P. Robinson, Susan Welch, James F. Sheffield, Lee Sigelman, Peter Eisinger, Gary Copeland, Grace Hall Saltzstein, Michael Goldstein, Michael Preston, Frank J. Thompson, F. Chris Garcia, Michael Olivas, Cynthia Brown, and Chandler Davidson. Robert E. England, our sometime coauthor, gave us a great deal of advice and performed some bibliographic work for us. The College of Arts and Sciences at West Virginia University provided summer support for Joe Stewart and also provided Ken Meier with the designation "Visiting Scholar" during his time there. David Hedge, the acting chair, provided all the amenities that he could within the limits of his authority. The West Virginia legislature deserves our thanks for providing us with the following disclaimer: "Notwithstanding any language formerly inadvertently remaining undeleted in this [manuscript] contrary to [authors'] intent and which language and date is hereby retroactively expunged to the time of its unintended inclusions as a technical correction without intervening effect." Were it not for this disclaimer we would have to blame Paul Sabatier for any remaining errors.

—Milwaukee, Wisconsin and Dallas, Texas
April 1990

Preface

The dramatic struggle of black Americans to achieve equal access to education is well known. The corresponding struggle of Hispanic Americans has been relegated to a sidebar or ignored completely. Hispanics, the second-largest and fastest-growing minority in the United States, have been and continue to be denied access to Anglo institutions of education. They have higher dropout rates, lower levels of educational attainment, and receive education of distinctly inferior quality. This book is an in-depth examination of 142 United States school districts with at least 5,000 students and 5 percent Hispanic enrollment. It uses quantitative, historical, and legal analysis to understand Hispanic inequities in education and what can be done about them.

Four major arguments are presented. First, segregation is not necessary to deny Hispanic students access to equal educational opportunities. While Hispanic students are more segregated than black students, other more subtle methods are equally effective in denying access to education. Academic grouping including special education, ability grouping, curriculum tracking, and segregated bilingual education can be used to separate Hispanic students from their Anglo schoolmates and to limit Hispanic educational opportunities. Similarly, ethnic disparities in discipline can be used to discourage Hispanic students from remaining in school. Discriminatory use of academic grouping and discipline has been termed "second-generation educational discrimination." Through the use of such techniques, Hispanic students can be induced to drop out of school, resulting in lower levels of educational attainment. Those Hispanics who remain in school receive a lower quality education.

Second, education is a political process. Second-generation discrimination exists because Hispanics lack the political power to prevent such actions. School districts with greater Hispanic representation on the school board and among teaching faculty experience significantly less second-generation discrimination against

Hispanic students. Representation on the school board results from mobilized Hispanic political resources and a favorable school district political structure (ward rather than at-large elections). Greater school board representation, in turn, leads to greater Hispanic representation in administrative positions, which leads to more Hispanic teachers. Increases in Hispanic representation, then, produce educational policies that benefit Hispanic students.

Third, discrimination against Hispanic students results from both race and social class. Using the power thesis of intergroup relations, this analysis argues that intergroup differences generate intergroup hostility. Discrimination against Hispanic students is a function of both their ethnicity and their lower social class background. As Hispanics become more middle-class, the level of discrimination decreases. Similarly when blacks attend the school system in large numbers, the prime focus of discrimination is against blacks; and Hispanic students are subject to less discrimination. The racial and class patterns in the school system simply mirror those in the political process. Hispanics achieve their greatest political successes in districts with larger proportions of lower-class Anglos and larger proportions of blacks.

Fourth, politics and the policy process differ greatly among the various subgroups of Hispanics. By examining Mexican-American, Cuban-American, and Puerto Rican school districts, generalizations are made about each. Cuban Americans have the economic and political resources to avoid most negative aspects of second generation discrimination; as a result, they do well in the educational system. Mexican Americans' educational experiences are a function of their political resources. Where they have extensive political representation, they have been able to reduce the level of discrimination. Where they do not, they are a subordinate racial minority. Puerto Ricans fare the worst; their educational experiences resemble those of black Americans, but they do not have the compensating political resources that blacks possess. The situation of Puerto Ricans is especially grim for lower-class Puerto Ricans.

Chapter Outline

Chapter 1 presents our political theory of educational policy. Representation in policy-making position is viewed as a function of political resources (numbers and education), social class, race, and district political structure. The theory links representation in policy-making positions to differences in public policy, with policy a function of representation, political resources, race, social class, and school district size. Chapter 2 presents an overview of the politics in different Hispanic communities. The unique patterns of immigration, incorporation, and politics for Mexican Americans, Cuban Americans, and Puerto Ricans are discussed.

Chapter 3 is an historical overview of Hispanic efforts to gain access to equal educational opportunities. Educational policies have evolved from exclusion to segregation to the current use of second-generation educational discrimination. Chapter 4 examines the political representation of Hispanics on school boards, in administrative positions, and in teaching positions. The empirical analysis also assesses the prospects for black/brown coalitions in educational politics.

Chapter 5 documents the inequities in access to education. It argues that these patterns are consistent with the notion of discrimination and shows that political action can counter discrimination. Chapter 6 looks at the linkages among various aspects of second-generation discrimination. In addition, the relationships between second-generation discrimination and segregation and between second-generation discrimination and white flight from school systems are investigated. Chapter 7 provides a summary of the book's findings and a series of policy recommendations.

Chapter 1

Hispanic Representation and Equal Education

The Hispanic[1] quest for equal educational opportunities has paralleled that of black Americans, but the Hispanic movement was and remains clearly separate from the black movement. Hispanics were not part of the classic *Brown v. Board of Education* (1954) case that struck down the doctrine of separate but equal. The absence of Hispanics from this case should not be taken to imply that Hispanics were not segregated; separate Mexican schools were maintained by both Texas and California (Fernández and Guskin 1981, 112; San Miguel 1987; Cooke 1971). To gain access to local public schools, Hispanics fought a series of political and legal battles (see chapter 3). In states that maintained de jure segregated school systems, Hispanics filed suits to be declared "white" so that they could attend white schools (see San Miguel 1987). After desegregation became a reality, Hispanics sought the legal designation "minority" to avail themselves of remedies under the federal Civil Rights Acts. Not until 1975 did the U.S. Supreme Court recognize that educational discrimination against Hispanics must be considered in suits to desegregate public education (*Keyes v. Denver*).

The emphasis on desegregation and a more recent concern with bilingual education has shifted the focus somewhat from the original goal of obtaining equal access to educational opportunities. This study examines a series of actions that school districts can take to limit minority student access to education; these actions have been labeled "second-generation educational discrimination." Second-generation discrimination is the use of academic grouping and discipline in a discriminatory manner so that Hispanic students are separated from Anglos.[2] With this separation, Hispanic students are denied educational opportunities that are offered to Anglo students.

This chapter presents our theory of educational policy-making that we use to examine school district policies of academic grouping, discipline, and access to equal educational opportunity. After briefly stressing the fundamental importance of education as a method of combating discrimination, education is presented as a distinctly political process. By using a political focus for educational policy, we imply that Hispanics must gain access to political and administrative policy-making positions to affect educational policies directed at Hispanic students. A theory of minority representation that has been used to account for black representation on school boards, in administrative positions, and on faculties (see Meier, Stewart, and England 1989) is adapted to Hispanics. Finally, Hispanic representation is integrated into a theory of public policy-making that includes Hispanic political resources, social class pressures, racial competition, and school district size.

The Crucial Nature of Education

Discrimination on the basis of race or ethnicity can affect an individual's employment, level of income, quality of housing, access to health care, etc. Of all the forums for discrimination, discrimination in education is the most invidious. In a nation that prides itself on the ideal of upward social mobility, the ability to rise above one's social origins is heavily dependent on attaining a quality education. If Hispanics are denied equal access to education and, as a result, receive less formal education or receive education of inferior quality, then discrimination in other areas is much easier. Without education, a person may not be hired because he or she is not qualified. Without a job, inadequacies in income, housing, health care, and countless other amenities of life are exacerbated.

The linkage between education and income is not new; it forms the backbone of the human capital approach to economics. Human capital proponents argue that the primary determinant of a person's income is that person's investment in education, either in formal education or on-the-job training (Schultz 1961; Becker 1975). In the University of Michigan's longitudinal study of poverty, Greg Duncan reports that "differences in the level of education can account for a substantial share of the long-run earnings differences between individuals" (1984, p. 109). Although Duncan can explain only 15 percent of the variation in earnings with education, this is five times the variation that can be explained by other factors such as work experience, test scores, achievement motivation, father's education, and personal efficacy.

Human capital studies often produce what is called a rate of return on education: the percentage gain in income that results from an additional year of education. Cotton found that the rate of return on education for Mexican Americans in 1980 was 6.25 percent (1985, p. 875). This figure is significantly above his estimate of the rate of return for blacks (3.89 percent) and approximately equal to the rate of return for Anglos (6.72 percent). Using a different methodology, Bean and Tienda estimate that the returns on investment in education are 4.5 percent for Mexican Americans, 5.6 percent for Puerto Ricans, and 4.3 percent for Cuban Americans (1987, p. 380). Unfortunately, Bean and Tienda do not provide a return on investment estimate for Anglos.

Although other studies of Mexican American workers do not indicate that they receive the same returns on education as Anglos (e.g., Verdugo and Verdugo 1983, 421), many of these studies are limited because they do not distinguish the quality of education that individuals receive (see Penley, Gould, and de la Vina 1983, 445). As we argue in this research, the quality of education received by Hispanics in the United States is not equal to that received by Anglos (see chapter 5). Penley, Gould, and de la Vina (1983, p. 449) circumvented this problem by studying only graduates of accredited business schools; they found no difference in the earnings of Mexican Americans and Anglos when one controlled for sex, age, experience, college grades, and industry of occupation.

An additional way to examine the relationship between education and income for Hispanics is to examine these variables for the school districts in this study. Using the percentage of Hispanics with high school diplomas in 1980 to predict average Hispanic income, Table 1–1 shows a strong positive relationship. Education by itself explains 45 percent of the variation in Hispanic incomes across the school districts.

Table 1–1   The Relationship Between Hispanic Education and Income

Hispanic Median Income = $9,184 + $193.55 x Percent High School Grads
$r^2 = .45$ $F = 110.74$
$N = 137$

Education not only improves a person's ability to earn an income, it also improves access to specific types of jobs. Access to professional jobs—doctors, lawyers, accountants, etc.—is limited to individuals with the requisite education. Education is also important in gaining access to government jobs, particularly those with higher pay and greater responsibility (Meier and Nigro 1976). In this case, Taylor and Shields' (1984, p. 386) study of federal civil service jobs found that education produced a higher return for Mexican Americans than it did for Anglos.[3]

Educational achievement is perceived as the key to upward mobility. Cohen and Tyree credit education as the single most important variable in allowing intergenerational escapes from poverty; they conclude, "Education . . . matters more for the poor" (1986, p. 811). In the educational process, students learn about the social and political institutions that operate in society. Education provides students with the potential tools to influence such institutions and provide a better life for themselves (Sleeter and Grant 1985, 54; Friere 1970; Everhart 1983; Barbagli and Dei 1977).

The Hispanic community clearly recognizes the crucial nature of education. A 1989 survey of Milwaukee area Hispanics ranked educational limitations as the main problem facing their community (Bauer 1989, 4B). In a 1980 survey of Houston, Hispanics ranked public education as the most important problem that they faced (MacManus and Cassel 1988, 209). A study of Hispanic legislators in Texas revealed that these representatives introduced more legislation related to education than for any other policy area (Mindiola and Gutierrez 1988, 352).

Our stress on education should not be interpreted as downplaying discrimination against Hispanics. Even if access to education were equalized in the United States, we would still expect to find some discrimination against Hispanics in employment and other areas. We would expect the disparities between Anglos and Hispanics, however, to be less in such a situation. If educational opportunities are equalized, then discriminatory actions are more difficult to hide since a person discriminating must find reasons other than a lack of education to deny Hispanics jobs or other opportunities. Equalizing educational opportunities, therefore, implies that discrimination must become more overt to be effective. Overt methods of discrimination are more readily noticed and easier to combat.[4]

Education and Politics

The overwhelming bulk of educational literature goes to great lengths to avoid discussing politics. In most cities, formal mechanisms were established to isolate the school system from the influence of partisan politics. As part of the progressive tradition of political reform, school systems were operated by independent school districts (Tyack 1974; Davidson and Korbel 1981).[5] Independent school districts were given budget autonomy and taxing authority separate from that of other local governments. To further isolate the school district from politics, a multimember, nonpartisan school board was created to govern the system. Since board members were normally part-time, public-oriented citizens, day-to-day authority was delegated to a professional administrator who was responsible for the school district's actual operation.

The structural separation of school districts from local politics succeeded in isolating schools from the impact of local *partisan* politics, but it clearly did not eliminate politics from the school system. Politics, according to Harold Lasswell (1936), is the determination of "who gets what?" A school system separated from the pressures of local partisan politics still must make the same decisions that a system not so separated would make. Taxes must be raised, school buildings must be built, teachers must be hired, and curricula must be designed. The determination of who benefits from education policies is an exercise in politics, whether the decision is made by a politically motivated mayor or by an independent school board and a professional administrator. Contending that the public education system is above politics at the same time it consumes $185 billion a year in tax dollars (1988) is a fiction that simply cannot be maintained (Tucker and Zeigler 1980).

The view of nonpolitical education contrasts dramatically with the perceptions of Michael Olivas. Olivas argues that the educational disadvantages of Hispanics are so intertwined with their political powerlessness that "it may be impossible to disentangle the educational problems stemming from Hispanic political disenfranchisement, inasmuch as educational policy is political both at local and higher levels" (1983, p. 112). To Olivas, the lack of political power and unequal access to education are the same problem.

To influence educational policy decisions affecting equal access to education, Hispanics must be able to influence three key decisions—the determination of overall school district policy, the translation of overall policy into administrative rules and procedures, and the application of rules and procedures to individual students. Each of these decisions is dominated by a separate group of decision-makers. Overall school district policy, including policies on equal education, are set in theory by the school board.

While school administrators, especially the superintendent, play a role in forming overall policies, they dominate the translation of these policies into specific administrative rules and procedures. Teachers then take the administrative rules and procedures and apply them to individual students.

At each stage of the process, decision-makers exercise discretion. Although a school board faces numerous constraints on its actions, such as the district's tax base, federal laws, state regulations, etc., it still has substantial discretion to affect district policies. State and local laws may limit the type of school buildings the board can build, for example, but the exact placement of the buildings and how the building is structured is up to the board. School board members, in our view, are autonomous decision-makers who are somewhat but not totally constrained by economic, political, and social forces (Nordlinger 1981). We assume that school board members, when exercising discretion, will act just like other decision-makers, that they will attempt to maximize their own policy preferences.

School boards, as legislative units, cannot make policies so specific that no discretion is left to administrators. The policy implementation literature illustrates countless situations where legislative policies were altered by the bureaucracy that implemented them (Pressman and Wildavsky 1973; Bullock and Lamb 1984; Mazmanian and Sabatier 1983). The school superintendent and school administrators also have policy preferences; and when possible, they will exercise discretion so that policies will reflect those preferences.

Finally, most policies as they descend the administrative hierarchy are changed and adapted to individual situations (Downs 1967). Teachers are akin to what Lipsky (1980) calls street-level bureaucrats.[6] They exercise discretion in using discipline, encouraging or discouraging students, recommending placement in various academic groups, and countless other ways. Although "objective" rules have been established for many of these actions, the teacher still retains discretion. Most situations calling for action can be interpreted differently or even ignored. By exercising discretion in this way, the teacher can alter the policies established by school administrators.

All three decision-makers, we argue, exercise discretion and use that discretion to influence policies to be consistent with their own policy preferences. This book does not directly measure policy preferences, but rather it uses ethnicity as a surrogate measure of policy preferences. We assume that Hispanic school board members, administrators, and teachers favor polices that provide greater educational equity for Hispanic students and oppose polices that reduce access to quality education for these students. Our concern is whether or not Hispanic access to positions of decision-making authority results in educational policies that benefit Hispanic students (see Lineberry 1978, 175).

The Politics of Representation

A political theory of representation is used to explain Hispanic access to school board seats, administrative positions, and teaching positions. The selection method varies for each group; most school boards are elected (those for dependent school districts are appointed); administrators are hired by the school board or by other administrators; and teachers are hired by administrators using merit criteria. Despite differences in selection, the same political theory of representation can be used with some modifications to explain Hispanic access to these positions. The theory contains four political forces—Hispanic political resources, district political structure, social class, and Hispanic access to other decision-making positions. Since our representation measures change somewhat for each set of decision-makers, three variations of the model will be discussed.

Access to School Board Seats

1. Hispanic Political Resources. To win school board elections, Hispanics must have political resources that can be converted into electoral victories. In a democracy, the most obvious political resource is Hispanic votes measured as the percentage of Hispanic residents in the school districts.[7] Hispanics have seen many of the same efforts to prevent them from voting as blacks have. English literacy tests were used in most southwestern states, white primaries often excluded Hispanics, poll taxes disenfranchised poor Hispanics, and intimidation and violence to discourage voting were common (Crow 1971; Shockley 1974; de la Garza 1979). Votes, in fact, are probably the most important political resource the Hispanic community has.

Although registered voters are a necessary condition for electing Hispanic representatives, they are not a sufficient condition. Election victories require credible Hispanic candidates. Studies of

urban politics generally suggest that ethnic groups, including Hispanics, produce viable candidates for political office once the ethnic group contains members who are middle-class (Garcia and
Arce 1988, 127; Wolfinger 1965; Banfield and Wilson 1963). Middle-class status for Hispanics could be operationalized by income,
occupation, education, or business ownership. We use the percentage of Hispanics with high school diplomas as the measure of
middle-class status.[8]

   2. Electoral Structure. Translating Hispanic resources into
Hispanic membership on the school board has been hampered by
electoral structures that grew out of the urban reform movement.
Education systems, if anything, were more affected by the reform
movement than were city governments. Education was viewed as
a technical process that should be left to experts to determine the
best way to educate children (Tyack 1974). Control of policy by
experts meant that political influences had to be minimized. The
result was a school system run by a professional administrator
with public input restricted to a school board of civic-minded people. To make sure only citizens with the right views served on the
school board, elections were usually nonpartisan, held in the
springtime when no other elections were contested; individuals
were elected at-large for staggered terms. All these reforms were
designed to isolate school boards from the wrong type of partisan
activity (Wakefield 1971; Cistone 1975).[9]

   Of the political reforms, the most detrimental to minorities,
including Hispanics, is at-large elections (Davidson and Korbel
1981; Fraga, Meier, and England 1986; Mindiola and Gutierrez
1988, 350). At-large elections allow all voters in a school district
to vote for all candidates for the school board; ward elections, on
the other hand, divide the school district into smaller election
wards and elect individual board members from each ward with
voting restricted to ward residents. At-large elections require
greater political resources to win than ward elections because
candidates must run school district-wide rather than in a smaller
ward (Heilig and Mundt 1984). At-large elections are particularly
harmful to minority candidates when voting is polarized by ethnicity (a frequent condition: see Stowers 1987a; de la Garza 1974;
Garcia 1979, 174).

   Three types of general selection plans are used to fill school
board seats. In addition to at-large and ward elections,[10] dependent school district board members are appointed by other elect-

ed officials (the mayor, the county commission, etc.). The politics of an appointed board differs greatly from the politics of elected boards (Robinson, England, and Meier 1985, 981). Representation on an appointed board depends on participation in the winning electoral coalition of the individual(s) who appoint the board members. Usually minorities are given a "fair share" of the school board seats allocated to supporters of the winning candidates. Our measure of district structure, therefore, includes a measure that distinguishes between ward, at-large, and appointed school districts.

3. Social Class and Social Status. The group competition or power thesis view of groups in society is that groups compete with each other for tangible benefits, including those in the political process (Coser 1956; Schermerhorn 1956; Wilson 1973). The potential for conflict or cooperation between groups is a function of the differences and similarities between the groups (Giles and Evans 1985, 1986; Feagin 1981). If a minority group is similar to the majority group, the majority group will feel less threatened by minority demands and will be less likely to oppose minority access to governing institutions. Giles and Evans (1986) use the power thesis to argue that discrimination is less likely against middle-class blacks than against lower-class blacks because middle-class blacks share many of the values of middle-class whites. They imply that discrimination has as much to do with social class as with race.

The power thesis is directly applicable to Hispanic efforts to achieve political representation. In 1985 the Hispanic median family income was only 70 percent of the Anglo median family income; Hispanic high school graduation rates were only 63 percent of Anglo rates. If social class differences are a reason why Anglos might react negatively to Hispanics, then Hispanics who have made it in Anglo society would be perceived as less of a threat.[11] By analogy, middle-class Anglos would prefer to be represented by middle-class Anglos rather than by lower-class Anglos. If social class differences are the prime concern, then, Anglos might prefer representation by middle-class Hispanics who share their political views to representation by lower-class Anglos who do not.

The Giles/Evans power thesis receives some support from events in Crystal City, Texas. Crystal City was the site of working-class Mexican-American electoral victories in 1963 and again in

1970. Mexican Americans were able to elect all members of the city council, and eventually members of the school board (Shockley 1974). The tactics of the Anglo population, when confronted with a working-class Mexican-American political revolt, are revealing. Rather than continue to run Anglo candidates, they ran Mexican-American candidates with business ties and higher levels of education. Anglo support went overwhelmingly for middle-class Hispanic candidates rather than those perceived as lower-class.

Stowers' (1987a) analysis of Miami also reveals the class nature of urban politics in regard to minorities. She found that voting for Hispanic candidates was inversely related to socioeconomic status in Hispanic precincts. The class nature of politics changed, however, as the community's class composition changed. Middle-class Cubans were more likely to vote for candidates who did not make direct ethnic appeals (see also Garcia 1979, 176). The ability of moderate Mexican-American candidates, such as Federico Peña in Denver (Hero 1987) and Henry Cisneros in San Antonio, to attract Anglo votes is also consistent with the power thesis.

By using the class-based power thesis, we are arguing that middle-class Anglos are concerned more about lower-class candidates than they are about middle-class Hispanic candidates. As a result, in a school district with a large lower-class Anglo population, middle-class Anglos will be more supportive of Hispanic candidates (particularly those who make middle-class appeals). To tap this social class dimension of politics, we will use the percentage of the Anglo population who resides in poverty; this measure should be positively related to Hispanic school board representation.

If school board politics were only a contest between Hispanics and Anglos, the above presentation of the power thesis would be adequate. In many urban school districts, however, this is not the case. The school districts in this study have an average of 10 percent black population. Applying the power thesis to three groups is revealing. From the perspectives of the dominant Anglo coalition, Hispanics are more similar to Anglos than are blacks. Middle-class Hispanics, because they can "pass" as Anglo, are less likely to be perceived as a threat than blacks, regardless of the social class of blacks. This logic suggests that the Anglo community is likely to prefer Hispanic candidates to black candidates if given the choice. We hypothesize, therefore, that as the percentage of black population increases (a black resource that influences their ability to elect black candidates), Hispanic representation will increase as Anglos vote for Hispanic candidates.

Our hypothesis of Anglo support for Hispanic candidates in preference to black candidates directly challenges the Browning, Marshall, and Tabb (1984) incorporation thesis. Using ten northern California cities, they argue that Hispanics need to form coalitions with blacks and liberal whites to gain political representation (the equivalent of a rainbow coalition). The Browning, Marshall, and Tabb view stresses the cooperation of minority groups rather than competition. In chapter 4, we will present a critical test between the power thesis and the Browning, Marshall, and Tabb incorporation thesis.

In sum, Hispanic political representation of school boards should be affected by Hispanic political resources, district structure, and social class. In terms of specific indicators, we would expect that the level of Hispanic representation would be positively correlated with Hispanic population, Hispanic high school education, ward rather than at-large elections, the proportion of Anglos living in poverty, and the percentage of black population.

Access to Administrative Positions

The crucial role of minority administrators in the educational system has been demonstrated for blacks (Meier, Stewart, and England 1989). In contrast, the role of Hispanic school administrators has not been assessed. Most studies of Hispanic representation in administrative positions stress either a patronage argument or a representative bureaucracy argument. The patronage argument is simple: Hispanics should have the same share of positions that they have of the population. Such a distribution would be consistent with notions of fairness and equity (e.g., Dye and Renick 1981; Mladenka 1989a). A representative bureaucracy view of equity stresses the discretion of administrative officials. An Hispanic administrator is assumed to be more likely to make decisions that benefit other Hispanics (see chapter 4 for a more elaborate discussion of representative bureaucracy). Hispanic administrators should be more sensitive to the cultural norms and mores in the Hispanic community. In addition, an Hispanic school administrator is likely to become a leader in the Hispanic community (for an illustration see Shockley 1974).

Hispanic access to school administrative positions uses the same model of political representation as the school board seats model with a few modifications. Because our concern is with administrators rather than elected officials, the various forces represented by the indicators might change. The direction of impact, however, remains the same.

1. School Board Members. The one variable that must be added to the political model of representation when applied to Hispanic administrators is school board members. Districts with a higher percentage of black school board members employ a larger percentage of black school administrators (Meier, Stewart, and England 1989, 73). A similar relationship should hold for Hispanics for two reasons. First, the school board hires the superintendent. The school board could either hire a Hispanic superintendent or an Anglo superintendent who strongly supports minority hiring (see Thompson 1978 on the importance of personnel hiring values). Second, the school board could enact affirmative action policies for lower-level administrative positions or could put informal pressure on higher-level administrators to hire more Hispanics at lower levels.

2. Hispanic Resources. Hispanic resources were measured as the Hispanic population percentage and the proportion of Hispanics with high school diplomas. These resources could affect school administrative hiring in two ways. First, they could operate as political resources; as surrogates for the Hispanic community's political clout, they measure the ability of Hispanics to pressure the school district for favorable policies. Second, they also represent favorable labor-pool characteristics. School districts where the Hispanic population is numerous and well educated should have more Hispanic individuals who are qualified to be teachers (Sigelman and Karnig 1977, 1976, make a similar argument for public-sector employment in general).[12]

3. District Structure. The selection structure for the school district will not be used in the administrators' model. While district structure is directly related to school board access, it should not affect the ability to attract Hispanic school administrators. Any impact of district structure on the level of Hispanic administrators should operate indirectly through Hispanic school board members.

4. Social Class. The group competition view of racial groups again predicts that the Anglo community would prefer Hispanic administrators from middle-class backgrounds to Anglo administrators from lower-class backgrounds. The percentage of Anglos living in poverty also represents a labor-pool constraint; districts with more Anglo poverty will have fewer qualified Anglos for administrative positions, thus generating more opportunities for Hispanics.

Access to Teaching Positions

1. Hispanic Administrators. By modifying the Hispanic administrators' model slightly, it can be used for Hispanic teachers also. Teachers are normally hired by administrators. Because the literature shows that public managers frequently hire individuals with characteristics similar to their own (Saltzstein 1983; Thompson 1978; Dye and Renick 1981), we hypothesize that school districts with a large percentage of Hispanic administrators also will hire a large percentage of Hispanic teachers. Since the school districts under consideration are large, school board members should play only an indirect role in hiring teachers. Accordingly, the proportion of Hispanic school board members is deleted from the model.[13]

2. Hispanic Resources. A large Hispanic population and an educated Hispanic population can have two separate impacts on the percentage of Hispanic teachers. They can operate as political resources that allow the Hispanic community to place pressure on the school district to hire more Hispanic teachers. They can also represent favorable labor-pool characteristics that increase the pool of Hispanic teaching candidates.

3. Social Class. Anglo poverty also can perform two functions in the attraction of Hispanic teachers. A large lower-class Anglo population is an unfavorable pool for recruiting Anglo teachers. The power thesis also holds that the Anglo community would prefer Hispanic teachers from middle-class backgrounds to Anglo teachers from lower-class backgrounds.

Public Policy Impact

Measuring the impact of minority representation on public policy has been hindered by the lack of good policy measures. Three qualities are necessary for a measure of public policy to be useful in linking minority representation to policy. First, measures must represent policies that policy-makers can influence. Second, the policies must be tied closely to minority interests so that policy-makers can see the benefit of certain policies for their constituents. Third, the policies need to be measured over a wide variety of school districts so that the findings can be generalized.

Much of the work on the impact of minority representation has failed to meet one or more of these criteria. Early studies of black representation focused on the impact of black mayors on public policies of the 1960s and 1970s (e.g., Keech 1968; Campbell and Feagin 1975; Levine 1974; Nelson 1972; Nelson and Meranto 1976; Poinsett 1970; Stone 1971). A similar set of Hispanic case studies does not exist, probably because Hispanics have only recently won mayoral elections and insufficient time has passed to assess their impact (Hero 1987). One excellent case study that does exist is Shockley's examination of Crystal City, Texas. After the election of an Hispanic majority to the city council and the school board, a variety of policies were changed. In the school system, bilingual-bicultural education programs were implemented, and more Hispanic teachers and administrators were hired. At the national level, de la Garza (1984, p. 9) also attributes policy changes to President Carter's appointment of Hispanics to positions in the federal bureaucracy. In contrast, Hero and Beatty's (1989) case study of Mayor Peña's first term and reelection in Denver found that Peña was highly constrained by his need to form a governing coalition; his policies, particularly in economic development, resembled those of his predecessor.

Still, the case study methodology, despite its ability to provide rich detail in a politically informed study, has limitations. The case study method does not permit the use of control variables to ensure that findings are not spurious. Nor are the results of case studies necessarily generalizable to other jurisdictions. Browning, Marshall, and Tabb (1984) attempt to overcome this problem by doing ten case studies of northern California cities. They find that minority representation (both blacks and Hispanics) resulted in the creation of police review boards, appointment of minorities to commissions, and more minority business contracts with government (Browning, Marshall, and Tabb 1984, chapter 4). Despite the convincing nature of their analysis, the narrow base of their sample (northern California) limits generalizations (e.g., see Muñoz and Henry 1986; Travis 1986; Warren, Stack, and Corbett 1986).

A second set of studies examined the expenditures of cities with minority mayors and city council members. Although most of this research was on blacks (see Karnig and Welch 1980 for a review) and the findings have been modest, expenditure measures are not particularly good measures of public policy.[14] Expenditures at the city and school district level are difficult for public officials to affect in the short run. School district budgets are restricted by taxation limits, state funding formulas, federal aid, and other constraints. More important, the linkage between expenditures and minority interests is tenuous at best. Normally scholars assume that minorities favor greater welfare expenditures and less community development expenditures, yet logical arguments could be made for the other linkages.[15] For school districts, the Hispanic community is probably more concerned with the distribution of funds among schools and programs than the total level of spending.

An alternative to expenditure data that has been enthusiastically adopted by some social scientists is employment data (Dye and Renick 1981; Eisinger 1982a, 1982b; Browning, Marshall, and Tabb 1984; Mladenka 1989a, 1989b). Dye and Renick find that "the most important single determinant of Hispanic employment in cities is Hispanic representation on city councils" (1981, p. 483). This relationship is especially important for top-level jobs but not for lower-level jobs. In a similar study, however, Welch, Karnig, and Eribes did not find Hispanic representation to have a positive impact on the level of Hispanic municipal employment (1983, p. 671). Their results challenge Dye and Renick, and they suggest that Dye and Renick's findings were the result of many cities with only a negligible Hispanic population (Welch, Karnig, and Eribes 1983, 661).[16]

Hispanic representation in the bureaucracy, while important, is not the same as Hispanic impact on public policy. Using employment as a surrogate for public policy translates representation into a patronage context where elected officials seek jobs for supporters rather than policy changes. Welch and Hibbing take a step in the right direction; they found that Hispanic members of Congress had more liberal voting patterns than other members of Congress (1984, p. 332). Further progress is needed. This study will not use either expenditure or employment measures as policy measures because better measures of public policy in education are available.

Equal Educational Opportunity

This research addresses local public policies of access to equal educational opportunities for Hispanic students. Our definition of equal educational opportunity is similar to Weinberg's definition of integrated education (1983, p. 172). It is a situation where children are able to interact with each other and learn in a multiracial environment without barriers to academic achievement. It "embodies the concepts of parity and equity along with equal opportunities and access to the legitimate measures for exploiting the resources of a society" (Adair 1984, 2; see also Hughes, Gordon, and Hillman 1980; McConahay 1981).

Equal educational opportunities can be restricted by a variety of actions that segregate or resegregate classrooms. Although most overt methods of segregation such as separate schools, "Mexican rooms," and segregated buses have been eliminated, more subtle institutional methods of segregation are possible. Through the use of academic grouping and discipline, schools can limit interracial contact and deny minority students access to the best education available in a school district (see Rodgers and Bullock 1972; Children's Defense Fund 1974; Yudof 1975; Smith and Dziuban 1977; Ogbu 1978; Arnez 1978; Fernández and Guskin 1981; Hochschild 1984; Meier, Stewart, and England 1989). Practices that limit the integration of schools and deny minority students access to education have been collectively referred to as "second-generation educational discrimination" (Bullock and Stewart 1978, 1979).

Gaining equal access to education is a long-term goal of Hispanics. The G.I. Forum, the League of United Latin American Citizens, and other Hispanic organizations have been active for many years in stressing the need for access to good education (San Miguel 1982; Marquez 1987, 1989). As a result, the policies examined in this study are policies that should be apparent to Hispanic representatives; they are also policies that individual Hispanics can affect; and they are measured for a large number of school districts through out the United States by the Department of Education's Office for Civil Rights. Three types of policies are analyzed—academic grouping, discipline, and educational attainment.

Academic Grouping

Since the development of mass public education in the early twentieth century, schools have sorted students into homogeneous groups for instructional purposes.[17] At the elementary school level, ability grouping is common. Students are sorted by their perceived intellectual ability; ability grouping can take place within a classroom as "Bluebirds," "Robins," and "Magpies" are assigned

to reading, spelling, or math groups (Epstein 1985, 24). Other
schools might sort elementary students into different classrooms
ranked according to academic potential. In theory, each group is
taught similar materials, but the flight of the Bluebirds is faster
and covers more interesting terrain than that of the Magpies.

Curriculum tracking is generally a secondary school phenomenon; it involves assigning students by ability and/or interest
to different sets of classes or "tracks" of study that have different
curricula (e.g., college bound, general business, vocational). Curriculum tracking occurs both at the junior high and senior high
levels. In junior high curriculum tracks are generally based on
academic potential, while in senior high career or vocational aspirations also are considered (Epstein 1985, 23–24).

Students whom the schools cannot sort into various ability
groups or curriculum tracks within the regular academic programs can be classified as "special" or "exceptional" and placed in
special education classes. Special education class are designed for
children who are unable to benefit from the regular academic program (Heller, Holtzman, and Messick 1982, 3; Dunn 1968; Mercer
1973; Hobbs 1975). Special education students are in turn sorted
into classes for the educable mentally retarded (EMR), the trainable mentally retarded (TMR), the seriously emotionally disturbed
(SEMD), and specific learning disabilities (SLD), among others.

Schools also sort students via placements in compensatory
education. Compensatory education programs are designed to
remedy problems that result from economic or cultural depriva-
tion (Flaxman 1976; Ogbu 1978, 81–100). Students in these programs are given some type of additional or different educational
experiences with the goal of eventual return to regular classes.
Compensatory education programs became common as part of
the 1960s War on Poverty and were incorporated into federal
education funding programs.

Finally, schools sort students by their ability to speak English.
Bilingual education programs, as currently constituted, are a form
of compensatory education[18] intended to provide alternative
instruction until non-English-speaking students can join a regular
class and benefit from instruction in English. Although bilingual
education differs from other forms of sorting in its orientation
toward language, it shares the objective of homogeneous grouping
that characterizes other forms of academic grouping.

Academic grouping practices, such as ability grouping, tracking, and special education, gained prominence in the U.S. educa-

tion system when compulsory school attendance laws imposed a heterogeneous student population on the public schools (Tropea 1987a, 32; 1987b).[19] Later in the 1920s, along with advances in the art and science of psychometrics (Morgenstern 1966, 11), the current versions of academic grouping took shape.[20] Bilingual education also predates the current federal law; instruction in languages other than English was common for immigrant groups in several parts of the country. Federal government involvement in bilingual education started with the early Cuban refugee programs.

Academic grouping techniques are prevalent in most U.S. school districts. The National Education Association (1968) estimated that 85 percent of secondary schools make extensive use of curriculum tracking. About one-fourth of elementary schools use ability grouping to separate classes by ability (Rowan and Miracle 1983, 123) while 74 to 84 percent of elementary schools use within-class ability grouping (Austin and Morrison 1963; Wilson and Schmits 1978; Epstein 1985, 26). Virtually all large school districts have special education and compensatory education classes, and all schools with twenty or more language-minority students must provide bilingual education classes. Despite the massive use, academic grouping is controversial.

Although academic grouping techniques are considered useful pedagogical tools for creating homogeneous instructional groups, minority students can be denied equal educational opportunities through the use of academic grouping. Through the arbitrary and capricious selection and subsequent placement of Hispanic children in certain types of classes, Hispanic children can be denied access to quality education (Fernández and Guskin 1981). Special education students often receive an inferior education as the result of "dumbing down" the curriculum (Gartner and Lipsky 1987, 387). Education in lower ability group classes and vocational tracks is similarly less challenging (Oakes 1985). In addition, each of the sorting practices can separate Anglo students from Hispanics, thus segregating the school system (see Eyler, Cook, and Ward 1983; Damico and Sparks 1986). Academic grouping as a result has become highly controversial, with the debate over its utility focused on four issues—testing, separation, racial distributions, and quality of instruction.

1. Biases in Testing. Academic groups are determined through the use of tests, grades, and/or teacher reports. Classification systems have relied heavily on IQ tests to assign student groups. Such classification systems label a disproportionately large number of minority students as intellectually subnormal and a disproportionately small number as gifted (Hobbs 1975, 29). IQ tests in particular institutionalize the culture of Anglos as the single frame of reference for normal (Mercer 1972; Hobbs 1975, 29).

Biased tests are rarely the only method of assigning students to academic groups (Findley and Bryan 1975, 15–18). Teachers, counselors, school psychologists, and administrators make judgments to supplement these "objective" measures (Oakes 1985; Simmons and Brady 1981, 129).[21] If teachers and others hold racial, ethnic, or social class stereotypes, disparities in low-group placements for minorities or lower-socioeconomic children may be even greater than if tests alone were used as the placement criterion (Persell 1977; Metz 1978; Rosenbaum 1976; Lanier and Wittmer 1977).[22]

For Hispanic students with limited English proficiency, another problem occurs. Student placement tests are often given in English, even if the student's primary language is not English (Office of Special Education 1983, 9). As a result, students with limited use of English can be classified as mentally retarded and assigned to special education classes (Rangel and Alcala 1972, 316–32).[23]

Decisions to group children are crucial because academic grouping creates permanent educational routes for children (Oakes 1985, 3). Although 85 percent of students in college prep tracks go on to college, only 15 percent of students in other tracks do so (Jencks et al. 1972). Upward academic mobility from one level group to another, either during the academic year or between years, is rare (Groff 1962; Hawkins 1966; Mackler 1969; Rist 1978). Special education placements are especially permanent because such classes are assumed to be permanent rather than compensatory (Heller, Holtzman, and Messick 1982, 108). An Office of Education study concluded that fewer than 10 percent of children placed in special education classes are ever returned to regular classrooms (Gallagher 1972, 529). The Council of Great City Schools (1986) estimated that 5 percent of its special education students return to regular classes, but Gartner and Lipsky (1987, p. 375) challenged these numbers as inflated. Edgar and Maddox (1984) found 4 percent of special education students returned to regular classes over an eight year period; Walker et al. (1988, p. 397) found 1.4 percent left EMR classes in two years.

Permanent classification creates additional problems. Despite the scientific veneer of testing, students are often misclassified (Ysseldyke et al. 1983; Gartner and Lipsky 1987). In the Washington, D.C., school district, a study of special education students revealed that two-thirds belonged in regular classes (Kirp 1973, 719). In Philadelphia, a study of 378 EMR students determined that 25 percent clearly did not belong in EMR classes and another 43 percent might not belong (Garrison and Hammill 1971, 18; see also Dunn 1968). Shepard contends that 90 percent of the children served by special education are "indistinguishable from other low achievers" (1987, p. 327). Because students grouped in homogeneous units progress at different rates (Franseth 1966, 17), many students will not fit their initial classification after short periods of time.

2. Conflict with Integration. The process of school integration requires that students learn and interact in groups with students from other races and cultures. It requires equal educational opportunities, equal group status, and cross-racial contact (Allport 1954; Adair 1984). Academic grouping practices are in direct conflict with the goals of integration. In some cases the conflicts are obvious; the tradeoff between bilingual education and desegregation has long been noted (Eyler, Cook, and Ward 1983, 138; Cafferty and Rivera-Martínez 1981; Orfield 1978). Ability grouping, curriculum tracking, and special education create similar problems. In each case students are grouped with those who are similar to themselves and separated from those who are different. The groups created have unequal status; the goal of college is considered superior to jobs; honors classes are perceived as better than regular classes; and Bluebirds get more attention than Magpies (Rosenbaum 1976, 6).

3. Links to Discrimination. Related to the conflict between grouping and integration is the linkage of academic grouping to discrimination based on race and social class. Numerous studies have found that poor and minority students are disproportionately assigned to lower level academic groups, be they special education classes, ability groups, or curriculum tracks (Jones 1976; Ogbu 1978; Eyler, Cook, and Ward 1983; Adair 1984; Heller, Holtzman, and Messick 1982; Chinn and Hughes 1987; Meier, Stewart, and England 1989). Special education classes in California schools in 1966 had 27 percent Mexican Americans, even though Mexican Americans made up only 13 percent of the school population (Gre-

bler, Moore, and Guzmán 1970, 158). Although such disproportions have declined and Hispanics are not currently overrepresented in special education on a nationwide basis, they are significantly overrepresented in several states with large Hispanic
populations (Finn 1982, 367). Evidence exists that language difficulties were often used as a reason to assign students to classes
for the mentally retarded (Manuel 1965, 80). The National Center
for Education Statistics (Brown et al. 1980) reports that two of
every five Anglo students are in college prep tracks, while only
one of four Hispanic students are. About 30 percent of Hispanic
high school seniors report they are enrolled in vocational education tracks, compared to 22.5 percent of Anglo seniors (Brown et
al. 1980, 33).[24] Assignment to lower academic groups is associated with other negative effects on school children. It often results in
lowered self-esteem (see Jones and Wilderson 1976; Findley and
Bryan 1975; Metz 1978, chapter 5; Oakes 1985, chapter 7). Others
relate such assignments to increases in misconduct, delinquency,
and dropouts (Children's Defense Fund 1974; Findley and Bryan
1975; Rosenbaum 1976).

Discrimination is also implied by the initial implementation of
many academic grouping programs. Ogbu contends that the use of
IQ testing and academic grouping in some school districts intensi-
fied after the Supreme Court's decision to desegregate schools
(1978, p. 135). Trent (1981), using interviews with officials in
eighteen school districts, found increased use of curriculum tracking and ability grouping after court-ordered desegregation. The
California legislature repealed its law allowing the segregation of
Mexican-American students at approximately the same time it
authorized EMR programs (Mercer and Richardson 1975). In
Texas, those school districts that responded to the state attorney
general's order to desegregate Mexican-American students in
1950 often did so by creating "Mexican rooms" so that Mexican-
American children were taught in separate rooms from Anglo
children (Rangel and Alcala 1972).[25]

4. The Effectiveness of Grouping. The racial biases and associated problems linked to academic grouping mean that grouping
can be justified only if it produces significant positive benefits for
students. With the exception of bilingual education, the evidence
on the impact of academic grouping is clear. Kulik and Kulik
(1982) performed a meta-analysis of fifty-two valid studies of ability grouping, selected from over seven hundred existing studies.

They conclude that ability grouping does not have a positive impact on average and lower ability groups, but it does benefit higher ability groups.[26] Kulik and Kulik's conclusion about higher ability groups, however, is based on limited evidence since only ten of their studies produced significant results and not all of those favored the ability-grouped students. In addition, if higher ability groups benefit, the amount of benefit is small. Kulik and Kulik find that the positive impact is equivalent to improving performance from the 50th percentile to the 54th percentile, an especially modest improvement (1982, p. 421).

Studies of special education have produced similar results. Carlberg and Kavale's meta-analysis of fifty special education studies did not find benefits. They concluded that "special education class placement is an inferior alternative to regular class placement in benefiting children removed from the educational mainstream.... [There is] no justification for placement of low IQ children in special classes" (1980, p. 304). Other studies of EMR classes reach similar conclusions (Corman and Gottlieb 1978; Semmel, Gottlieb, and Robinson 1979; Dunn 1968; Gartner and Lipsky 1987).

For academic grouping, therefore, a consensus has merged. "Ability grouping, as practiced, produces conflicting evidence of usefulness in promoting improved scholastic achievement in superior groups, and almost uniformly unfavorable evidence for promoting scholastic achievement in average-or-low achieving groups" (Findley and Bryan 1975, 13; see also Goldberg, Passow, and Justman 1966; Heller 1982; and Franseth 1966). Or in the more direct language of Oakes, "No group of students has been found to benefit consistently from being in a homogenous group" (1985, p. 7).

The reasons why ability grouping and curriculum tracking have not produced positive benefits have been the subject of much study. One stream of research stresses that the group dynamics of lower ability groups is less conducive to learning (Alexander and Eckland 1975; Alexander and McDill 1976; Eder 1981, 159; Felmlee and Eder 1983). Another stream of literature stresses the role of the instructor, concluding that lower teacher expectations result in lower student achievement (Brophy and Good 1970; Rist 1973; Barr and Dreeben 1977). A third stream of research contends that lower curriculum tracked students receive less attention and advice from school counselors (Heyns 1974; Cicourel and Kitsuse 1963). The result of lower-quality education in lower academic groups means that initial differences between students are reinforced, and they actually widen over time (Alexander and McDill 1976; Chesler and Cave 1981; Felmlee and Eder 1983, 85).

Only for bilingual education does controversy still remain about the impact of academic grouping (see the discussion of bilingual education in chapter 3). Because bilingual education has become a salient political issue, the debate is more frequently conducted in political arenas than in research journals (for the discussion of the politics see San Miguel 1984). Three studies have received the most attention. A 1977 study by the American Institutes for Research examined thirty-eight bilingual programs and concluded that limited English-proficiency students assigned to bilingual classes did no better than those assigned to regular classrooms that did not have bilingual instruction. The U.S. Department of Education commissioned a study of bilingual education by Baker and de Kanter (1983). They concluded that special programs can improve achievement levels of limited English-proficient students, but that the case was generally weak. They argued that teaching a bilingual student in his or her home language was not necessary. Willig (1985), using different methods, reexamined some but not all of the studies that Baker and de Kanter analyzed. She concluded that bilingual education programs produced significant positive effects for students so assigned.[27]

Our study is not concerned with determining that bilingual programs are either effective or not effective. We are concerned with the segregative aspects of bilingual education, not the pedagogical aspects. Assignments to such classes based on ethnicity rather than need should be cause for policy concern. The American Institutes for Research, for example, found that "less than 30 percent of the participating children were actually limited in their English-speaking ability and that approximately 86 percent of the projects tended to keep children in bilingual education programs long after they were able to move into regular English-language classrooms" (1977, p. 511). Accordingly we will examine bilingual classes for their impact on Hispanic-Anglo segregation.

Disciplinary Practices

All schools use disciplinary procedures to maintain order in the school. If classrooms and corridors are disrupted by inappropriate behavior, then students are distracted and learning is difficult. If schools become a dangerous place to be, students are likely to stay away and fall behind in their studies.

Discrimination can be a factor in the use of discipline if disciplinary procedures are not uniformly applied to all students. Much literature supports the conclusion that discipline is used for purposes other than to maintain order. By selectively punishing minority students, they can be discouraged from attending school or from engaging in certain behaviors. Texas educational officials had a long history of punishing the use of the Spanish language among school age children (Banks 1982, 100). Disparities in punishment for black students have been found by a variety of researchers (Children's Defense Fund 1974, 1975; Southern Regional Council 1973; U. S. Commission on Civil Rights 1976; Arnez 1978; Meier, Stewart, and England 1989). Arnez contends such punishment was used to induce the most aware and aggressive black students to drop out of school (p. 31).

Although most studies do not show disproportionate discipline used against Hispanic students when aggregated at the national level (Eyler, Cook and Ward 1983, 142), the findings thus far are limited. Most research has focused on suspensions, with little attention given to corporal punishment and expulsions. This study examines all three of these measures. In addition, the use of discipline varies greatly from school district to school district. Simply because aggregate statistics for the entire nation do not reveal Hispanic disciplinary disproportions does not mean that such disproportions do not exist in any schools.

Discrimination in discipline can also occur in determining what actions are grounds for discipline. Research has shown that black students are suspended for offenses that are often permitted to Anglo students (Eyler, Cook, and Ward 1983, 144). Political activity on the part of Hispanic students was frequently used as grounds for punishment in an effort to keep the Hispanic student population in line (see Shockley 1974). Grebler, Moore, and Guzmán report that dress codes were more rigidly enforced against Hispanic students, especially in Texas schools (1970, p. 157).

Even if disparities in discipline do not occur, the disciplining of Hispanic students merits attention. Schools can use discipline to discourage Hispanic students from protesting inequitable conditions, to discourage their use of their native language, to encourage them to assimilate Anglo ways, and to encourage students to drop out of school. Even if all school districts do not practice such discrimination, the possibility exists that some do. Accordingly, disparities in discipline constitute a major part of this study.

Education Outputs

A school district that uses academic grouping and discipline in an effort to segregate the school system will deny Hispanic students access to the best educational experiences that the school district has to offer. A student who suffers such discrimination might pursue one of three paths. First, that student might become disillusioned with school, abandon all hope of ever pleasing the teachers, and drop out of school. Second, the student might continue to attend school but lose interest in the classes, fall behind in school, and fail to gain sufficient credits to graduate. Third, some students will be able to overcome discriminatory academic grouping and discipline and graduate, but they will not have had the same quality education that many Anglo students have had.

Two of these results—dropouts and high school graduates—can be measured and are included as the final two policy variables in this study. The third result is probably even more important than the other two. Unfortunately, any effort to compare the quality of education that minority students receive from different school districts is virtually impossible. Although student test scores are sometimes available from some school districts (see chapter 6), they are often not comparable because different tests are given or the tests are given at different times during the school year. Assessing the variations in the quality of education that individual minority students receive is important, and we encourage research in this area, but such an effort is beyond the scope of this study.[28]

Differences between Hispanic and Anglo students in terms of educational attainment have frequently been documented. Fernández and Velez note several studies of high Hispanic dropout levels (1985, p. 128). In Chicago for individuals twenty-five years old or older, the dropout rate was 31.3 percent for Anglos, 49.4 percent for blacks, and 56.7 percent for Hispanics. In New York, estimates are that five of ten Anglos who enter the ninth grade do not complete high school, compared to seven in ten blacks and eight in ten Hispanics (p. 137). Cervantes' examination of California high school data reveals a grade 9 to grade 12 attrition rate of 45 percent for Hispanics, compared to 21 percent for Anglos (1984, p. 285). National figures report an Hispanic dropout rate of 40 percent, compared to 14 percent for Anglos (Brown et al. 1980, 36). High Hispanic dropout rates have been attributed to peer pressure and poor grades; limited English proficiency does not appear to affect dropout rates (Valverde 1987, 324–26). Hispanic high school graduation rates nationwide are only 66 percent of Anglo rates and trail those of blacks by 20 percent (U.S. Bureau of the Census 1989, 131).

The Politics of Equal Educational Opportunity

Our goal in this research is to construct a political theory to explain Hispanic student access to equal educational opportunities. As a result, our explanatory variables are either highly political or are given political interpretations. We are less concerned with explaining second-generation discrimination per se as a result of nonpolitical forces such as the family, social factors, or other forces. The political theory of Hispanic access to equal educational opportunities follows closely the previous theory of political representation, using many of the same variables.

Hispanic Representation

The representatives most likely to affect policies regarding equal access to education are teachers (Heller, Holtzman, and Messick 1982, 38). Black teachers, for example, were the single most important factor in reducing second-generation discrimination against black students (Meier, Stewart, and England 1989, 106). Applying this logic to Hispanics, however, requires some modification. Blacks comprise approximately three times the proportion of public school teachers that Hispanics do (Fraga, Meier, and England 1986). As a result, most black students experience comparatively frequent contact with black teachers. Hispanic students, on the other hand, come into contact with Hispanic teachers a far smaller proportion of the time. We hypothesize, therefore, that to combat second-generation discrimination, Hispanic teachers must also have support from other policy-makers. Our model requires that Hispanic representation exist both on the school board and in the classroom (for a similar argument in regard to black representation, see Karnig and McClain 1988, 4). In short, without a critical mass of Hispanic representatives both in the legislative arena and in the bureaucracy, education policies will not be affected (see, for example, de la Garza 1984, 4).

The role of Hispanic school board members in combating second-generation discrimination is indirect, yet highly important. Hispanic school board members can provide a focus of pressure on the school district to minimize discriminatory action. They can do this by passing policies or simply by interacting with school district officials. Hispanic board members can also serve as a source of support for Hispanic teachers who wish to challenge school district policies in the classroom.

The role of teachers is more direct. The education literature consistently concludes that teachers affect student performance (Brophy 1983a; Evertson 1986). As Hawley and Rosenholt contend, "teachers have a significant impact on . . . the nature of the student's experiences, whatever the formal policies and curricula of the school might be" (1984, p. 4). Teacher expectations are highly correlated with student performance (Brookover and Erickson 1975; St. John 1975; Good and Cooper 1983; Holliday 1985, 76). This linkage is attributed to teacher behavior in that teachers provide more positive feedback to high achievers and more negative feedback to low achievers, thus accentuating the differences between the two groups (Rosenthal and Jacobson 1968; Heohn 1954; Good 1970).

The negative impact of teacher interactions with black students is well documented (Holliday 1985, 72; Rist 1970; St. John 1971; Brophy and Good 1974; Leacock 1969; Scritchfield and Picou 1982; Persell 1977; Dusek and Joseph 1983; DeMeis and Turner 1978; Marwit, Marwit, and Walker 1978; Rubovits and Maehr 1973; see also Brophy 1983b). Lomotey argues that black teachers improve the performance of black students (1987, p. 176). The literature on Hispanics is much less voluminous, but reasonably consistent. The U.S. Commission on Civil Rights (1974) documented that Anglo teachers treated Anglo students more favorably than they treated Hispanic students.[29] Buriel (1983) found Anglo students received more positive feedback from teachers than did Mexican-American students. Alvin So, using the High School and Beyond data set, concluded that "Anglo teachers had a more positive treatment of Anglo students than of Hispanic students . . . [and] Hispanic students received more positive treatment from Hispanic teachers than they received from Anglo teachers" (1987, p. 8). Tobias et al. (1982) found Anglo teachers were more likely to assign Hispanic students to special education classes than they would similarly achieving Anglo students (but see Tobias et al., 1983). Laosa contends such teacher discrimination is based as much on language as on ethnicity (1977b, p. 60). The only researchers not to find such differences, Muñoz-Hernández and Santiago Santiago, qualified their findings. While they did not find quantitative differences between Anglo and Hispanic students, they did find qualitative differences (1985, p. 101). Muñoz-Hernández and Santiago Santiago found Hispanic teachers tend to use indirect criticism of students rather than direct criticism, as Anglo teachers do. This indirect approach, they argue, is more consistent with Hispanic culture and values than is the more personal Anglo form of criticism (p. 108).

The ability of an Hispanic teacher to relate to Hispanic students is stressed by educators (for survey data see Genevie et al. 1988, 29). Hispanic students are found to be more oriented to learning via social interaction than to isolated task completion (Weinberg 1977b; Laosa 1977a, 27).[30] Hispanic teachers will be more likely to recognize Hispanic students' differences in cognitive style and devise methods of teaching that capitalize on it (Ramírez and Casteñeda 1974; Banks 1982, 98). The 1988 American Teacher Survey found minority teachers were significantly more likely to interact informally with students than were Anglo teachers (Genevie et al. 1988, 56). Hispanic teachers are also more likely to recognize language difficulties as such rather than characterize such a student as unable to learn (Fernández and Guskin 1981, 135).

Hispanic teachers can have a separate impact on Hispanic students simply by being in the classroom. An Hispanic teacher serves as a role model for Hispanic students. Hispanic students are exposed to other Hispanics who have been successful. A role model permits an Hispanic student to aspire to middle-class status yet retain an identity with other Hispanics, something that So finds is important in contributing to high scholastic achievement among lower socioeconomic status Hispanics (1987b, p. 19).

The first political hypothesis is that Hispanic representation on the school board and among the teaching faculty should be positively correlated with Hispanic student access to equal opportunities. We hypothesize that representation on both the school board and among teachers is necessary. Such representation should be positively correlated with gifted class enrollments and high school graduation. It should be negatively related to EMR assignments, TMR assignments, bilingual education assignments, dropouts, and disproportions in discipline.

Hispanic Resources

Greater Hispanic resources should be associated with greater access of Hispanic students to equal educational opportunities.

High levels of Hispanic resources indicate that the Hispanic community has the political resources necessary to place pressure on the school district for equal treatment of Hispanic students. It also indicates that individual Hispanic parents can resist a negative decision regarding their child.

Two measures of Hispanic resources will be used. The first, Hispanic education, was included in the representation models. The representation models also used Hispanic population as a resource, but that resource was linked to voting power rather than the ability to influence the implementation of equal education policies.[31] The second indicator of Hispanic resources will be the ratio of Hispanic median income to Anglo median income. This measure taps Hispanic resources relative to Anglo resources, relates to our power thesis argument, and has been previously used as a measure of Hispanic resources (Karnig and Welch 1979; Fraga, Meier, and England 1986).

The Power Thesis

The power thesis of Giles/Evans/Feagin argues that intergroup tensions are related to differences between groups. In terms of equal access to educational opportunities, the power thesis suggests two relationships. The first deals with social class. Since the power thesis holds that middle-class Hispanics are likely to be preferred by the Anglo majority to lower-class Anglos, class biases must be considered. Academic grouping has a long historical association with class biases (Heller, Holtzman, and Messick 1982, 28). Classifications are frequently based on standardized tests, and these tests have a known social-class bias. In communities with a homogeneous Anglo population, standardized tests will serve to separate Hispanic students from Anglo students. In a heterogeneous Anglo community, however, the use of standardized tests will adversely affect lower-class Anglo students as well. Hispanics, at least middle-class Hispanics, should fare better in such a school system because the discrimination will affect many more Anglo students (see, for example, Alexander and McDill 1976; Hauser, Sewell and Alwin 1976; Rosenbaum 1976).

The social-class indicator for the power thesis will again be the percentage of the Anglo population that resides in poverty. A large, poor Anglo class will be positively associated with Hispanic access to gifted classes and with higher graduation rates. It will be negatively associated with Hispanic enrollments in EMR,

TMR, and bilingual classes and with Hispanic disproportions in discipline.

The power thesis also has a racial component. Because Hispanics are more similar to Anglos than are blacks, a school district with both Hispanics and blacks will focus discrimination first on blacks and then on Hispanics. The presence of a large black enrollment, therefore, should limit the amount of second-generation discrimination against Hispanics. We hypothesize that, as more blacks are assigned to various academic groups, fewer Hispanics will be so assigned, and that as more blacks are disciplined, fewer Hispanics will be.

District Size

Finn found a negative relationship between minority EMR assignments and the size of the school district for large urban districts (i.e., those with more than thirty thousand students)(1982, p. 344). Such a finding can be explained theoretically. Large districts are more likely to attract attention from the Office for Civil Rights and are more likely to receive pressure from civil rights groups. In addition, large school districts are more likely to have regularized procedures for academic grouping and discipline. These factors make it less likely that a large district will engage in second-generation discrimination, all other things being equal.

The Nature of the Survey

The universe for analysis is U.S. school districts with a minimum enrollment of five thousand students and at least 5 percent Hispanic population as of 1976. Large districts were selected for two reasons. They represent the educational experiences of more Hispanic students, and they are more likely to keep the data required for our analysis.

Four separate data sources were used in this analysis. Measures of academic grouping, discipline, educational attainment, and student enrollment were originally gathered by the Office for Civil Rights (OCR) in the Department of Education as part of their "Elementary and Secondary School Civil Rights Survey." OCR conducted this survey every year from 1968 to 1974, and every two years thereafter. OCR does not survey every district every year; it uses a survey formula that stresses large districts. Three OCR data tapes were the major sources of data, a panel tape containing all surveys from 1968 to 1982, a second tape with the 1984 survey, and a recently released third tape with the results of the 1986 OCR survey.

Information on Hispanic income, education, Anglo poverty, and other similar demographic data were taken from the Bureau of the Census, *1980 Housing and Population Survey, File STF-3.* This file contains information aggregated by school district; it was released in 1985.

To gather information on Hispanic representation on school boards, administrative positions, and teaching positions, a survey was sent in the spring of 1986 by the authors to the superintendent of all districts with more than five thousand students and 5 percent Hispanic population. After a follow-up request, 67 percent of the surveys were returned. Limiting the survey to districts for which information was available from all sources reduced the number of districts to 145 usable districts. A listing of the school districts can be found in Appendix B.

A statistical profile of the school districts in the sample is shown in Table 1–2. The average district had approximately 39,000 students. One-half of these students were Anglo, three-tenths Hispanic, and one-sixth black. Notable in the statistical profile of districts is the range of variation on a wide variety of measures. Such variation gives us some confidence that these districts are representative of the educational experiences of most Hispanic students in the United States. In addition, we compared the survey districts with all large U.S. districts (more than five thousand students) on the policy measures used in this analysis. There were no appreciable differences between the two groups.

These districts have not had a stable enrollment composition over time. The average district increased its Hispanic enrollment by about ten percentage points since 1968 (Table 1–3). Some districts, of course, have become substantially Hispanic during this time period.

Our fourth data set contains historical data on the racial composition of school districts; it was collected by Franklin Wilson of the University of Wisconsin-Madison. The Wilson data set is the accepted source of measures on school desegregation in the United States. Because we wished to compare equal access to education with levels of desegregation (see chapter 6), this data set was merged with the other three.

Table 1-2   A Statistical View of the Districts in the Study

Characteristic	Mean	Standard Deviation	Low	High
Total Student Enrollment	38,963	100,671	3,927	932,880
Percent Anglo Enrollment	47.2	25.1	2.0	92.0
Percent Black Enrollment	15.7	17.8	0.0	83.4
Percent Hispanic Enrollment	30.6	24.6	5.0	96.0
Hispanic Graduates (Percent)	45.3	13.0	14.6	77.2
Anglo Graduates (Percent)	69.4	12.1	35.8	88.9
Hispanic Anglo Income Ratio	.77	.10	.40	.97
Percent Anglo Poverty	10.9	5.9	3.2	39.6

Table 1-3   Changing Student Enrollments in the Districts in the Study

Year	Percent Hispanic	Percent Anglo
1971	21.1	62.4
1972	20.4	63.8
1973	21.5	61.3
1974	22.0	60.2
1976	24.3	57.7
1978	24.7	55.3
1980	28.4	51.2
1982	24.8	50.0
1986	30.5	47.2

Notes

1. We use the term *Hispanic* when referring to all individuals of Spanish origin, regardless of their most recent country of residence. Mexican Americans will include those individuals of Spanish origin with previous residence in Mexico or its territories. Spanish Americans of northern New Mexico will be included as Mexican Americans. The terms Puerto Ricans and Cuban Americans will be used to describe those individuals who immigrated to the United States from those two islands respectively. To keep the terminology simple, only these terms for subgroups of Hispanics will be used.

2. We use the southwestern term *Anglos* to denote non-Hispanic whites. This term is more precise than the designation *whites* since most Hispanics are white.

3. Education was a significant predictor of salary for both Anglos and Mexican Americans, but the size of the coefficient was larger for Mexican Americans. The difference between the relative coefficients was not statistically significant.

4. This assumes, of course, that discrimination is illegal. As Stewart and De León (1985, p. 188) demonstrate using nineteenth-century data from Texas, education does not benefit Hispanics if employers are free to discriminate.

5. A few dependent school districts still exist, mostly in larger cities. A dependent school district is controlled by another jurisdiction, such as a city or a county. Several school districts in our sample are dependent school districts.

6. We use the term *bureaucrats* in a neutral manner to apply to individuals who are employed by large-scale formal organizations, in this case school districts (Weber 1946; Downs 1967). No negative connotations are intended.

7. We use percentage of all residents who are Hispanic rather than the percentage of the voting-age population. Although this overestimates the number of registered voters because many Hispanics are not citizens, it is consistent with past efforts to explain Hispanic representation (Fraga, Meier, and England 1986; Dye and Renick 1981; Welch, Karnig, and Eribes 1983). The younger age of the Hispanic population also makes this figure an overestimate. In chapter 4, the specific impact of immigration will be assessed.

8. The measure of middle-class status does not particularly matter. College education works about as well as high school education in most equations. Income measures are used in other portions of the theory to measure intergroup distance; income, therefore, was not used in this case to avoid collinearity problems. Hispanic business ownership data is difficult to find for a large number of communities because the Census Bureau only reports such data for large communities.

9. The wrong type of politics was partisan politics with its class-based appeals. By restricting participation in decisions, the remaining politics was limited to middle-class individuals. The process is still political; it merely restricts who participates in the educational policy process.

10. Some school districts use a combination of at-large and ward districts to elect school board members. This method has become more common as school districts have had at-large systems challenged in court. Often a compromise is negotiated that allows some board positions to be elected at-large and others to

be elected from wards. Because previous research on school boards (Robinson, England, and Meier 1985) revealed that mixed electoral systems produce results similar to ward systems, our analysis treats mixed systems as if they were ward systems rather than as a separate category. Using a separate category complicates the analysis but does not produce different results.

11. In support of this position is Denton and Massey's (1988) finding that middle-class Hispanics suffer less residential segregation than do lower-class Hispanics.

12. Individuals with only high school diplomas are probably not qualified to hold positions as school administrators. Hispanics with a college education would be a better measure. The two measures of Hispanic education, however, are highly collinear. Rather than change the measure of education in this regression, we decided that keeping the same measures was more important than the precise linkage of the measure to the theory. In no case did using high school rather than college graduates change the results.

13. Including school board members in the model did not produce statistically significant results. Whatever impact Hispanic school board members have on the hiring of Hispanic teachers operates through Hispanic administrators.

14. One exception is Saltzstein's research showing black mayors are positively associated with civilian control over the police force (1989, p. 536). For Hispanics, Hero (1986) linked greater expenditures in twenty-two Colorado cities to Hispanic economic disadvantages and the use of ward elections.

15. Federico Peña's primary strategy in Denver, for example, was to stress economic development. This would increase the tax base and permit some benefits to be redistributed to the minority community (see Hero and Beatty 1989). The Cuban community in Miami has also been a strong supporter of economic development.

16. Mladenka's (1989a) analysis using 1,200 cities supports the work of Dye and Renick.

17. We use *academic grouping* as a generic term for sorting students according to ability, needs, or aspirations. Academic grouping includes ability grouping, curriculum tracking, special education, bilingual education, and compensatory education.

18. The objective of the federal Bilingual Education Act is the

instruction of non-English-speaking children in their native languages until they are able to join a regular classroom. The "temporary" nature of the program is consistent with the notion of compensatory education. Those bilingual programs that seek to maintain competence in both languages would probably not be classified as compensatory (see Cafferty and Rivera-Martínez 1981). True bilingual programs that seek bilingual competence on the part of both language majority and minority groups would not use grouping to establish homogeneous groups.

19. Tropea found that Baltimore and Philadelphia created "special" schools in the year after compulsory school attendance laws were passed (1987a, p. 32). Vocational tracking first occurred in large numbers after the passage of child labor laws (Tropea 1987a, p. 35).

20. The social-class nature of academic grouping was apparent from its inception. Heller, Holtzman, and Messick contend that ability grouping was initially used to separate white middle-class children from lower-class ethnic children when public education became available to all children (1982, pp. 28–29; see also Edgar and Hayden 1984–85, p. 531).

21. Despite the use of such judgments to assign students to classes, Bickel finds that IQ tests are still the major reason for assigning students to EMR classes (1982, p. 197).

22. The impact of subjective biases is subject to dispute. Heller, Holtzman, and Messick (1982) in their analysis of black placements in EMR classes found that racial ratios were much smaller than those that would be predicted if only IQ tests were used.

23. Hispanic IQ scores increase dramatically when tests are given in Spanish (Chandler and Plakos 1969).

24. Given the much higher dropout rate for Hispanic students, these figures should be treated with caution. Many Hispanics are no longer in school by their senior year. If all high school students were used as the base, the Hispanic percentage in vocational education should increase dramatically.

25. In 1948 the Texas superintendent of instruction tried to enforce a court decision requiring desegregation of Anglo and Mexican-American students. The legislature responded by abolishing his position (Rangel and Alcala 1972, 339).

26. Oakes perceptively notes that ability grouping should benefit higher ability groups because such groups receive greater resources, better teachers, more individualized attention, more challenging curricula, and other educational advantages (1988, p. 43).

27. Positive findings sometimes depend on the goals for the program that the researcher has. Willig found that students in bilingual classes did much better when tested in their native language. While in some subjects those in bilingual classes did better when tested in English, overall results on English language tests were lower, though not significantly so. Willig does not discuss this finding but rather emphasizes her other findings.

28. One promising area is the percentage of students who are one or more grades behind in school. Analysis by Carter and Segura (1979) found that little of the variation in such rates could be explained by social and economic factors normally associated with poor performance in school, thus suggesting that variations in discrimination were the prime cause.

29. This data set also found that Mexican-American teachers were more supportive of Anglo students than of Mexican-American students. Durán suggests that this finding might be a result of the small number of Mexican-American teachers in the study (1983, p. 46).

30. Laosa further contends that research showing Hispanic students to be more attuned to cooperative learning approaches is linked to Hispanic child socialization patterns (p. 27).

31. Hispanic population was tried in the policy models in chapter 4 but had no impact on the results. Accordingly, it was deleted from the analysis.

Chapter 2

Politics in the Hispanic Communities

Perhaps the most common misperception about Hispanics is the view that they are a single, monolithic group. Hispanic residents of the United States have come from twenty-three different countries (Bean and Tienda 1987, 1). Each subgroup of Hispanics has a unique political and social history and was subjected to different influences before and after immigration to the United States. This chapter explores the politics of the three major groups of Hispanics in the United States—Mexican Americans, Puerto Ricans, and Cuban Americans. After presenting demographic information on the three groups, the political history of each is reviewed.

Demographic Diversity

Hispanic residents of the United States have immigrated from a variety of Latin American, Central American, and Caribbean countries. Entry into the United States depends on U.S. immigration laws, economic conditions in both countries, proximity to the United States, and a host of other factors. The 1980 U.S. Census designated 14.6 million persons as Hispanic (for a discussion of the definitions of Hispanic origin see Bean and Tienda 1987, chapter 2).[1] Of these, approximately 60 percent were Mexican Americans, 14 percent were Puerto Ricans, and six percent were Cuban Americans.[2]

The remaining Hispanics, often termed *other Hispanics,* comprise 20 percent of the total. Unlike some research, we will not consider other Hispanics in our analysis. The differences among Mexican Americans, Puerto Ricans, and Cuban Americans are fairly large, although they have some common experiences. Other Hispanics, on the other hand, have little in common with each other. The political experiences of an immigrant from the Dominican Republic differ greatly from those of an Argentine. The twenty-some identifiable subgroups within the other Hispanic category are demographically diverse and constitute small percentages of the population (see Bean and Tienda 1987, 95–102). As a result, other Hispanics are a residual category rather than an identifiable subgroup.[3]

Incorporation and Immigration

Mexican Americans were incorporated into the United States first by conquest and later by immigration. The Treaty of Guadalupe Hidalgo, ending the Mexican-American War, annexed Texas, Arizona, New Mexico, Colorado, and California to the United States. Mexican citizens residing in this territory were granted U.S. citizenship. Mexican immigration to the United States after the treaty was influenced by labor needs. As labor-intensive crops, including cotton, vegetables, and fruits, were planted in Texas, the demand for cheap labor produced large in-migrations of Mexicans (Pedraza-Bailey 1985b, 7). Mexican workers constituted approximately 85 percent of the common agricultural labor in the United States well into the twentieth century (Bean and Tienda 1987, 18).

Mexican immigration ebbed and flowed, depending on the demand for labor in the United States and the economic conditions in Mexico (Samora 1971). Until creation of the Immigration and Naturalization Service in 1924, immigration from Mexico was essentially unrestricted (Estrada et al. 1988, 41). Labor surpluses in the United States in the 1930s even led to forced emigration of more than 300,000 Mexican laborers back to Mexico (Barrera 1979; Acuña 1972, 190; Hoffman 1974). Mass deportations remained common through the 1950s (García 1980). Legal immigration to the United States reached its peak in the 1970s. Because wages are often seven times greater in the United States than in Mexico, strong incentives exist for illegal immigration (Estrada et al. 1988, 52). The Border Patrol apprehends more than one million persons a year seeking entry to the United States from Mexico (p. 58). Approximately 1.6 million illegal immigrants sought legal status under the Immigration Reform Act, and another 1.4 million sought access as temporary workers.

Puerto Rico became a U.S. territory following the end of the Spanish-American War and was designated a self-governing commonwealth in 1952. Puerto Ricans are citizens of the United States, although the meaning of their citizenship varies according to place of residence. Puerto Ricans residing on the island are not permitted to vote in U.S. presidential elections and are not represented in Congress except for a nonvoting member in the House of Representatives. They are also exempt for federal excise and income taxes.

Citizenship, however, does permit Puerto Ricans to move to the United States without restriction. Although Puerto Ricans have resided in the United States since the nineteenth century, they became a visible group only after World War II. Economic conditions are the prime influence on immigration. When the economy on Puerto Rico declines, migration to the United States increases.[4] When the Puerto Rican economy improves, more individuals move back to the island than move to the United States (Bean and Tienda 1987, 24). Between 1970 and 1977, 367,000 Puerto Ricans moved from the island to the mainland, and 338,000 migrated in the other direction (Brown et al. 1980, 3).

Cubans, unlike Mexican Americans and Puerto Ricans, were not added to the United States by conquest, nor does their immigration rate respond to economic conditions. Large numbers of Cubans immigrated to the United States when Fidel Castro overthrew the Batista dictatorship in 1959. The initial wave of Cuban immigrants included well-educated, wealthy supporters of Batista. Although the initial exiles arrived with their wealth intact, those arriving after the Bay of Pigs invasion had their assets confiscated in Cuba. Successive waves of exiles, including those of the aerial bridge era (1965–73) were younger, less well educated, and less likely to be professionals than the early arrivals (Bach 1980, 44; Pedraza-Bailey 1985b, 15).

Early arrivals from Cuba thought their stay in the United States would be temporary until the Castro regime was overthrown. When the Cuban Revolution established its stability, residence in the United States became permanent. The diversity of the Cuban-American population increased dramatically with the Mariel boatlift in 1980.[5] Approximately 125,000 Cubans were permitted to leave Cuba in 1980 (Silva 1985, 13); most eventually settled in the Miami area. Many of these individuals had relatives in the United States or were political prisoners; others were criminals, mental patients, and other individuals whom Castro did not want in Cuba. For the first time, Cuban immigration included blacks as well as whites (Pedraza-Bailey 1985b, 23). Cubans are currently the second-largest foreign-born minority in the United States (Portes and Mozo 1985, 35).

The immigration experience of Cuban Americans is unique among Hispanics in that they were accorded favored status. Federal funds were provided to help resettle Cuban refugees, and financial assistance was made available for education or to gain occupational certification for professionals (Pedraza-Bailey 1985a).

Government policies assisted Cubans in attaining middle-class status, in direct contrast to the cheap labor policies that economically restricted Mexican Americans and Puerto Ricans.

Geography

Each major Hispanic subgroup is geographically concentrated in a different region. Mexican Americans are located primarily in the southwest, where the original demand for farm workers was greatest. Three of every four Mexican Americans reside in either Texas or California. Fully 85 percent live in the five southwestern states—Texas, New Mexico, Colorado, Arizona, and California (Bean and Tienda 1987, 142). Despite their image as a rural people, 80.9 percent of Mexican Americans live in metropolitan areas, a figure that exceeds the percentage for Anglos (see Table 2–1). Of the three major groups of Hispanics, Mexican Americans are the youngest (24.5) with the lowest percentage of foreign born (26 percent) and the least likely to use Spanish as their primary language at home (86.1 percent).

Table 2–1   Demographic Variation Among Hispanic Groups

Characteristic	Mexican Americans	Puerto Ricans	Cuban Americans	Blacks	Anglos
Metro Residence	80.9%	95.8%	93.8%	81.9%	73.3%
Median Age	24.5	24.6	37.0	24.9	30.6
Foreign-Born	26.0%	50.6%	77.4%	3.1%	3.0%
Spanish Language	86.1%	90.7%	94.4%	NA	NA
Fertility Rate	1.72	1.66	1.07	1.57	1.23
Median Education	9.1	10.0	11.7	12.0	12.0
High School Grads	39.4%	42.3%	57.0%	61.8%	77.1%
College Grads	5.7%	6.3%	17.5%	11.8%	21.0%
Males in Labor Force	83.5%	73.8%	85.0%	73.3%	84.6%
Unemployment	9.7%	12.6%	6.9%	10.8%	5.4%
Family Income	$14,510	$11,168	$18,650	$13,558	$21,235
Poverty Rate	26.8%	28.2%	13.1%	28.3%	7.8%

Source: U.S. Census, compiled by Bean and Tienda, 1987

Puerto Ricans are concentrated in the northeastern United States. Nearly one-half reside in New York, with most of those residing in New York City. Three of every four Puerto Ricans live in the five states of New York, New Jersey, Pennsylvania, Connecticut, and Massachusetts (Bean and Tienda 1987, 142).[6] Table 2–1 reveals that Puerto Ricans are almost exclusively an urban people, with 95.8 percent residing in metropolitan areas. Puerto

Ricans are younger than the Anglo population (24.6 years old). Given the free flow of migration to and from Puerto Rico, the 50.6 percent foreign-born figure (individuals born on Puerto Rico are counted as foreign-born for this table) and the 90.7 percent Spanish language figures are to be expected.

Cuban Americans are highly concentrated on the east coast of the United States. Fully 58.4 percent live in Florida, with over half of all Cuban Americans located in the Miami metropolitan area (Bean and Tienda 1987, 143). Other states with large Cuban-American concentrations are New York, New Jersey, and California. Unlike Mexican Americans and Puerto Ricans, Cuban Americans are becoming more concentrated geographically rather than less. The distinctive nature of the Cuban-American population is revealed by Table 2–1. Cuban Americans are significantly older than the other two Hispanic groups (37.0 years), have a greater percentage of foreign born (77.4 percent), and are more likely to use Spanish at home (94.4 percent). Since these figures are for the 1980 census, they do not reflect the impact of the Mariel migrations.

The relative youth of the Puerto Rican and Mexican-American population, along with their higher fertility rates and continued immigration, means that Hispanics are a rapidly growing portion of the public school population. In 1980 Hispanics were 6 percent of the population, but 13.4 percent of school enrollments (Arias 1986, 33). The relative poverty and language problems suggest that Hispanics will also have greater educational needs. Their concentration in major urban areas, thus, will place a great deal of pressure on major urban school districts that already face resource constraints.

Education

A prime characteristic of minority groups in the United States is a lack of access to the educational system. For both Mexican Americans and Puerto Ricans, levels of formal education are lower than those for black Americans (see Table 2–1). Mexican Americans have the lowest levels of formal education, followed by Puerto Ricans. Cuban Americans do not fit the pattern of a minority group. Their college graduation rates are three times higher than those for Mexican Americans and exceed those of blacks by more than five percentage points. In terms of education, Cuban Americans resemble Anglos more than they resemble other Hispanics.

The educational attainment of Hispanics is also changing rapidly. Census Bureau estimates for 1987 (see Table 2–2) show that Mexican Americans improved their high school graduation rates by 13.7 percent, Puerto Ricans by 27.2 percent, and Cuban Americans by 8.1 percent. College graduation percentages improved slightly for Mexican Americans and Puerto Ricans and declined for Cuban Americans. The latter decline probably reflects the impact of the Mariel immigration.

Table 2–2	March 1987 Census Data on Hispanic Americans			
Variable	All Hispanics	Mexican Americans	Puerto Ricans	Cuban Americans
Population (000)	18,790	11,762	2,284	1,017
Median Age	25.1	23.5	24.3	35.8
% High School Grads	50.9	44.8	53.8	61.6
% College Grads	8.6	5.8	8.0	17.1
In the Labor Force	65.0	66.4	53.9	66.7
Unemployment Rate	10.0	11.7	11.0	5.5
Family Income	19,995	19,326	14,584	26,770
% Below Poverty	24.7	24.9	38.1	13.3
% Managers & Prof.	12.3	10.4	13.9	21.6

Source: U.S. Bureau of the Census (1987)

Income

The relationship between education and income is well documented (see chapter 1). The use of Mexican Americans and Puerto Ricans as cheap sources of labor means that most immigrants possessed few skills. As a result, unemployment rates for Mexican Americans and Puerto Ricans are approximately double those for Anglos and, in the case of Puerto Ricans, exceed that of blacks. Cuban Americans experience less unemployment, yet not so little as Anglos. This lower unemployment rate has been attributed to the Cuban economic penetration in Miami, which allows the Cuban community to absorb low-skill labor within the community (Bean and Tienda 1987); later waves of immigrants have essentially served as a working class for the earlier waves (Bach 1980, 40).

Median family income levels reveal a familiar pattern. Puerto Ricans have a family income barely one-half the Anglo median income (Table 2–1). Mexican-American incomes are higher and, in fact, exceed those of blacks. Cuban Americans have incomes much higher than those for other Hispanic groups. Their incomes are more similar to those of Anglos than they are to those of other minority groups. From 1980 to 1987, median family incomes grew by 33 percent for Mexican Americans, 31 percent for Puerto Ricans, and 44 percent for Cuban Americans. Income differences thus are increasing, not decreasing. Patterns for poverty are similar to those for income.

The economic status of Cuban Americans merits some elaboration. Estimates suggest that eighteen thousand, or one-third of all businesses in Miami, are Cuban-owned (Bach 1980, 44) as is 40 percent of manufacturing. Cuban Americans control thirty of the city's banks (Warren, Stack, and Corbett 1986, 629) and have sixteen bank presidents and 250 vice presidents (Wilson and Portes 1980, 303). The Census Bureau (1987) estimated that 21.6 percent of Cuban Americans held managerial or professional jobs, compared to 10.4 percent of Mexican Americans and 13.9 percent of Puerto Ricans. Relative to other Hispanic groups, the economic resources possessed by Cuban Americans are far greater than simple comparisons of income would suggest.

The Politics of Hispanic Communities

The different forms of politics within the various Hispanic communities have a variety of origins. Differences in geographic location, in immigration patterns, in preexisting political systems, in timing of arrival, and in method of incorporation into the United States result in different political reactions to Hispanics. These different reactions mean that the pattern of political development for each group is somewhat different. Even though in each case Mexican Americans, Cuban Americans, and Puerto Ricans are political minorities, their roads to political power have varied in length and difficulty.

Cuban-American Politics

Foreign policy concerns have greatly shaped the political actions of Cuban Americans. Initial refugees from the Cuban revolution devoted their political activities to the overthrow of the Castro regime. Although this position in retrospect might seem unrealistic, in 1960 it did not. The U.S. government had actively participated in the overthrow of a left-wing government in Guatemala in 1954 (Moore and Pachon 1985, 192), and presidential candidates from both parties pledged support to the Cuban community. A political infrastructure developed as Cuban refugees formed exile organizations devoted to the overthrow of Castro (Boswell and Curtis 1983, 169)

Dreams of reconquest were dashed with the Bay of Pigs fiasco and the Cuban Missile Crisis. In exchange for a Soviet promise to remove offensive weapons from Cuba, President Kennedy agreed not to invade Cuba. Because Kennedy was blamed for the lack of air support during the Bay of Pigs invasion, the Cuban Missile Crisis was seen by Cubans as a sellout of their interests (p. 170). Early Democratic failures plus the strong anticommunist rhetoric of Republican candidates during the 1960s attracted the Cubans to the Republican party (Moore and Pachon 1985, 192).

As the prospects for returning to Cuba dimmed,[7] and as a result of favorable naturalization procedures, Cubans rapidly became U.S. citizens.[8] Portes and Mozo (1985, p. 40) report Cubans had a higher naturalization rate than most other immigrants. The favored status of Cuban immigrants and the nature of the immigrants themselves greatly influenced their orientation to politics. Unlike Mexican Americans, Puerto Ricans, or most other immigrant groups, the federal government committed substantial aid to resettle the Cuban population; Moore and Pachon estimated these expenditures at $1 billion in the 1970s alone. The political nature of the immigration meant that early immigrants were better educated and of higher economic status than later immigrants. Rather than having to await the development of a middle class for political action (see, for example, Wolfinger 1965), the middle-class nature of early refugees permitted almost immediate political successes.

Miami city politics best illustrates the success pattern of Cuban Americans. Only seven years after the initial influx of refugees, the first two Cuban-American candidates ran for city council positions in 1967. The first successful candidate for city council was elected in 1973, and a second Cuban American joined the council in 1979 (Stowers 1987a, 2). In 1985 Cuban Americans elected a majority to the city council; in 1985 both the mayor as well as the city manager were Cuban Americans. Prior to winning a governing majority in Miami, Cuban Americans were an integral part of the previous governing coalition. In 1989 Ileana Ros-Lehtinen won a special election to become the first Cuban-American member of Congress.

Cuban Americans have not been nearly as successful in school board politics. Dade County operates a county-wide school system with school board members elected in at-large elections. Because Hispanic Americans make up only 42 percent of Dade county compared to 64 percent of the city of Miami (Brierly and Moon 1988b, 3–5), they have not had significant electoral successes in school board elections.[9]

Stowers (1987a, p. 9), in an analysis of local Miami elections with Hispanic candidates, reveals that voting patterns are highly polarized by ethnicity although this declines as more Cuban-American candidates run for office against other Cuban-American candidates. Ethnic polarization has increased the salience of politics for Cuban Americans, and as a result turnout percentages for Cuban Americans exceed those of Anglos by five to ten percentage points (Stowers 1988, 6). This high turnout compensates for the lower registration rates among Cuban Americans (Brierly and Moon 1988b, 6; see also Portes and Mozo 1985, 50).[10]

Stowers (1987a, 1987b, 1988) attributes the rapid political mobilization of the Cuban-American community to the middle-class status of the initial refugees. Although lower-class Hispanics provided stronger support for early Hispanic candidates, later candidates were strongly supported by middle-class Hispanics (Stowers 1987a, 14). The middle-class, conservative nature of many Cuban-American candidates is less threatening to the Anglo community than are black candidates (Warren, Stack, and Corbett 1986). Warren, Stack, and Corbett (p. 629) argue that the business orientation of the Cuban-American elite has served to create ties with dominant Anglo economic interests. These common economic interests have led to an Hispanic takeover that is supportive of "downtown" interests rather than in opposition to them.

Although the initial fervor has dampened, Cuban-American politics remains characterized by an unusual concern for foreign policy. The recency of immigration and the strong anticommunist orientation mean issues such as Contra aid, the funding of Radio Marti, and similar cold war disputes are more important in the Cuban-American community than they are in other Hispanic communities. These positions, plus the historical events of the Cuban Missile Crisis, have led to solid Republican voting (see Portes and Mozo 1985, 35). An estimated 90 percent of Cuban-born Dade County voters cast ballots for Ronald Reagan in 1980 and 1984 (de los Angeles Torres 1988, 93).[11]

Puerto Rican Politics

Although Puerto Ricans have resided in the United States for centuries, only since World War II have large numbers moved to the United States. Because Congress unilaterally granted U.S. citizenship to Puerto Ricans, Puerto Ricans did not have to first become citizens before voting in U.S. elections.[12] Despite the large numbers of Puerto Ricans residing in electorally strategic major cities, their political development has been slow for at least four reasons.

First, migration patterns flow both from Puerto Rico to the mainland and back again. Initially, Puerto Ricans were recruited as cheap labor; during "Operation Bootstrap," intended to industrialize Puerto Rico, migration to the mainland was seen as a safety valve for displaced agricultural workers. These migration patterns reveal a continued attachment of mainland Puerto Ricans to the island politics (Jennings 1984a, 6). Many Puerto Ricans, until recently, planned to return and retire on the island (p. 11). With Puerto Rico seen as home, island political developments, including movements for independence or statehood, take on greater salience than local mainland politics.

Second, Puerto Ricans immigrated to major cities in the northeast and midwest. Many of these cities, such as New York, Chicago, and Boston, were governed by organized political machines. Although Democratic political machines in times past served to integrate ethnics into mainstream American politics, they did not do so in the case of Puerto Ricans. Because the machines were able to control city government with their white ethnic base, they saw no need to appeal to Puerto Ricans, especially since the inclusion of Puerto Ricans might alienate their Anglo support. Not only were the political machines unresponsive, they were also in a period of decline. With the creation of urban bureaucracies to administer welfare programs, the machine no longer had excess benefits to distribute to new arrivals.

Third, Puerto Rico created the Office of the Commonwealth to assist Puerto Ricans in New York and other cities. The Office became the focal point of Puerto Rican organizational interests, representing the position of Puerto Ricans in a variety of governmental forums. Despite its good intentions, the Office retarded the political development of Puerto Ricans because Puerto Ricans relied on a government agency rather than developing independent political institutions to articulate political demands (Jennings 1984b, 83–84). By providing social services through an agency linked to the island, the Office prevented Puerto Ricans from focusing on other, more political solutions to their problems within the United States.

Fourth, the cheap labor status of most Puerto Ricans contributed to their lack of participation in the political process. Perhaps the best-known linkage to political participation is socioeconomic status; lower-status individuals simply participate less in American politics (Verba and Nie 1972). Puerto Rican immigrants are often from marginal economic positions in Puerto Rico and are employed in low-paying jobs in the United States. The end result is a predictable low level of political participation.

The conditions hindering the political development of Puerto Rican communities in the United States are being gradually overcome. Entrance to politics, as a result of these conditions, has not been the same as it has been for white ethnics. In contrast, the political incorporation of Puerto Ricans has been through marginal political forces rather than through mainline Democratic politics. These marginal forces perceived benefits that could be gained from political appeals to Puerto Ricans, while the mainline Democratic party did not.

The first Puerto Rican elected official, Oscar García Rivera, for example, was elected to the New York legislature in 1937 as a Republican when that party attempted to make inroads into the Democratic strongholds of East Harlem (Falcón 1984, 32). When the Republican party found García Rivera too liberal for its tastes and nominated someone else for his seat, he won reelection for another term as a candidate of the American Labor Party. U.S. Representative Vito Marcantonio was one of the few Democratic politicians to make direct appeals to Puerto Ricans. Marcantonio employed Spanish-speaking workers in his district office, defended Puerto Rican nationalists in court, and advocated independence for Puerto Rico (Falcón 1984, 34–38). Although Marcantonio was a Democrat, he was identified with the far left wing of the Democratic party.

Perhaps the most successful Puerto Rican politician of recent times, Herman Badillo, also gained access to power through "marginal" political movements. Badillo, stymied by the Democratic machine, worked through reform Democratic organizations (Baver 1984, 46). Badillo became the first Puerto Rican elected to the U.S. Congress and was later deputy mayor of New York City.

The most recent, and perhaps the most successful, non-mainline political avenue for Puerto Ricans was the poverty programs of the 1960s. Part of the poverty programs' effort was maximum participation by poor people in political action. Just as the poverty programs produced a series of young black leaders, they also produced a new generation of Puerto Rican politicians. Ramon Valez, the best known of these "poverty-crats," built a Puerto Rican political machine in the South Bronx (Baver 1984, 48).

The lack of responsiveness of mainstream political organizations, the working-class status of most Puerto Ricans, and the ties to political events on the island explain the continued association of mainland Puerto Ricans with radical politics. Puerto Rican cigar rollers were active in early American labor organizations (Falcón 1984, 23). Puerto Rican nationalists were involved in an assassination attempt on President Truman in 1950 and a 1954 attack on the U.S. House of Representatives.[13] In the 1960s the militant Young Lords party became the Puerto Rican equivalent of the Black Panthers with their involvement in political confrontations and social service delivery (Lucas 1984, 106; Baver 1984, 49).

Despite the unwillingness of the mainstream Democratic party to embrace Puerto Ricans, Puerto Ricans vote loyally for Democratic candidates. Falcón (1984, p. 38) cites estimates that 80 percent of voting Puerto Ricans in 1940 cast ballots for Franklin Roosevelt. Although Puerto Ricans could be expected to gravitate to the Democratic party as result of their socioeconomic status, some political events have encouraged this loyalty. The 1928 Democratic party platform called for Puerto Rican statehood, the New Deal included Puerto Rico in its programs, and the War on Poverty provided funds for the island.

Although one might assume the concentration of Puerto Ricans in major northeastern cities would provide the same stimulus to political development that aided Cubans in Miami, such is not the case. The Puerto Rican share of the electorate is fairly small in most cities; for example, only 16 percent of New York voters are Hispanic. In addition, concentrations of Puerto Rican voters are often intermixed with concentrations of Mexican-American, Dominican, or Panamanian voters; only 60 percent of New York Hispanics, for example, are Puerto Ricans (Moore and Pachon 1985, 191).[14]

Access to school board positions has been especially difficult. In New York, the school district most likely to have Puerto Rican representation, such efforts have been hindered by labor union opposition, campaign slating practices, district gerrymandering, and extensive legal challenges to Puerto Rican candidates (Fuentes 1984). In other school districts, at-large elections have prevented

Puerto Ricans from winning school board elections. More success-ful have been nonelectoral tactics such as the New York school boycott in support of a school superintendent who supported bilingual education (Jennings 1984a, 8; see also chapter 3 in this book). In 1989 Joseph Fernández, the superintendent of the Dade County school system, became the first Puerto Rican to be the New York City school superintendent.

Mexican-American Politics

The southwestern United States was added to the union after the conclusion of the Mexican War. Open conflict between Anglos and Mexicans, however, continued for many years after the war ended (see Navarro 1974, 59–61). Because Mexican settlers in these regions were isolated by great distances from the central government in Mexico City, they developed local political institu-tions for governing. California, in particular, had developed popu-larly elected institutions at the local level (Hyink, Brown, and Thacker 1985, 17). With the American acquisition, the Mexican dominance of the political institutions lasted until Anglo in-migra-tion produced an Anglo majority. At that point the Anglo majority reduced and even eliminated the political power of the Mexican-American community.

The relative accessibility of various settlements affected the ability of Anglos to establish political dominance. In Texas, sparse Mexican settlements meant a four-to-one Anglo majority at the time of annexation. Anglo dominance was almost immediate. In northern California, the gold rush brought an Anglo majority; but in southern California, Mexican Americans retained a numerical majority until the 1870s. When the balance of population shifted, Anglo politicians asserted control over the government (Camarillo 1979). In the more isolated regions of New Mexico, Anglos were unable to gain a population majority. At a result, Mexican Ameri-cans have played a continuous role in governing that state.[15] Ang-los in Arizona, to avoid sharing power with New Mexico Hispan-ics, pressed for the creation of a separate Arizona territory in the nineteenth century (Acuña 1972, 93). Statehood for both Arizona and New Mexico was delayed, according to Estrada et al., owing to their large Hispanic populations (1988, p. 45).

The ability of Anglo settlers to seize political control of the con-quered regions was aided by the class structure of the existing Mexican community. Mexican settlements were highly structured,

with the large land owners at the top of the socioeconomic ladder. Among individual landowners, status was enhanced by birth
in Spain and the lack of intermarriage with the Indian population. Further down in social status were mestizo artisans and
workers. At the bottom were the common laborers and Indians.
Because the Mexican community had a preexisting political system, the major threat to Anglo supremacy was the large Mexican
landowner.

Anglo political domination was driven as much by economic
concerns as by political concerns. To establish control over the
local government, the large Mexican-American landowners had to
be eliminated or coopted into the Anglo political system. In Texas,
Anglos used the new Anglo court systems and fraudulent practices
to claim title to land owned by Mexican Americans (Barrera
1979). When legal tactics failed, violence was frequently used
(Acuña 1972, 39), including encouraging Indian raids in Arizona
(p. 83). In California, a land commission invalidated 25 percent of
Mexican land titles and imposed substantial legal costs on the
remainder via court challenges (Robinson 1948, 106). In southern
California, the prosperity of the gold rush for the Mexican-American cattle rancher delayed Anglo control over the land because
the income from beef sales was large enough to fight Anglo
takeover efforts in the courts (Camarillo 1979).[16] With the reces-
sion of 1873 reducing incomes and Anglos willing to lend money
at excessive interest rates, many southern Californian Mexican
Americans also lost their land to Anglos. In New Mexico, change
in land taxation policies (Estrada et al. 1988, 32) and later National Forrest Service acquisitions were used to take control of Mexican-American lands. Only in more remote parts of New Mexico
did Mexican Americans retain economic power and come to an
accommodation with Anglo interests that led to a sharing of
power between Anglo and Mexican-American elites.[17]

With Anglo control of the land and political institutions, the
Mexican-American population became a cheap source of labor for
farming and mining. Since the labor needs were unskilled, the
prime objective was to procure a willing and docile labor force.
The use of the Texas Rangers, the California Highway Patrol, and
other law enforcement personnel to keep the Mexican-American
population in line is well documented (Gutiérrez and Hirsch 1974,
86; Grebler, Moore, and Guzmán 1974, 188; McWilliams 1968; de
la Garza 1979, 103; Acuña 1972, 38–41). Despite pockets of resistance (Navarro 1974, 59–61), the Mexican-American population

for the most part was reduced to a subordinate political and economic minority group.

In Texas, the one-party rule of the Democratic party resulted in tactics to restrict Mexican-American voting similar to those used against blacks in other southern states. Literacy tests disqualified a large number of Mexican Americans,[18] and poll taxes were used to discourage others from voting (de la Garza 1979, 107).[19] The more "loyal" Mexican Americans were integrated into rural political machines run by Anglo bosses. A boss would then vote his voters as he saw fit. Intimidation, coercion, and outright violence were not uncommon.

The turning point in Mexican-American politics was World War II. Numerous Mexican Americans served in the armed forces and were exposed to ways of life different from those in rural Texas and California. After returning from the service, many took advantage of veterans' benefits to further their education or to buy homes. The wartime economy produced a major economic boom in the southwest, and the scarcity of labor in the cities led many Mexican Americans to move to urban areas (Montejano 1987, 268). Urbanization, by increasing contact, and the return of the World War II veterans provided the catalysts for individuals to attempt changes in the political system.

Post–World War II political efforts spawned Mexican-American interest groups to press for political changes. While the Mexican-American community has always had a modest number of multifunctional organizations, the post–World War II era saw the development of distinctly political groups (Tirado 1970). The League of United Latin American Citizens, a middle-class organization, sought assimilation and greater political participation. The G.I. Forum stressed gaining access to equal educational opportunities as a method of upward mobility. The Los Angeles Community Service Organization helped Edward Roybal in 1949 become the first Mexican American to be elected to the Los Angeles city council (Tirado 1970, 63). Henry Gonzales ran unsuccessfully for governor of Texas and later successfully for the U.S. Congress.

Mexican-American voters played an especially crucial role in the election of 1960. The Víva Kennedy effort under the leadership of Roybal, Gonzales, and Senator Dennis Chávez of New Mexico attempted to turn out Hispanics in large numbers for the Kennedy-Johnson ticket. Hispanic voters provided the margin of victory for Kennedy in Texas and New Mexico and, therefore, in the election (Levy and Kramer 1974, 241). The movement also produced the Political Association of Spanish Speaking Organizations (PASSO) which had some success in electing Hispanics to local offices (Tirado 1970, 70).

Further political development of the Mexican-American community was delayed by structural barriers. Although local Texas governments could hardly be termed "reformed," they adopted many trappings of reform government, including at-large, nonpartisan elections. In California, the reform nature of government meant few patronage positions to reward loyal followers. Gerrymandering was common. California congressional districts in 1960s divided the East Los Angeles Mexican-American community into six congressional districts without producing a single district with a Mexican-American majority (Juarez 1974, 305). The City of Los Angeles apportioned council districts based on registered voters rather than population until 1971 (Padilla and Ramírez 1974, 202). Legal victories were fought and won by the Mexican-American Legal Defense and Education Fund (MALDEF) and others, but the progress was on a city-by-city basis and therefore slow. The extension of the Voting Rights Act in 1975 to Mexican Americans by permitting bilingual ballots eliminated many of the formal barriers to registration and voting (Montejano 1987, 289).[20]

The one exception to the slow political development of Mexican Americans occurred in New Mexico. As a result of its isolation and lower levels of Anglo in-migration, Mexican Americans in New Mexico have long shared power with Anglos.[21] New Mexico never used an English literacy test to restrict voting; the state constitution contained a bilingual provision from its inception as the result of the actions of the Fraternal Order of Penitent Brothers (a politically active Mexican-American religious and fraternal organization [Holmes 1967, 51]). Hispanic voter turnout in New Mexico equals and often exceeds that of Anglos (Garcia and Wrinkle 1971, 37).

Hispanic political power in New Mexico is concentrated in the north in both urban and rural counties (p. 37). In 1950 New Mexico had twenty Mexican-American legislators, while the four other southwestern states had none (Moore and Pachon 1985, 185). From 1849 to 1973 New Mexico elected a total of 1,169 Hispanic legislators, compared to 68 in Colorado and 33 in California (Padilla and Ramírez 1974, 190). New Mexico elected Dennis Chávez to the U.S. Senate in 1935 and followed him with Joseph Montoya. Congressional seats in New Mexico have frequently been held by

Mexican Americans, starting the Benigno Hernández in 1915 (Vigil 1988, 284). During the 1980s both members of Congress were Mexican American.

Isolation and concentration also permitted Mexican Americans to play a continuous, albeit minority, role in Colorado politics. Mexican Americans held political control in four southern Colorado counties for nearly 100 years until the in-migration of Anglos after 1950. By 1956, however, the Mexican-American power base had shifted to Denver and Pueblo (Padilla and Ramírez 1974, 205). Some Mexican-American political representation, as a result, almost always existed in Colorado.

Mexican Americans in contemporary politics are heavy supporters of the Democratic party (Garcia 1979, 172). Freeman's study of Mexican Americans in South Tucson showed that Democrats outnumbered Republicans by 27.7 to one (1974, p. 61). Levy and Kramer estimated that Lyndon Johnson won 90 percent of the Mexican-American vote in 1964 and that Hubert Humphrey won 87 percent in 1968 (1974, p. 242). Although the Republican party has made recent appeals to Mexican Americans, they have not been rewarded with commensurate voter loyalty (see Padilla and Ramírez 1974; Garcia and Arce 1988, 129).

Although the strategic location of Mexican Americans in the key electoral states of California and Texas has increased their role in national politics, Mexican Americans have not been able to capitalize fully on this. In part, Mexican Americans are unable to maximize their impact because one out of three adults is not a citizen of the United States (*National Journal,* January 24, 1987, 224). Turnout among registered voters is also perceived to be low, 10 to 20 percent less than Anglos (Garcia and Arce 1988, 129); Wrinkle and Miller found turnout in Hildago County, Texas, negatively correlated with Mexican-American residence after 1968 (1984, p. 310), confirming earlier work of McClesky and Merrill (1974, 130; but see MacManus, Bullock, and Grothe 1986, 607). Much of the low turnout levels can be explained in terms of citizenship and low socioeconomic status (Garcia 1979, 169; Welch, Cromer, and Steinman 1975, 376).

Mexican Americans flirted briefly with radical politics in the 1970s before returning to mainstream political participation. La Raza Unida, a militant Mexican-American third party, was able to take political control of Crystal City, Texas, and a few other small communities and played a role in statewide electoral politics in both Texas and California (Juarez 1974, 304; Shockley 1974).

Ramsey Muñiz, running on the La Raza Unida ticket, captured 6 percent of the vote for governor of Texas in 1972 (Montejano 1987, 289). In the 1960s other Mexican Americans, led by Reies Lopez Tijerina, seized control of part of Kit Carson National Forest in New Mexico. School walkouts and protest marches were common tactics (Acuña 1972, 227; Hyink, Brown, and Thacker 1985, 226; Culver and Syer 1984, 258). And the story of Cesar Chávez and his nonviolent efforts to organize farm workers is well known.[22]

With the passage of the turbulent 1960s, the dying of the anti-Vietnam War movement, the collapse of the radical student movements, and the demise of the radical black power movements, the more radical Mexican-American political movements also declined. La Raza Unida became paralyzed by internal dissension and rapidly lost its electoral clout (Montejano 1987, 291; Muñoz and Barrera 1988, 218). Restrictive election laws and greater responsiveness to Hispanic issues by the two major parties also played a role in La Raza's decline (Estrada et al. 1988, 55; Muñoz and Barrera 1988, 231). Mexican Americans could also point to successes in traditional electoral politics. Voter registration increased with federal provisions for minority language ballots and locally organized voter registration drives (Culver and Syer 1984, 260). President Jimmy Carter actively sought Hispanic votes and was the first president to make a large number of Hispanic appointments (de la Garza 1984, 9). Moore and Pachon estimate the number of Mexican-American state legislators in the five southwestern states quadrupled between 1950 and 1983 (1985, p. 185). Despite these gains, Table 2–3 shows Hispanics remain significantly underrepresented in state legislatures. Nine Hispanics currently serve in the U.S. Congress (seven are Mexican American, one is Cuban American, and one is Puerto Rican). Both New Mexico and Arizona have had Mexican-American governors, and San Antonio and Denver have had Mexican-American mayors (for a discussion of the election of Federico Peña in Denver, see Hero 1987).

Although most Mexican Americans live in the southwest, substantial numbers live in large cities outside the southwest. William Emilio Rodriguez, for example, was elected to the Chicago city council in 1915 (Santillan 1988a, 104). Santillan contends that Mexican-American political power in the midwest, however, was severely crippled by the forced repatriation policies of the 1930s.

Table 2–3   State Legislatures' Hispanic Representation Ratios

State	Percent Hispanic Population	Number of Hispanic Legislators	Representation Ratio*
Connecticut	4.0	1	.13
Rhode Island	2.1	1	.32
New York	9.5	8	.40
New Jersey	6.7	1	.13
Ohio	0.9	1	.90
Pennsylvania	1.3	1	.30
Indiana	1.7	1	.42
Illinois	5.6	3	.20
Kansas	2.7	3	.72
Florida	8.8	9	.64
Louisiana	.8	2	1.74
Texas	21.0	25	.60
Montana	1.3	1	.53
Colorado	11.8	9	.76
New Mexico	36.6	38	.93
Arizona	16.2	10	.68
California	19.2	7	.30
Nevada	7.3	1	.23
Oregon	2.6	1	.43

Source: U.S. Bureau of the Census, 1989: p. 256.

*Percent of Legislators who are Hispanic ÷ Percent Hispanic Population

The forces dominating Mexican-American politics in the southwest also affected Mexican Americans in other parts of the country. Víva Kennedy organizations were active in Illinois, Indiana, Michigan, Nebraska, and Iowa (Santillan 1988a, 108). La Raza Unida organized in midwestern states but generally took the form of a pressure group rather than a political party (Santillan 1988a, 109). Mexican Americans have also had some modest success in local elections in midwestern cities.

Although this chapter stresses differences among Cuban Americans, Puerto Ricans, and Mexican Americans, we should also note that substantial variation in political attitudes, actions, and impacts exists within each Hispanic subgroup. Frank Gilliam's analysis of California respondents shows that Mexican Americans become significantly more conservative as they earn higher incomes, grow older, lose group consciousness, and reside in the United States for longer periods of time (1988, Table 4). Demographic cleavages affect Hispanics just as they do Anglos. Despite such impacts, Mexican-American political attitudes remain significantly different from those of blacks or Anglos (Gilliam 1988, Table 3).

Conclusion

This chapter examined demographic and political variations among Hispanic communities in the United States. Although Hispanics are often perceived as a single minority group, in reality they are composed of numerous, distinct groups. Because this study focuses on the three largest Hispanic groups—Mexican Americans, Cuban Americans, and Puerto Ricans—only those groups were discussed in this chapter. Even though the politics of Cuban Americans, Mexican Americans, and Puerto Ricans differ greatly, they have some commonalities. Unlike other ethnic minorities, immigration of Hispanics continues, so problems of language and acculturation persist (Arias 1986, 40). Each group can correctly be characterized as a political minority group. Puerto Ricans and Mexican Americans have faced a long history of political and economic exploitation. Despite recent political gains in most parts of the county, Hispanics remain significantly underrepresented in the political process. Political limits have, in turn, restricted the ability of Hispanics to gain equal access to Anglo institutions of education. The struggle for equal access to education is the topic of the following chapter.

Notes

1. Nineteen eighty-nine estimates by the Census Bureau placed the Hispanic population at 20.1 million. There were 12.6 million Mexican Americans, 2.3 million Puerto Ricans, and 1.1 million Cuban Americans. The Hispanic population in the United States is growing at a rate five times faster than the population as a whole.

2. The census count does not include those who are in the United States illegally. Estimates of the number of illegal aliens range from 2 million to 5 million, depending on the source (Arias 1986, 28).

3. The small numbers involved would not permit us to examine, say, the educational politics of Costa Ricans. Our sample is limited to large school districts; and when analysis is done by subgroup, only those subgroups of Hispanics large enough to make up a majority of the district's Hispanics can be used. The aggregate nature of the analysis, therefore, limits us to the three largest Hispanic groups.

4. The movement creates problems for school children whose schooling is disrupted. Cafferty and Rivera-Martínez (1981, p. xxi) report that from 1950 to 1980 250,000 children in Puerto Rican schools transferred to New York City schools. Another 200,000 Puerto Rican children transferred from New York City schools to schools in Puerto Rico.

5. These recent immigrants arrived too late to be included in the 1980 Census.

6. Both Puerto Ricans and Mexican Americans have a substantial population residing in Illinois.

7. A 1966 poll of Cubans living in Miami found that 83 percent said they would return to Cuba after a successful counterrevolution. A 1977 Miami survey found that 93 percent intended to remain in the United States permanently (Boswell and Curtis 1983, 173).

8. Specifically, Cubans did not have to leave the country to apply for status as permanent resident aliens (see Prohias and Casal 1980, 55).

9. As Brierly and Moon (1988a, p. 4) demonstrate, the Hispanic population of Dade County is not universally Cuban. Only 70 percent of Hispanic residents claim Cuban origin. Substantial portions of Dade County Hispanics claim Mexican, Puerto Rican, Nicaraguan, and other origins. We are skeptical, however, that the diversity of the Hispanic population affects its ability to gain political representation. See our analysis concerning the diversity of the Hispanic population in chapter 4.

10. Lower registration rates are likely a function of citizenship. As more Cuban Americans become citizens, the electoral majorities of the Cuban-American population will increase. Brierly and Moon's (1988a) data suggest that Cuban-American voting power might double with increases in registration.

11. De los Angeles Torres contends that Cubans outside the Miami area are not as conservative. She estimates that only 65 percent of New York-area Cubans and 68 percent of Chicago-area Cubans voted for Reagan in 1984.

12. The Jones Act was passed despite opposition from the Puerto Rican legislature. This has led many scholars to conclude that citizenship was imposed on the Puerto Rican people (see, for example, Jennings 1984a). The Jones Act can be viewed as an

attempt to preempt independence movements by Puerto Ricans.

13. Baver (1984, p. 45) feels that these events, the subsequent investigations of Puerto Rican organizations by the House Un-American Activities Committee, and the cold war anticommunist movement are reasons why mainline Democrats were hesitant to appeal to Puerto Rican voters.

14. We examine the impact of the heterogeneity of the Hispanic population on school board representation in chapter 4. Our analysis does not indicate that heterogeneity reduces the amount of representation that Hispanics achieve.

15. Arizona was sparsely settled as a result of isolation and Indian hostility (Bancroft 1962, 475). It did not have either a large Mexican population or a large influx of Anglos.

16. California land laws placed the burden of proof on the landowner to prove that the land was his or hers (Acuña 1972, 105). This burden required the Mexican landowner to spend far more in defending a land claim than a person seeking to invalidate the land claim would spend.

17. Many New Mexico land records were destroyed in 1870, thus making the defense of land claims difficult (Acuña 1972, 63).

18. Literacy tests were, of course, given only in English rather than in Spanish. Even if literacy in Spanish were allowed, arbitrary grading of the tests could have served the same purpose.

19. English literacy tests were also used in Arizona (Crow 1971, 29) and California to restrict the number of Mexican-American voters.

20. The impact of bilingual ballots might be more symbolic than real. Rodriguez and Christman (1988) found that only one-third of one percent of voters in Santa Clara County California requested voting materials in Spanish.

21. Acuña (1972) condemns this power sharing in New Mexico as class-based. Many Hispanics in New Mexico are known to distinguish themselves from Mexican Americans by claiming Spanish descent.

22. For a discussion of earlier Mexican-American efforts at unionization, see Navarro 1974, pp. 64–66.

Chapter 3

Hispanics and Education Policies

In contrast to the wealth of scholarship on blacks in the United States, little research has focused on the civil rights and education of Hispanics (Fernández and Guskin 1981). The Anglo power structure's lack of interest in the topic has been striking. When Senator Walter Mondale chaired a public hearing of the U.S. Senate Select Committee on Equal Educational Opportunity in 1970 he noted, "I . . . [used to think] that the fastest way to empty a hearing room was to announce hearings on Mexican-American educational problems. But I have now found a way to clear a hearing room even faster, and that is to discuss Puerto Rican educational problems" (U.S. Senate 1970, 3795). Missing even from Senator Mondale's frame of reference was any concern about the experiences of Cuban Americans. The education of the three largest subgroups of Hispanics in U.S. school systems (Brown et al. 1980, 42), despite intergroup differences, shares problems arising from differences with the dominant culture, discrimination, and language-based curricula and testing.

This chapter examines the educational experiences of students of Mexican-American, Puerto Rican, and Cuban ancestry in the United States. Education is especially important for Hispanics for three reasons. First, Hispanics are more likely to live in poverty and, without access to education, poverty perpetuates itself (see chapter 1). Second, Hispanics as a group are much younger than Anglos (see chapter 2), so they are both more likely to need and to use more education. Third, immigration of Hispanics to the United States continues; as a result, problems of recent immigrants will persist for Hispanics long after other immigrants have adapted to American culture and education. This chapter first examines the educational history of Mexican Americans, Puerto Ricans, and Cuban Americans. Closely related are efforts in judicial, executive, and legislative arenas to define and improve the educational status of Hispanics. Next, some studies shed light on the educational experiences of these groups. Of particular interest is the issue of language and how language differences contribute to different educational experiences for Hispanics and Anglos. Discussion then turns to what has become a popular strategy for dealing with Hispanic educational problems, bilingual education. Finally, special attention is paid to how the totality of these circumstances suggests that Hispanics are being subjected to what, in other contexts, has been dubbed "second-generation educational discrimination." Attention cannot be equally divided among these topics because the existing evidence on the issues is not equally voluminous. In some instances, few if any studies address important questions.

Historical Background

Mexican Americans

Given the Anglo efforts to dominate Mexican Americans politically and economically (see chapter 2), we should not be surprised that education was used for similar purposes. Economic and political domination is enhanced when the educational system reproduces and reinforces the inequities in society. Policies of denying equal access of Mexican Americans to educational opportunities, therefore, were consistent with the overall relationship between Mexican Americans and Anglos in the United States.

Mexican Americans, while not subject to "separate, but equal" laws in quite the same form that blacks were, were routinely denied access to education or were provided with only inferior segregated education. Texas residents of Mexican ancestry felt pointed discrimination in education when, only four years after creating a fund to help support public education, the state legislature in 1858 designated English as the principle language of instruction in public schools.[1] In 1870, Texas went further and *mandated* English as the language of instruction in public schools (Kloss 1977, 177).

"Mexican only" schools, established by local school boards, were present, if not common, in Texas by the advent of the twentieth century (Rangel and Alcala 1972). Where Mexican Americans had sufficient numbers to exert pressures on local officials, schools of some ilk were usually provided. Some Mexican-American children, for example, were able to attend public schools in Brownsville and San Antonio after 1875 and in El Paso after 1883, but these schools were generally segregated, overpopulated, inferior to the facilities available to Anglos, and available only to relatively wealthy Mexican-American families (San Miguel 1987, 10–12).

Until the 1920s, even where Mexican-American youths attended schools in Texas, they were frequently denied access to secondary education. Elementary schools were deemed sufficient (Rangel and Alcala 1972, 315; Weinberg 1977a, 286). Those seeking additional education were taught a trade. A Texas study of education for the 1927–28 school year concluded that about 40 percent of the Mexican-American school-age population were not provided any schools, while only 9 percent of the Anglos were in the same situation (Manuel 1930, 95). As late as 1944 Allsup (1977, p. 27) contends that 47 percent of Mexican-American school-age children in Texas received no education. San Miguel summarizes the status of education for Mexican Americans in Texas into the early 1930s in this way: "The condition of economic subordination and political powerlessness among the Tejano population as well as the prejudice of Anglos toward them assured their continued exclusion from and denial of equal public education" (1987, p. 25). Despite adverse conditions, Mexican Americans took advantage of whatever educational opportunities existed in Texas. Private nonsectarian and parochial schools provided an alternative for some (pp. 9–10).

As the twentieth century progressed, the policy of limited education evolved into a policy of Americanization; education was to transform Mexican Americans into "Americans." As a result, more Mexican-American children were admitted to public schools (pp. 33–37). As these students stayed in school longer, attending higher grades even into secondary school, vocational training was provided to equip them to work in local economies (p. 46).

While these assimilationist pressures came from the state level, local officials often took actions at odds with these forces. Compulsory school attendance laws were often ignored if Mexican-American children were involved. These children were counted in the school census that was used to obtain funds from the state, but local school districts did not need to spend money on truant children. Even if Mexican-American children did attend schools, funds were not apportioned on anything resembling an equitable basis. Provision of unequal education was possible because most school districts established separate classes for Mexican Americans within Anglo-dominated schools. Such segregation was based on local school board policies, not on any constitutional or statutory grounds as was the case with blacks (San Miguel 1987,

47–55). "Segregation of Mexican elementary school-age children originated at the turn of the century but flourished during the period from 1920–1942 . . . " (p. 55). By 1942, one estimate showed that 122 school districts in 59 Texas counties throughout the state maintained segregated schools for Mexican Americans (Little 1944, 59–60). One segregated elementary school was reported as late as 1970 (Weinberg 1983, 206).

Studies published in 1944 and 1945 documented the plight of Mexican-American students in Texas schools and provided ammunition for advocates of reform (San Miguel 1987, 97). This led to a redefinition of the "Mexican problem" in Texas schools and the genesis of the acceptance, at least among professional educators, of the desirability of bilingualism (pp. 103–08).[2] Implementation of bilingual education, however, had to wait until the federal programs of the late 1960s.

Further west in Arizona, the First Territorial Legislature appropriated limited funds in 1864 for schools on the condition that instruction occur in English. Since no schools actually opened in the state until the next decade, their action did little more than express the prevailing sentiment (Claridge 1972, 329). When schools became common, however, English instruction was mandated. When many Mexican-American students, the largest non-Anglo ethnic group in Arizona, could not speak English, they were labeled "slow learners" and assigned to classes for those so designated.[3] Dropping out as soon as a student attained age sixteen was common. Only with an increase in the number of Hispanic educators and the advent of bilingual classes was this pattern altered in any way (Claridge 1972, 338).

In California, segregated "Mexican schools" were established as soon as a locale had enough students to hold classes. The explicit goal in these schools, as in Texas, was the "Americanization" of Mexican-American students. An 1855 state ruling mandated instruction in English (Weinberg 1983, 197). A Los Angeles public school with instruction in Spanish was abolished two years earlier, and instruction was conducted by Anglos in English. Three petitions presented during the 1850s for bilingual schools in Los Angeles were rejected. Only a private, Catholic school established in 1861 offered bilingual education in that city (pp. 194–95).

In some areas with few Mexican-American students, segregating students was too expensive and awkward. Even in districts with officially segregated schools, segregation was not total (Wollenberg 1978, 111–13, 116–17). Integration might be allowed on the basis of "apparent prosperity, cleanliness, the aggressiveness of parents, and the quota of Mexican Americans already in the mixed school" (Tuck 1946, 185–86). Segregation was less common at the secondary school level because the "Americanization" rationale no longer held (if students were to be "Americanized," that should have occurred in the elementary grades), because many school districts could not afford two secondary schools and because the Mexican-American dropout rate was so high that few Hispanic students stayed in school that long (Wollenberg 1978, 117–18).

Even into the 1950s, many Mexican-American students were offered a segregated education, either with separate schools or within formally desegregated schools. Postwar protests by Mexican Americans and repeal in 1947 of the California statute that made it legal to segregate an ethnic group had no impact on segregation (although Mexican Americans were not specifically mentioned in the code [Cooke 1971]; see *Romero v. Weakley* 1955, 836).[4] Intraschool segregation was taken to such lengths, for example, that Mexican-American and Anglo junior high school graduates might have ceremonies on separate days (Weinberg 1977a, 286).

Among the southwestern states, only New Mexico's educational system lacked the tradition of mandated discrimination on the basis of language. Before statehood, New Mexico had very little public education, leaving wealthy Hispanics to send their children to private schools (Weinberg 1983, 199). The original state constitution included provisions that called for the "training of teachers proficient in both the English and Spanish languages, to qualify them to teach English speaking pupils" and prohibited the denial of "children of Spanish descent . . . the right and privilege of admission and attendance in the public schools . . . and they shall never be classed in separate schools" (Wiley 1965, 30; Holmes 1967, 51). Thus, while the clear intent was to have students taught English, the concern for bilingual teachers was decades ahead of its time.

The overriding issue in New Mexico's educational politics seems to have been school financing arrangements (Wiley 1965), and this issue was not cast in strictly ethnic terms. This framing of the issue is undoubtedly due, at least in part, to the work of Dr. George Sánchez, who saw "school finance [as] a professionally technical problem" (quoted in Wiley 1965, 44). So, even though Sánchez, in his major study of New Mexicans, showed that counties with higher proportions of New Mexicans had less money to spend on education per "classroom unit" (1940, p. 72), his definition of "New Mexicans" was limited to "descendants of the Spanish colonials who settled this region in the sixteenth, seventeenth, and eighteenth centuries" (p. vii). Sánchez did not extend his concern generally to "Spanish-speaking people."

This more benign history does not mean that Hispanics in New Mexico did not suffer discrimination. Public schools were slow to develop because the more prosperous Hispanics preferred private education (Weinberg 1983, 199). Lower-class Mexican Americans had few schools to attend until the twentieth century. As late as 1974, one observer reported that "lots of old-fashioned type segregation" remained in New Mexico, particularly in rural areas (quoted in Orfield 1978, 211–12), but the legal infrastructure supporting discrimination seems to have been less well developed than in other states. The degree of actual discrimination, as in other southwestern states, was more a result of local actions than state laws.

Puerto Ricans

The educational history of Puerto Ricans in the United States is much briefer than that for Mexican Americans. On their home island, Puerto Ricans were educated under a classic colonial system. Under United States rule since 1898, Puerto Ricans were expected by the U.S. government to fund their own educational system but run it as the U.S. desired. The primary requirement was to conduct instruction in English. Teaching English was considered a symbol of loyalty to the United States (Bou 1966).

Education in Puerto Rico was not universal, nor was it extensive for those who received it. Not until the early 1960s were nearly all elementary-age children in school; but even then, "more than 60 percent attended for only 3 hours a day. In 1967, just under half of rural students still attended for less than a full day" (Weinberg 1977a, 298).

Given the poor educational system in Puerto Rico and the migration patterns to and from the island, the low achievement levels of Puerto Rican students in U.S. public schools are not surprising. Puerto Rican enrollments in the New York City schools rose from 12 percent in 1956 to 22.2 percent in 1969 (Fitzpatrick 1971, 132; Weinberg 1977a, 298), but achievement lagged owing to language difficulties. Achievement problems were also reported in other cities with significant Puerto Rican enrollments (Margolis 1968; Connecticut Advisory Committee 1973).

The achievement problems of Puerto Rican students in New

York City schools may well have been exacerbated by tracking. In 1963, only 1.6 percent of the academic diplomas awarded went to Puerto Ricans; and in 1969, only 14.2 percent of the Puerto Rican students were in academic high schools, enrolled in the traditional college-prep curriculum (Fitzpatrick 1971, 132–33). Most Puerto Ricans were in the less demanding basic high schools.

As with other Hispanic populations, language difficulties are a key problem in the educational process of Puerto Ricans. As an indicator of the severity of this problem among Puerto Ricans, the New York City school system's policy of not administering standardized achievement tests to students "who have not reached a reasonable level of English-speaking ability" meant that in 1967 more than 16 percent of the students in the schools with the heaviest concentrations of Puerto Rican students were not tested (Fitzpatrick 1971, 134).

Cuban Americans

The educational history of Cuban Americans is even shorter than that of Puerto Ricans, for reasons detailed in chapter 2. The upper- and middle-class status of early immigrants had important implications for the educational levels they brought with them. Despite the fact that prerevolutionary Cuba was highly ranked among Latin American countries in its investment in education and in literacy (Blutstein et al. 1971, 143), in absolute terms it had serious problems. The upper and middle classes, distrusting the corrupt public educational system, sent their children to private schools. Those who could not afford private education, the working and lower classes, were left with the public school system (Boswell and Curtis 1983, 26). It was from the classes that had educated their children in private schools that many of the first immigrants came. Among the first wave of Cuban immigrants between 1959 and 1963, over one-third (36 percent) had completed high school or some college. In contrast, only 4 percent of the Cuban population attained this level of education according to the last available (1953) Cuban census (Fagen, Brody, and O'Leary 1968, 19).

For the Mariel-era immigrants, the postrevolutionary educational system in Cuba is relevant. Consistent with the ideological underpinnings of the revolution, all private schools were nationalized, and more effort was invested in rural areas where in prerevolutionary days the illiteracy rate had been almost four times that of urban areas (Boswell and Curtis 1983: 26). Although educational opportunities are now more widely available than before the revolution, and although Cuba invests about 10 percent of its gross national product in education (Ward 1978, 112), questions have been raised about the quality of the current Cuban educational system. Critics charge that the lack of qualified teachers and the limited amount of time spent on the study of traditional academic subjects (vis-a-vis Marxist-Leninist thought) cannot but hurt the quality of Cuban education (see Boswell and Curtis 1983, 27–28 for a brief discussion of this issue).

Given the background of the first Cuban immigrants, Cuban Americans have a marked preference for private schools. The disdain in which public schools were held in Cuba has been transferred to the United States (García, 1982). Schools operated by the Catholic Church have tried to meet this demand but have been only partially successful. Data indicate that almost two-thirds of the over nineteen thousand students enrolled in Catholic schools in Dade County for the 1982–83 school year were Hispanic—largely Cuban (Boswell and Curtis 1983, 127). A local church official estimated that "we could double the enrollment today if we could build the schools fast enough . . . " (quoted in Boswell and Curtis 1983, 127).

Litigation, Regulations, Legislation, and Change

Efforts to change the educational system should be expected first among those communities with the greatest political development. Since Puerto Ricans were slow to develop a political power base, action by Puerto Ricans was unlikely. Because Cuban Americans were recent and privileged immigrants, they would be less likely to perceive the need for change. Mexican Americans, with their longer history in the United States and their greater political development, should be the first group of Hispanics to press for changes in education. Policy issues in the Hispanic community generally paralleled those of black Americans but were resolved much later than they were for blacks.

For Hispanics, the litigation campaign challenging segregated schools was spearheaded by the League of United Latin American Citizens (LULAC), a group of vocal middle-class Mexican-American citizens. LULAC's initial challenge of segregation was a class action suit brought against the Del Rio, Texas, Independent School District, alleging that Mexican-American students were being denied equal protection of the law under the U.S. Constitution by being placed in segregated facilities (*Independent School District v. Salvatierra* 1930). For the first time "the courts were asked . . . to determine the constitutionality of the actions of a local school district with respect to the education of Mexican Americans" (San Miguel 1987, 78). The court agreed that Mexican Americans could not be segregated based simply on their ethnicity but found that the school board was not engaged in this practice. The school board could continue to segregate Mexican Americans on the grounds of irregular attendance and, more importantly, language. The court found this was permissible segregation on educational grounds. Thus the first foray into the courts was unsuccessful, and LULAC resolved to emphasize other tactics (San Miguel 1987, 81).

Litigation was not used again until 1945, when LULAC came to the aid of several Mexican Americans who were challenging the segregation of Spanish-speaking pupils in Orange County, California. Alleging denial of equal protection of the laws under the U.S. Constitution, a favorable ruling was obtained and upheld in the Circuit Court of Appeals (*Méndez v. Westminster School District* 1946, 1947). For the first time, a federal court found segregation of Mexican Americans in public schools to be a violation of state law and a denial of the equal protection clause of the U.S. Constitution. This latter finding meant that the decision was relevant to Mexican Americans elsewhere. Thus, the attorney general of Texas issued an opinion banning segregation of Mexican-American students except for "language deficiencies and other individual needs and aptitudes demonstrated by examination or properly conducted tests . . . through the first three grades" (quoted in San Miguel 1987, 120). The amount of actual change, however, varied. In Texas, with the absence of implementation guidelines, segregation continued (pp. 120–21). In California, many school systems desegregated, but de facto segregation in large urban areas led one observer to suggest that Mexican-American students in California were more segregated in 1973 than they were before *Méndez in* 1947 (Wollenberg 1978, 132–34).

The legal battle shifted back to Texas in 1948. LULAC, in conjunction with a newly organized group of Hispanic World War II veterans, the American G.I. Forum, supported a lawsuit by several Mexican-American parents. They charged officials in several central Texas school districts with unconstitutional segregation. The decision in this case, *Delgado v. Bastrop Independent School District* (1948), enjoined local school officials from segregating Mexican-American students. The decision in *Delgado* went beyond the one in *Méndez* to clarify that segregation of Mexican-American students, even in the absence of articulated regulations or policies, was not permissible. The decision also held state school officials responsible for "condoning or aiding" segregation of Mexican Americans (San Miguel 1987, 125). Unlike the aftermath of *Méndez,* implementation guidelines were issued by the state superintendent of public instruction,[5] but the results were much the same—massive noncompliance (pp. 125–26). When pressure from the Mexican-American community convinced the state superintendent to withdraw the accreditation of the noncompliant Del Rio school district, the state legislature abolished this position and appointed another person to the newly created position of commissioner of education. Needless to say, the new commissioner was less than energetic about dismantling dual schools for Mexican Americans and Anglos. In fact, his first decision was to reverse the disaccreditation of the Del Rio schools (pp. 128–30).[6]

Throughout the 1950s, particularly after the *Brown* (1954) decision struck down segregation of blacks, cases were brought before the judiciary, occasionally resulting in a favorable decision or settlement. In *Hernandez v. Driscoll Consolidated Independent School District* (1957) the court found that Hispanics had been unconstitutionally assigned to separate classes on the basis of ancestry, but allowed their assignment to such classes if individuals lacked English language skills.[7] Actual dismantling of dual schools for Anglos and Mexican Americans was rare, and litigation was again temporarily abandoned by Hispanic interest groups as a tactic because of its perceived futility (Rangel and Alcala 1972, 345).

Litigation was revived as a major tactic in support of equal educational opportunity for Mexican Americans with the formation of the Mexican-American Legal Defense and Education Fund (MALDEF) in 1968 (O'Connor and Epstein 1984). MALDEF participated in litigation raising a wide range of issues, and even when its victories were limited in terms of the numbers of people directly affected, or even in defeat, MALDEF's actions were important symbolically, both to its potential constituents and to its opponents (San Miguel 1987, 173). In MALDEF's litigation, education was an important focus. The most common type of education litigation sought to eliminate segregated schools, but MALDEF also defended Mexican Americans "punished by school officials" for exercising their civil, constitutional, or political rights. It also took the offensive in cases raising questions about school board member selection systems, discriminatory employment in public education systems, discriminatory school financing arrangements, and bilingual education (pp. 172–74).

Segregation was a necessary focus for MALDEF because the federal government's school desegregation enforcement agency, the Office for Civil Rights (OCR), originally treated Hispanics as white for desegregation purposes. Because OCR defined Hispanics as "white," they could remain segregated without arousing federal interest. In addition, local school districts could send black students and Hispanic students to the same schools to achieve some "desegregation," leaving other schools all-Anglo (Rangel and Alcala 1972, 365–72).

This policy formally changed in 1970 when Stanley Pottinger of OCR issued his now famous "May 25th memo," announcing that the agency would henceforth be concerned with discrimination on the basis of national origin.[8] As applied to school districts, the memo stated: "Where inability to speak and understand the English language excludes national origin minority group children from effective participation in the educational program offered by a school district, the district must take affirmative steps to rectify the language deficiency in order to open its instructional program to these students" (quoted in Weinberg 1977a, 287). Thus, the agency shifted from being solely concerned with black-white desegregation in southern schools (Bullock and Stewart 1984) to include national origin discrimination as defined by language (Orfield 1978, 207).

A second weapon MALDEF needed in the fight against segregation was provided by the courts in *Cisneros v. Corpus Christi Independent School District* (1970). In this case, not filed by MALDEF, the plaintiffs asked the court to apply the principles of *Brown,* the case that stuck down "separate but equal" schools for blacks, to Mexican Americans. Such a finding would require that Mexican Americans be recognized by the courts as a separate class. The U.S. district court obliged, and for the first time Mexican Americans were declared to be an identifiable group within public school systems and protected by the Fourteenth Amendment.

The thrill of victory was short-lived, however, because in the same month the Fifth Circuit Court of Appeals handed down a decision in the Houston desegregation case which allowed local authorities to treat Mexican Americans as whites for desegregation purposes, leaving Anglos unaffected by the process (*Ross v. Eckels* 1970). Another decision had also allowed school officials in Miami to use Cubans as whites for desegregation purposes

(Orfield 1978, 203). Thus, the task facing MALDEF was to get higher court acceptance of the *Cisneros* decision. In pursuit of this goal, MALDEF filed amicus curiae briefs in a number of Mexican-American school desegregation cases pending before the Fifth Circuit. MALDEF's position was basically "[w]e want to know where we stand" (quoted in San Miguel 1987, 180).

Despite the fact that this was the same court that had issued the *Ross* decision holding that Mexican Americans were not an identifiable group for desegregation purposes, the Fifth Circuit, in appeals from Corpus Christi and Austin cases, found that Mexican Americans were such a group and had been denied their constitutional rights in these instances (*Cisneros v. Corpus Christi Independent School District* 1971; *U.S. v. Texas Education Agency* 1972). MALDEF got a victory, but the waters were still muddy. There was an intracircuit difference of opinion that had to be resolved.

The resolution came in the *Keyes* case, the Denver desegregation case decided in 1973. The decision in this case, filed by blacks, required taking a position on the status of Mexican Americans. Denver had significant populations of blacks, Anglos, and Hispanics, so the court had either to lump the Hispanics in with Anglos or recognize Hispanics as a separate group. The latter tack would lead to the conclusion that Hispanics had also been illegally segregated and require a plan to desegregate them also. The U.S. Supreme Court decided that Mexican Americans were an identifiable minority group and constitutionally entitled to recognition as such for desegregation purposes (*Keyes v. School District Number One, Denver, Colorado,* 1973). School officials in systems found to be unconstitutionally segregated could not treat Hispanics as whites for the purpose of desegregating schools. Subsequent decisions extended the logic of *Keyes* to Puerto Ricans in New York and Boston (*Hart v. Community School Board of Brooklyn District #2* 1974, 733; *Morgan v. Hennigan* 1974, 415).

The *Keyes* case did not spawn a wealth of Hispanic desegregation. Even though Hispanics as a whole were more segregated than blacks in the mid-1970s (National Institute of Education 1977a; Orfield 1978, 205–06), MALDEF turned its attention from desegregation to other methods of achieving equal educational opportunities. The remedy MALDEF stressed in its fight for equal educational opportunity was bilingual education (discussed below).

Educational Funding

Providing equal educational opportunities for all students is limited by the structural nature of the American school system. Local control is an important value in the mythology of public education, and school districts routinely disregard other political boundaries when establishing their own. With only a few exceptions, local school districts raise a large portion of their own funds. Relying heavily on property taxes, local funding for education can vary greatly from district to district within a given state.

Hispanics and other minorities are greatly affected by the variation in school district funds. Hispanics are primarily an urban people in the United States; they generally reside in poor, inner-city districts with small and declining tax bases. In California in 1970, some districts could spend 2.5 times as much per pupil as neighboring districts (Dominguez 1977, 175). Texas, with its ability to tax oil-producing property, had even larger interdistrict financial disparities.

The fiscal inequality of districts was exacerbated by the proliferation of school districts, particularly in Texas. District boundaries followed no logical pattern and, in fact, divided up other political jurisdictions. The Dallas Independent School District and the Houston Independent School District both encompassed only a small portion of the metropolitan area of these cities. San Antonio had thirteen separate school districts in and around the city (Flaxman 1976, 459). In most cases, Hispanics lived in the poorer districts, and Anglos lived in the wealthier ones.

This interdistrict financial inequality was challenged as a violation of the U.S. Constitution's equal protection clause. Parents from the predominantly Hispanic Edgewood School District won a federal district court case in Texas, declaring the property tax base of funding unconstitutional. In 1971, California Hispanics won a similar suit (*Serrano v. Priest*). Cases in seven other states also questioned the constitutionality of school finance (Dominguez 1977, 176). Hopes for a more equitable redistribution of school funding, however, were dashed when the U.S. Supreme Court in *San Antonio v. Rodríguez* (1973) held that citizens did not have a constitutional right to equally funded education.

In the wake of this litigation, some legislative efforts were made to provide some equalization of school funding. Texas adopted a state aid formula that distributed more funds to districts with smaller property taxes bases. In California, the State Supreme

Court had held the school finance provisions also violated the state constitution, thus requiring state efforts at equalization. In 1989, the Texas Supreme Court recognized the problem that the U.S. Supreme Court did not and struck down property tax funding as a violation of the Texas constitution's guarantee of an "efficient" public school system (*Edgewood v. Kirby* 1989). Courts in nine other states made similar rulings, thus requiring state efforts to equalize school finance.

Language and the Educational Experiences of Hispanics

Clearly much of the controversy about education for Hispanic students centers around language. Spanish has proven to be the most long-lasting foreign language introduced into the United States, probably because immigration from Mexico and other Latin American countries has been continuous over an extended period of time (Grebler, Moore, and Guzman 1970, 428–32). Only 14.3 percent of Hispanics in the United States are estimated to have an "English-language background" (Brown et al. 1980, 27). Language is often the cue for discrimination against Hispanics, although some of the discrimination directed toward Hispanics may be based on physical variations (Ogbu 1978, 227). The linkage between language and education is simple; students with limited ability to communicate in English are at a disadvantage in most U.S. schools.

Language is more than a medium of communication; it serves as a storehouse of cultural values and an emblem of group identity (Stoddard 1973, 107–51). Thus, for both school systems and Hispanics, language has symbolic and practical importance. For Hispanic peoples, the Spanish language serves as a link to the culture of one's forbearers. Practically, the inability to speak Spanish leaves one at a serious disadvantage if one travels between the United States and Mexico or Puerto Rico.

For schools, the inability to control the language used by students, or the inability to teach effectively in one language, threatens the image of the school as a "melting pot" and the efficiency of schools as "producers" of "educated" people.[9] The problem is exacerbated by mandatory attendance laws. At earlier points in U.S. history, when schools were called upon to assimilate large numbers of students from non-English-speaking families, students "who could not learn English . . . got out before their problems became too noticeable" (Glazer and Moynihan 1963, 127). Legal requirements now foreclose this option. With current mandatory attendance laws, both students and schools often become frustrated.

With Puerto Ricans especially, the relationship between language and culture is highlighted. "It has become increasingly clear that a major reason for the failure of [Puerto Rican students in] the schools rests in cultural differences: the school system presupposes a cultural style and preparation which are different from those which characterize the Puerto Ricans" (Fitzpatrick 1971, 139). In particular, studies show that Puerto Rican family life stresses social interaction while middle-class Anglo children are reared in an atmosphere that emphasizes task completion (Weinberg 1977a, 299). This cultural difference, combined with school experiences which seem to retard the development of reading skills among Puerto Rican students (p. 299), yields a problematic situation for the education of Puerto Ricans.

Among Hispanics, Puerto Ricans are the most interested in having their children literate in Spanish. More than other Hispanics, Puerto Rican parents aspire to return to their native land, where fluency in Spanish and knowledge of Puerto Rican culture is important (Zirkel 1973). Thus, bilingual-bicultural education is highly prized among Puerto Ricans.

The situation among Cuban Americans is somewhat different. Relatively fewer native-born Cubans (i.e. those born in Cuba) consider English their native language compared to Mexican Americans born in Mexico or Puerto Ricans born on the island, yet income data show that this has not hampered their economic status. The presence of this anomaly arises from the combination of the occupational status of the first immigrants, the large government commitment of resettlement aid, and the ability to establish a thriving enclave within which solely Spanish-speaking persons are not at an employment disadvantage (Boswell and Curtis 1983, 117). Further, the evidence suggests that Cuban Americans have adopted English as their primary language much quicker as a group than either Mexican Americans or Puerto Ricans despite the stronger attachment to Spanish among the Cuban-born, noted above. The proportion of second-generation Cuban Americans who speak English primarily is estimated to be as high as two-thirds (p. 118). Young Cuban Americans have been notable for their development of a hybrid "Spanglish," leading one foreign language professor in the Miami area to estimate that the average Spanish vocabulary of Cuban-American children contains only about five hundred words (pp. 122–23).

Given the language difficulties, that Hispanics do not fare well on standardized intelligence tests should not be surprising. A long list of studies since the 1920s, when social scientists and educators began to invest a great deal of faith in IQ tests, examine the language issue and IQ tests. They generally show either that Mexican Americans score significantly lower on such tests than do Anglos or raise questions about the validity of using such exams for Hispanic children (Mercer 1973; Padilla and Ruiz 1973; De Avila and Havassy 1975). Results from studies of Puerto Ricans are more mixed (see Anastasi and Cordova 1972 for a review of early studies; Stodolsky and Lesser 1971; Sexton 1972; Loehlin, Lindzey, and Spuhler 1975). Some find Puerto Ricans scoring at the national norm, at least on some tests. Most find Puerto Ricans scoring below the national norm; one study reaches this finding irrespective of whether the exam is given in English or Spanish (Anastasi and Cordova 1972, 326). Because Hispanics students have differing degrees of fluency in both Spanish and English, however, an exam totally in either language can fail to reveal a student's capabilities.

Bilingual Education

Language conflicts in education now focus primarily on bilingual education programs. Spanish-English bilingual education has become a major issue in U.S. education policy. It is "often presented as a plausible or even preferable alternative to desegregation" (Orfield 1978, 206), and major debates rage about exactly what form bilingual education should take. Bilingual education has become the policy of choice among Hispanic educators, while many Anglo educators remain skeptical of its value.

Bilingualism as a policy gained national status with the passage of the Bilingual Education Act of 1968. This act, amending the Elementary and Secondary Education Act, recognized the "special educational needs of the large numbers of children of limited English speaking ability in the United States" and declared it to be national policy "to provide financial assistance to local educational agencies to develop and carry out new and imaginative elementary and secondary school programs designed to meet these special educational needs" (P.L. 90–247, Sect. 702). No specific programs were mandated, and $15 million was authorized for the first year (Fitzpatrick 1971, 148). Bilingual education was intended to be compensatory for students who came from economically and linguistically "disadvantaged" households. Bilingual education programs were to be offered at the option of local school boards (San Miguel 1984, 506).

The Senate hearings on the bill focused mainly on Hispanics in the southwestern part of the United States. The legislation was supported by Mexican Americans, particularly because they saw it as an opportunity to include some Mexican-American cultural heritage in public school curricula. In short, bilingualism could be a remedy for the Anglo culture's domination of the educational system. As noted above, bilingual-bicultural programs were sought as remedies in suits brought or supported by MALDEF.

The idea of promoting biculturalism, even though it was advanced in the hearings, was deemphasized in the final legislation. Predominant was the view that English was the national language which should be taught as effectively as possible to assimilate non-English speakers into the mainstream of U.S. life as quickly as possible (U.S. Senate 1967). Bilingual education was designed as a policy emphasizing transition, not one creating bicultural education.

The divorce of bilingualism and biculturalism was important because it allowed educational officials to retain claims to expertise and to control of the school systems. Acceptance of bicultural education would suggest that school systems were failing children, not vice versa, and that school systems should be responsive to localized communities. Given the lack of expertise extant in school systems on the nondominant subculture, some control of education matters would have to be surrendered by professional educators. This conflict was often couched in terms of "decentralization" of schools, and Hispanics were often involved (e.g., Puerto Ricans in New York City [Fitzpatrick 1971, 152–53]).

The May 25th memo issued by OCR (discussed earlier) further involved the federal government in bilingual education. In addition to weighing the federal government in opposition to discrimination against Hispanic students, the memo specifically focused on language as a defining characteristic. It prohibited the use of language deficiencies as a rationale for academic grouping of students, particularly in classes for the mentally retarded. It also imposed on local school districts the responsibility for overcoming the language deficiencies of their students so that all educational programs were accessible to language minority students (San Miguel 1984, 507).

More dramatic than legislation or administrative action in policy impact was a case filed on behalf of Chinese students in San

Francisco. In that case, *Lau v. Nichols* (1974), the Supreme Court affirmed the May 25th memo of OCR and required that school districts "take affirmative steps to rectify the language deficiency [of national origin minority students] . . . to open [their] instructional program[s] to these students." The Court found that the failure of school districts to provide non-English-speaking students instruction that they could understand denied them their right to equal educational opportunity. The court required the school district to take action but stopped short of mandating bilingual education.

Even though bilingualism had been given its impetus by litigation involving Chinese students, Hispanics were clearly the largest group of potential beneficiaries. Data from the National Center for Education Statistics (1975) showed that 96 percent of elementary school-age Hispanics (ages 6–13) lived in homes where some Spanish is spoken; in the 14 to 18 age range the comparable figure was 78 percent. A later publication of the National Center for Education Statistics (1978) reported that 70 percent of the estimated 3.6 million children in the United States with limited English proficiency were Hispanic.

Problems with implementing bilingual education programs, however, were already apparent. MALDEF's plan for a bilingual-bicultural educational program in a desegregated Denver school system was rejected as working at cross purposes with desegregation (*Keyes v. School District No. 1, Denver, Colorado* 1975, 480): "Bilingual education . . . is not a *substitute* for desegregation" [emphasis in the original]. While bilingual programs could be made part of a remedy for unconstitutional segregation, the court did not believe that they could be a remedy in and of themselves (Fernández and Guskin 1981, 113). Thereafter, court decisions generally chose between desegregation, i.e., dispersing students throughout a school system, and bilingual programs, which seemed to promote segregation based on language or national origin within schools (for an example of the latter, see *Serna v. Portales Municipal Schools* 1974), although in some cases the court did adopt a bilingual education plan as part of a remedy for segregation (see *Bradley v. Milliken* 1975, 1144).

While MALDEF remained nominally committed to both desegregation and bilingualism (Orfield 1978, 211–14), it emphasized the establishment of bilingual classes. Hispanic students boycotting East Los Angeles high schools in 1968 asked not for desegregation, but for bilingual programs, inter alia (Wollenberg 1978, 134–35). And when OCR moved against discrimination against

Hispanics, bilingualism was often the preferred remedy, even if segregation remained (Orfield 1978, 207). Partly as a result, a larger proportion of Mexican-American students were attending segregated schools in 1980 than in 1970 (Carter and Segura 1979, 128–44). Desegregation had clearly taken a back seat to bilingual education in the Mexican-American community.

The Puerto Rican Legal Defense and Education Fund (PRLDEF), a relative latecomer to the civil rights struggle for Hispanics, never argued for desegregation. Perhaps because language and culture are more salient for Puerto Ricans, and perhaps because Puerto Ricans are concentrated in urban areas where desegregation is impractical owing to the scarcity of Anglos, bilingualism was the organization's primary goal from the beginning (Orfield 1978, 214–15). PRLDEF sued or intervened in cases in New York City; New Jersey; Boston; Wilmington, Delaware; Buffalo; Philadelphia; and Waterbury, Connecticut (p. 215). It negotiated an out-of-court settlement to establish the nation's largest bilingual educational program in the New York City school system (pp. 211, 217). The general thrust of legal intervention became even more specific by the late 1970s. When Hispanic legal organizations took action, they usually intervened in cases at the remedy stage for or in defense of bilingual programs.

In the wake of *Lau,* OCR used its regulatory authority to require that school districts test non-English-speaking students and place them in bilingual education programs. Despite provisions designed to prevent the "existence of racially/ethnically identifiable classes" within such programs (Teitelbaum and Hiller 1977, 160), segregation is common. Orfield (1978, p. 220) gives three reasons for the prevalence of segregated bilingual programs:

1. Hispanic students normally attend schools with considerable segregation;

2. Though [OCR] has brought heavy enforcement pressure on school systems to provide bilingualism, it has done virtually nothing about desegregation;

3. The regulations in the various programs are full of loopholes so large that they make a mockery of the policy statements about segregation. The regulations permit segregation of groups defined by linguistic ability where local school officials say it is educationally necessary.

Orfield concludes that "in practice there have been almost routine segregation at the local level and no federal enforcement of integration policies" (p. 220).

Even though bilingualism and segregation has become an "either-or" proposition, it need not be so (Cardenas 1975; Teitelbaum and Hiller 1977; Roos 1978). Integrated bilingual programs working with the goal of mainstreaming children as quickly as possible are not unimaginable; they are simply seldom tried because they, with some truth, are perceived to be expensive and to require administrative innovation. True bilingual-bicultural programs that expose all students to different languages and cultures have similar restrictions.

The potential harm that bilingual education programs as currently structured can have when inserted into the American school system is evident. Bilingual education becomes another form of academic grouping. While integration and bilingual/ bicultural education are not antithetical, it is not uncommon for implementation of bilingual classes to produce segregated Hispanic classes. At least part of this occurs in response to federal government incentives. Reimbursement to local school boards for the education of students in bilingual classrooms is usually tied to the number of limited English-proficient (LEP) students in the classes, creating a disincentive to include anyone other than LEP students in such classrooms (Fernández and Guskin 1981, 121). Bilingual education, as a result, emphasizes grouping students in homogeneous units and teaching different students with different curricula. Such a program fits the pattern of academic grouping but uses language rather than IQ as the grouping criterion.

Bilingual programs were also implemented before sufficient numbers of bilingual teachers were trained. Bilingual classes in many cases became remedial work rather than programs that enriched the education of students. Bilingual classes as remedial classes stigmatize the students enrolled because they group these students into a category with inferior status within the school (Fernández and Guskin 1981, 132–33). In such "inferior" classes, equal educational opportunity is not provided. The end result can be segregated education that reinforces rather than eliminates inequities in educational opportunities.

Distinguishing between the promise of bilingual education and the reality of programs that currently exist is the key. Bilingualism is an important asset in an increasingly interdependent world economy; and biculturalism could not but improve intergroup relations. Becoming a "bi-illiterate" (Stoddard 1973, 111), however, is hardly better than having the same lack of ability in one language.

Second-Generation Discrimination

When blacks were able to overcome the legal obstacle of segregation, they were faced with second-generation educational discrimination in the form of inequitable academic grouping and discipline. The development of second-generation discrimination
against black students was predictable once the objective of the
civil rights movement became desegregation rather than integration (see Meier, Stewart, and England 1989). Educational policies
that affect Hispanic students are not nearly so developed. Hispanics did not achieve major desegregation victories in court until
after the last great wave of school desegregation cases was won.
Because Hispanic students remained highly segregated and
because bilingual education seemed to encourage continued segregation, the second-generation educational discrimination faced
by Hispanics was more rudimentary than that faced by blacks.

The academic research on academic grouping and discipline is
fairly limited concerning Hispanics; only in the area of educational
attainment have a modest number of studies detailed the unequal
access of Hispanics to educational opportunities. A pattern, however, can still be discerned. Hispanics are consistently underen-
rolled in classes for gifted students (Fraga, Meier, and England
1986, 862). Both Mexican-American and Puerto Rican students
are overrepresented, often inappropriately, in low-ability or mentally retarded classes (Illinois Advisory Committee 1974, 32–39;
U.S. Commission on Civil Rights 1974, 23). Finn (1982) found disproportionate EMR assignments for Hispanic students in some
states with large Hispanic populations. Historical evidence suggests that grouping Hispanic students was prevalent as early as
the 1920s (Weinberg 1983, 196) with as many as half of all Mexican-American students assigned to slow-learner rooms or to
development centers.

Grouping was often based on the student's inability to use the
English language. Regardless of whether or not one finds significant differences in exam scores for Hispanic students depending on
whether they take the exam in Spanish or in English, the results of
research consistently raise questions about the wisdom of grouping
students based on "judged ability to use English" (Davis and Personke 1968, 233). Chandler and Plakos, for example, find that,
among a group of Spanish-speaking students in classes for the educable mentally retarded, retesting these students with a Spanish-
language instrument raised the median score by thirteen points,

raising many of these students to scores that would not justify their placement in EMR classes (1969, pp. 30–31).[10]

Academic grouping of elementary school students often results in tracking Hispanic secondary school students. One author argues that Puerto Rican students are consistently tracked into vocational programs (Cordasco 1972, 342). Mexican-American students were historically funneled into vocational training or agricultural training rather than academic programs. Nationwide among high school seniors in 1972, 30.1 percent of Hispanics were in vocational or technical programs, compared to 22.5 percent of white, non-Hispanic seniors (Brown et al. 1980, 60). A study of Chicago argues that tracking among high schools is so severe that many minority students cannot get the science, math, and foreign language courses that they need in order to be admitted to college (Fernández and Velez 1985, 130).

While classes for the mentally retarded and other forms of academic grouping are often defended as benefiting the student, suspicions are raised by the fact that, for example, the California legislature first provided for such classes in the year that it repealed the clause permitting racial/ethnic segregation of the state's schools (Weinberg 1983, 34). In addition, a substantial body of research (see chapter 1) questions the academic and social benefits of these classes.

The assignment of Hispanic students to remedial classes, especially those for the educable mentally retarded, has been challenged in the courts. As early as 1968, Mexican-American parents challenged assignments to mentally retarded classes in Santa Ana, California (Weinberg 1983, 321). A compromise settlement was reached in a similar California case in *Diana v. California State Board of Education* (1970, 1973). The state agreed to use bilingual testing procedures before placing Hispanic students in special education classes. In *Larry P. v. Riles* (1979), the court established additional procedural protection for students assigned to special education classes; many of these protections were then incorporated into law with the passage of P.L. 92–142.

Disproportionate discipline can also be a problem (Fernández and Guskin 1981, 126). Hispanic students can be disciplined more frequently than Anglo students, thus discouraging them from continuing to attend school. Hispanic students might be punished more severely or punished for offenses that are permitted to other students. Of particular concern was the punishment of Hispanic students for speaking Spanish on school grounds

(Weinberg 1983, 201) and punishment for political activities (Shockley 1974).

Academic grouping and discipline experiences undoubtedly have contributed to the historically high dropout rate among Hispanic students. Classes with little content and arbitrary discipline encourage Hispanic students to leave school. In the late 1960s, the average Mexican-American student dropped out of school by the seventh grade. Dropout rates of Hispanic students before completion of high school were estimated to be almost 80 percent in Texas and 73.5 percent in California (Bernal 1971, 367). Another study by the U.S. Commission on Civil Rights estimated that in five southwestern states, 91.1 percent of the Mexican-American students entering the first grade remained in school through the eighth grade, but only 60.3 percent through the twelfth grade (1971, p. 11). The evidence is even more distressing for Puerto Rican students. A New York study shows that only 43 percent of the Puerto Rican tenth-graders in 1966 were seniors two years later (Fitzpatrick 1971). Later data estimated the dropout rate among Hispanics between the ages of fourteen and thirty at 25 percent, with about 45 percent of this number being from Spanish-speaking homes. A special study of students who were high school sophomores in 1980 shows that 27.1 percent of the Hispanics subsequently dropped out of school—a higher proportion than for any other ethnic/racial group—and that only 30.3 percent of those dropouts had completed requirements for a high school diploma or its equivalent by the fall of 1984—a lower proportion than for any other ethnic/racial group (Center for Education Statistics 1987, 28–29). Puerto Rican and Mexican-American dropout rates generally exceed the Hispanic average, while the rate for those of Cuban ancestry is over ten percentage points lower than the Hispanic average (Brown et al. 1980, 101, 105).

As might be expected, Hispanic students lag behind Anglos in academic achievement. Anglo high school seniors generally are awarded higher grades than their Hispanic counterparts (p. 68). From the most recently available National Assessment of Educational Progress, Hispanics trail Anglos at each tested grade level in writing and reading (Center for Education Statistics 1987, 18–19, 131–32, 135–37, 146–48). Turning to specific subgroups of Hispanics, studies consistently show that Mexican Americans trail Anglos in reading and math scores, in grade point averages, and in writing performance (Coleman et al. 1966; Carter 1970; U.S. Commission on Civil

Rights 1974). The pattern is similar for Puerto Ricans who consistently score below grade level on reading exams (Sexton 1972).

The result is that Hispanics have had and continue to have significantly lower educational attainment levels than Anglos. A comparison of school enrollment levels by age groups in five southwestern states, using 1960 census data, showed that for thirty-nine of forty comparisons the percentages of Spanish-surnamed trailed the percentages of Anglos enrolled in school (Manuel 1965, 55). Nationwide data from October 1978 showed slightly lower enrollment levels of Hispanics than Anglos at all age levels. Hispanic youths, particularly males, were consistently more likely to be two or more years below their expected grade level in school (Brown et al. 1980, 20, 80, 82). Non-English speaking contributes to this grade lag (Brown et al. 1980, 88).

In New York, only 16 percent of Puerto Rican students earned academic high school diplomas, qualifying them for admission to college (Fitzpatrick 1974). The situation was much the same for Puerto Ricans in Boston and Chicago (Illinois Advisory Committee 1974, 43; Ogbu 1978, 221). Nationwide data on the proportion of those aged twenty-five or older who have completed at least four years of high school show Hispanics trailing non-Hispanics by about twenty-six percentage points (see chapter 1). The proportion of Hispanics entering college in five southwestern states was estimated by the U.S. Commission on Civil Rights to be less than one-half that of Anglos (1971, p. 11). From the negative perspective, adult Hispanics are approximately five and one-half times as likely as adult non-Hispanics to have attended school less than five years. Almost one-fourth (23.1 percent) of Mexican Americans fall into this category, as do 15 percent of Puerto Ricans and 9.3 percent of Cubans (Brown et al. 1980, 24).

Despite all these difficulties, Hispanics have continued to make modest gains in educational attainment. The Bureau of the Census reports that 36.5 percent of Hispanics over the age of twenty-five were high school graduates in 1974. By 1987 this figure had increased to 50.9 percent. Approximately one-fourth of Hispanic high school graduates attend college.

Concern with dropouts and levels of educational attainment is not misplaced. Such a concern, however, should not distract us for examining the quality of education that Hispanic students receive when they remain in school. A complete documentation of second-generation educational discrimination against Hispanic students is needed. Chapter 5 provides these data.

Second-generation educational discrimination as an issue rarely reaches the political agenda when issues of Hispanic education are discussed. The lack of concern can be explained. Hispanics appear to have accepted the professional norms of educators more than blacks have; they have not mounted legal challenges to academic grouping with the same intensity that black groups did. We need to also remember that Hispanic Americans have a much shorter history of combating educational ills than black Americans. While Hispanics have been active in fighting discrimination for an extended period of time, they have not had a *Brown* decision that raised their expectations only to dash them when new methods of discrimination arose. Finally, Hispanics appear willing to accept bilingual education in lieu of desegregation. Because bilingual education as currently designed is consistent with the grouping notions that underlie second-generation discrimination, grouping per se is less likely to be challenged.

Conclusion

Political minorities in the United States face limited opportunities for educational equity, and Hispanics are no exception. Although the educational history of Mexican Americans, Puerto Ricans, and Cuban Americans shows a great deal of variety, some common themes exist. In all three cases, Hispanic students have not been given full, unlimited access to the benefits of the American educational system. Second, the American educational system has tried to Americanize Hispanics, thus undercutting support for their language and culture. The final and most important similarity is that educational policies affecting Hispanic students reflect the realities of the political system. Education, in our view, is merely another policy that reflects the differences in political power among groups in the United States. This thesis suggests that the solutions to problems of education can be found in the political process. The following chapter examines the access of Hispanic Americans to political positions of power in the educational system.

Notes

1. This occurred just over a decade after the legislature chartered a university in which German was to be the language of instruction.

2. Bilingual education was also attractive to Hispanic educators because it held out the promise that more Hispanic teachers would be hired.

3. This early form of academic grouping is remarkably similar to current uses of the phenomenon.

4. This clause was repealed as a direct response to *Mendez v. Westminster* (1947), discussed below. Interestingly, the repeal was signed into law by then-Governor Earl Warren, the person who would later lead the U.S. Supreme Court in striking down segregation in the nation's schools (Wollenberg 1978, 108).

5. These regulations clearly noted that segregation was still mandated for "members of the Negro race or persons of Negro ancestry," but not for "members of any other race" (quoted in San Miguel 1987, 126).

6. In Arizona, a similar case banned the segregation of Mexican-American students in 1951 (see *Gonzales v. Sheely*).

7. The plaintiffs in this case challenged the local school board's practice of segregating Mexican-American students for the first two grades of schooling and requiring these students to spend four years in these first two grades regardless of academic achievement. Thus, Mexican-American youngsters could not enter the third grade until their fifth year of school. The school board counter sued, asking that the parents of the children involved in the suit be enjoined from speaking any language other than English in the presence of school-age children and that the parents keep their children from associating with anyone who did not speak English. The federal judge dismissed the defendants' counter claim in a terse footnote.

8. This occurred during a time of growing awareness in the federal government of the problems of Hispanics. Congress established the Cabinet Committee on Opportunity for the Spanish Speaking on December 30, 1969. A year and a half later that Committee was able to report such progress as the growth in number of Spanish-speaking employees in the Office of Education from zero to forty-six (Cabinet Committee 1971, 29). Perhaps more informative of the condition of Hispanics in the federal government was the listing by the Committee of all thirty-one Spanish-surnamed/Spanish-speaking federal officials in top level executive positions in the federal government (pp. 118–20).

9. Tuck (1946) has argued that language can be an effective, subtle instrument of social control of non-English-speaking people, making overt discrimination less necessary to achieve the same end.

10. This criticism assumes that the tests themselves are valid. In the case of IQ tests, there is ample reason to believe that they are not valid indicators of potential (see chapter 1).

Chapter 4

Hispanic Representation in Educational Policy-Making Positions

Defining representation has occupied political scientists since the time of Aristotle (Pitkin 1967; Kuklinski 1979). Theorists of representation distinguish between two forms of representation, *passive* and *active*. Passive representation concerns the similarity between representatives and the represented in regard to demographic characteristics. Usually an entire set of representatives is compared to all citizens rather than direct comparisons between individual representatives and their constituents (Weisberg 1978). One such comparison might be between the percentage of Hispanic representatives on a school board and the percentage of Hispanic voters in the population. Hanna Pitkin (1967) terms this view of representation *descriptive representation.*

Implicit in the notion of passive representation is the idea that passive representation leads to other forms of representation (i.e., that electing more Hispanics to political office will produce benefits for Hispanic people). One need not make this assumption to study passive representation. Passive representation is an important topic of study because it concerns equity and equal access to positions of influence. Political positions and possession of them should be equitably distributed, a piece of the pie/patronage view of representation.

Despite the logical defense for passive representation, most scholars seek to link passive representation with active representation. Representation, according to Pitkin should not focus on "being something rather than doing something" (p. 67). Representation, she contends, should be viewed as one person "acting in the interests of the represented" (p. 209). Eulau and Karps extend Pitkin's active view of representation by asking how a representative should act. They argue that a representative can act in the represented's interests in four ways. First, *policy congruence* implies the representative makes decisions consistent with the policy preferences of the represented. Second, *service responsive-*

ness indicates the representative secures individual benefits for the individuals who are represented (e.g., an exemption from a regulation). Third, *allocative responsiveness* requires the representative to seek benefits for his or her constituency that benefit the entire constituency (e.g., a pork barrel project). Fourth, *symbolic representation* means the representative takes actions that build constituency trust and general support for the representative (1977, p. 235).

Although all four forms of representation are active representation, our concern is with public policy. Accordingly, we are interested in only the first form of active representation—policy congruence. Service responsiveness, allocative responsiveness, and symbolic representation remain important to the process of representation, but their discussion is beyond the scope of this research.

If active representation is defined as representatives acting in the policy interests of the represented, how might passive and active representation be linked? Two linkages have dominated the literature—the *electoral linkage* and the *socialization linkage.* The electoral linkage assumes a rational representative who desires to remain in office. Traditionally, representatives had a choice between two roles: a delegate who would vote consistent with constituency wishes regardless of his or her own views *and* a trustee who would vote his or her conscience (Eulau et al. 1959; Miller and Stokes 1963; applied to school boards, Mann 1974).[1] If representatives fear the loss of their position through electoral defeat, a rational representative would act as a delegate.

The electoral linkage has two limitations. First, many elected positions lack electoral competition, and as a result some representatives have little fear of electoral defeat (Prewitt 1970). Second, using elections to enforce representatives' responsiveness has little utility if one wishes to examine the representative behavior of nonelected individuals such as bureaucrats.[2]

The alternative linkage between representatives and the represented is the socialization model. The socialization model of representation is most developed in the arguments for representative bureaucracy (Long 1952; Levitan 1946; Mosher 1968). According to advocates of representative bureaucracy, a bureaucracy (or any other institution) is representative to the extent that the social origins of the representatives mirror the social origins of the represented (Mosher 1968).

The linkage between social origins (passive representation) and policy congruence requires several intermediate steps. Policy congruence suggests that a representative acts as the represented would act if the represented could somehow participate in the process and make the decisions. One way to ensure such policy congruence is to require the representatives and the represented to share the same political attitudes and values (Uslaner and Weber 1983; Meier and Nigro 1976).

To achieve congruence in political attitudes, then, requires that both the represented and the representatives be subjected to the same influences on their political attitudes. The political socialization literature (Dennis 1968) argues that socialization patterns are related to demographic origins—to race, sex, social class, religion, etc. A bureaucracy that mirrors the social origins of the population, therefore, should share the population's socialization experiences, have similar political attitudes, and make policy decisions similar to those that the populace would make if it participated in all decisions (Meier and Nigro 1976).

Unfortunately for the socialization linkage to representation, social origins are weak predictors of political attitudes. Meier and Nigro (p. 465) found that eight demographic origin variables could explain only 2 to 9 percent of the variance in the policy attitudes of adult federal bureaucrats. Why social origins do not predict political attitudes (and thus likely policy congruence) well is explicable. Socialization is nothing more than a learning process; as such, it does not suddenly cease at age twenty-one but continues throughout one's life (Brim and Wheeler 1966, 17). As a result, simply by being a representative means that an individual has had different socialization experiences from other individuals. For bureaucrats, as opposed to elected officials, the bureaucracy itself performs some additional socialization that can overwhelm many preexisting attitudes (Meier and Nigro 1976, 466; Miles 1978; Romzek and Hendricks 1982).

The socialization linkage survives, however, in certain specific situations. The demographic origin that remains the best predictor of attitudes and is likely to have adult experiences that reinforce it is race (Free and Cantril 1968). As Alan Monroe contends, "Race constitutes the greatest social cleavage in America, at least as far as political opinions are concerned" (1975, p. 87). The impact of Hispanic ethnicity is also strong. Frank Gilliam's (1988) study of political attitudes shows Mexican Americans hold distinctly different opinions from either Anglos or blacks on issues salient to Mexican Americans. In a bureaucratic context, Mann's survey of school administrators found minority administrators twice as likely as white administrators to see their roles as delegates or politicos rather than trustees (1974, p. 310). The socialization linkage of representation, therefore, is appropriate to this study if policy indicators are used that can be directly linked to ethnicity.

This chapter examines the descriptive representativeness of three groups of individuals—school board members, school administrators, and teachers. In each case the linkage between passive and active representation is somewhat different. For school board members, the most likely linkage is from elections (but see Prewitt 1970). Since high-level school administrators serve at the pleasure of the school board but lower-level administrators are isolated from this direct electoral pressure, the linkage for administrators is likely a combination of elections and socialization. For teachers, protected by tenure, union contracts, or other civil service rules, the representation linkage operates through socialization. This chapter only examines passive representation; active representation is covered in chapter 5.

School Board Representation

Levels of Minority Representation

Compared to the massive literature on black representation in urban governments, the representation literature for Hispanics is modest. Notwithstanding the few studies, both city councils and school boards have been examined to determine if they are representative of Hispanics in a passive sense. These representation studies measure passive representation in two ways. Initially, virtually all studies calculated the *representation index*. The representation index is merely the percentage of Hispanics on the city council or school board divided by the percentage of Hispanics in the jurisdiction's population (Subramaniam 1967). The attractiveness of this index is its interpretation. When Hispanics have political representation exactly equal to their population percentage, the index equals one. When Hispanics are underrepresented, the index is less than one and specifies the exact percentage of underrepresentation. Similarly, when Hispanics are overrepresented, the index is greater than one, and shows the exact percentage of overrepresentation.

The representation index is a useful measure, but it has one significant flaw. When the percentage of Hispanic population is small, any representation at all results in extremely large numbers that distort the index. Gradually, the consensus approach has shifted from the representation index to the Engstrom/McDonald regression approach. Engstrom and McDonald (1981) estimate the representation relationship by using the minority population percentage as an independent variable in a regression that predicts the percentage of minority representation. The regression slope for this regression is similar to the representation index but is less sensitive to extreme values.

If the intercept of this regression is close to zero, then the regression coefficient can be interpreted similarly to the representation index. A slope of 1.0 means that Hispanics hold exactly the percentage of seats that their population warrants. A slope of less than one indicates underrepresentation, and a slope greater than one implies overrepresentation.

To provide a comparative context for our results, the meager past research in this area merits noting. Using the central cities associated with the nation's SMSAs in 1970, Taebel (1978) examined the sixty cities with sufficient Hispanic population to constitute a majority in one electoral district if the city were divided into electoral wards. Taebel found a mean representation index of .44 for Hispanics on the city councils of these cities (that is, Hispanics had approximately 44 percent of the representation that one would expect given their numbers) (p. 145). Using a mail survey of 124 cities of 25,000 people with at least 10 percent Hispanic population in California, Arizona, Colorado, New Mexico, and Texas, Karnig and Welch calculated a city council representation ratio of .45 (1979, p. 469).[3]

The only study to examine Hispanic representation on school boards is Fraga, Meier, and England (1986). Their sample includes school districts with 25,000 or more students and at least 5 percent Hispanic population. This sample limits them to thirty-five extremely large school districts in all parts of the country. Using the Engstrom/McDonald regression approach, they estimate the representation index at .77 (p. 858).

The seats-population relationship for our set of school districts is shown in Table 4–1. The equation shows Hispanics doing significantly better than other studies have shown. The slope indicates that Hispanics attain 86 percent of the school board seats that one would expect, given their population percentage. In short, Hispanic representation on these school boards falls short by only 14 percent. This representation level, however, is qualified by a threshold effect. A significant intercept (-5.5) implies Hispanics receive no representation when their numbers are small (e.g., when population is less than 6.5 percent, or 5.5 ÷.859). At any given level of Hispanic population, therefore, Hispanic representation is 5.5 percentage points less than the expected 86 percent of the population.

Table 4–1   Hispanic School Boards: The Seats-Population Relationship

School Board Seats = -5.55 + .859 (Hispanic Population)
$r^2 = .60$ F = 205.46   N = 137

Representation and Political Reform

Perhaps no aspect of urban representation is more controversial than electoral structure. As part of the progressive era reforms of urban governments in the early twentieth century, an effort was made to take politics out of city government. Elections are held at times different from national elections, many local elections are nonpartisan, and city manager government and at-large elections were adopted (Lineberry and Fowler 1967; Davidson and Korbel 1981). If anything, the reform movement was more successful with school districts than it was with cities. Independent school districts were created to sever the political ties of cities to schools. Virtually all school district elections are nonpartisan, and the overwhelming majority use at-large elections. The separation of partisan politics from education was completed by hiring a professional administrator to run the schools (Tyack 1974, 127).

Much research has documented the harmful effects of the urban reforms on minority representation. The focus of criticism has been the use of at-large elections. By requiring candidates to run at-large rather than in smaller electoral districts, a candidate must attract a majority from the entire school district/city rather than a smaller electoral ward. Since Hispanics are segregated somewhat in urban areas, at-large elections often mean an Anglo majority, whereas ward elections would have at least some wards with an Hispanic majority.[4]

Almost every study to examine the impact of at-large elections has found that they have a detrimental impact on minorities.[5] Taebel correlated minority representation with electoral structure and found a positive correlation of .285 for Hispanics (1978, p. 147).[6] He interprets this finding to mean that a weak relationship exists between ward elections and more Hispanics on the city council.[7] The detrimental impact of at-large elections, further evidence shows, is not as great for Hispanics as it is for blacks. Taebel attributes this finding to a lower level of residential segregation for Hispanics than for blacks (see Lopez 1981 on residential segregation). Examining ten Texas cities that shifted city council elections from at-large to ward, Polinard and Wrinkle (1988) found that the change to ward elections increased Hispanic representation.

The Fraga, Meier, and England study of school boards uses the regression approach to examine the impact of electoral structure on school board representation (1986, p. 858). They find that compared to ward elections, at-large elections reduce Hispanic representation by 2.6 percent while appointive systems reduce Hispanic representation by 6.3 percent. Neither coefficient is statistically significant. Polinard, Wrinkle and Longoria, on the other hand, find that district elections have a statistically significant positive impact on Hispanic school board representation when Hispanics are a minority of the population (1988, p. 11).

Engstrom and McDonald (1982) have argued that population and electoral structure have an interaction effect on representation. The appropriate way to assess this relationship, they contend, is to set up dummy variables for various electoral structures, multiply these dummy variables by the percentage of minority population, and observe the difference in regression coefficients.[8] Such a regression is presented in Table 4–2. Interpreting each slope similarly to the interpretation from Table 4-1, provides a striking conclusion. Subject to a threshold effect of 5.87 percent, ward elections result in a six percent overrepresentation of Hispanics on school boards, and appointed systems produce a five percent overrepresentation. As predicted, at-large elections retard representation, with Hispanics underrepresented by 21 percent in at-large systems in addition to a 5.87 percent threshold. The difference in regression coefficients between the ward systems and the at-large systems is statistically significant.[9]

In chapter 1 we argued that Hispanic representation on school boards is a function of four variables. Two of these variables have already been introduced—Hispanic population and selection plan. The other two variables are Hispanic resources and social class. Hispanic resources, in theory, are needed for political mobilization. Although Karnig and Welch did not find that Hispanic resources were related to Hispanic election to city council seats (1979, p. 471), a logical relationship between the two exists.[10] Hispanic resources other than pure numbers are operationalized as the percentage of Hispanics over the age of twenty-five with a high school education. Since educational attainment has long been linked to increased voting participation (Verba and Nie 1972), this resource should indicate greater voter mobilization. The percentage of Anglos living in poverty is our social class indicator for the Giles/Evans/Feagin power thesis, which argues that the Anglo establishment will seek to isolate itself from poor Anglos as well as poor Hispanics (Giles and Evans 1985; Giles and Evans 1986; Feagin 1980; Denton and Massey 1988).

Table 4–2   The Impact of Electoral Structure on
                   Hispanic Representation

Dependent Variable = Percent Hispanics on School Board

Independent Variable	Slope	t-score
Ward * (Hispanic Population)	1.064	12.00
Appointed * (Hispanic Population)	1.049	3.48
At-Large * (Hispanic Population)	.794	12.77

R^2 =	.63
Adjusted R^2 =	.62
F	75.62
N	137
Intercept	-5.87

Table 4–3 presents the five-variable model of Hispanic political representation. Although the level of explanation does not greatly improve and the threshold (e.g., the intercept) jumps dramatically, each variable is statistically significant in the correct direction. Each additional one percentage point of the Hispanic population that graduates from high school is associated with a .24 percentage point increase in school board representation. An increase of one percentage point in Anglo poverty produces a .80 percentile increase in Hispanic representation. The findings of electoral structure interacting with population remain generally the same; the representation coefficients are .96 for ward elections, .88 for appointive systems, and .68 for at-large election systems. The detrimental impact of at-large elections remains even with controls for Anglo poverty and Hispanic resources.

Table 4–3   Hispanic Representation as Function of
                   Electoral Structure and Hispanic Resources

Dependent Variable = Percent Hispanics on School Board

Independent Variable	Slope	t-score
Ward * (Hispanic Population)	.96	9.00
Appointed * (Hispanic Population)	.88	2.80
At-Large * (Hispanic Population)	.68	8.13
Hispanic High School Education	.24	2.45
Percent Anglos Below Poverty	.80	2.70

R^2	.65
Adjusted R^2	.64
F	49.72
Intercept	-22.66
N	137

Minorities and Selection Plan

The literature linking electoral structure to minority representation has always assumed that the racial/ethnic minority in question is a numerical minority. Since our concern is with the Hispanic representation as a way to explore theories of political
representation, we did not limit our analysis to only school districts with a Hispanic minority. In fact, fourteen of our districts are
more than 50 percent Hispanic. Table 4–4 shows that Hispanics
do fairly well in districts where they constitute a majority of the
population, even if at-large elections are used.[11] If Hispanics attain
a voting majority in school board elections, then at-large elections
should help them gain additional representation, just as it does for
other groups with a majority of voters.

Defining when Hispanics have a majority of school district voters is not straightforward. Using the percentage of Hispanics
among those eligible to vote may not be the best way. Although
low turnout for Hispanic voters has often been cited (Wrinkle and
Miller 1984, 310), other evidence suggests that Hispanics are as
likely to vote as Anglos are (MacManus, Bullock, and Grothe 1986,
607). The more important political factor is that school board elections have extremely low turnout. Taebel discovered that only 4.6
percent of eligible voters cast ballots in the Texas school board
elections that he studied (1977, p. 157); Minar found 8.7 percent
turnout in forty-eight Illinois school board elections (1966, p.
824).[12] Crow estimated about 10 percent turnout for Arizona
school board elections (1971, p. 33).

Table 4–4   **School Districts with Hispanic Majorities**

District	% Hispanic Population	% School Board Seats Hispanic	Selection Plan
Montebello Unified, CA	67	20	At-Large
Edgewood Independent, TX	79	86	At-Large
San Antonio, TX	62	71	Ward
El Paso Independent, TX	57	29	Ward
Baldwin Park Unified, CA	59	20	At-Large
Bassett Unified, CA	64	50	Ward
El Monte, CA	50	0	At-Large
El Rancho Unified, CA	75	71	At-Large
Gadsden Independent, NM	71	60	At-Large
Santa Fe Public, NM	56	80	At-Large
Kingsville Independent, TX	54	14	At-Large
Pharr-San Juan-Alamo, TX	85	100	At-Large
South San Antonio, TX	73	86	Ward
Weslaco Independent, TX	83	57	At-Large

Given such low turnout levels, a school district with fewer than 50 percent Hispanic voters may well have an Hispanic voting majority if many Anglos do not go to the polls. Turnout is a function of interest in the election (Wolfinger and Rosenstone 1980, 8). Just as black candidates increase the interest of blacks in an election (Pettigrew 1976), the presence of Hispanic candidates likely also increases Hispanic turnout.[13] Perhaps the greatest motivating factor in increasing turnout in a school board election is for an individual to have children in the school system.[14] An individual without children, or with children in a private school system, has little reason to vote in a school board election. In the only study of individual voters in a school board election, Taebel found 52.1 percent of the voters had children in the school system (1977, p. 158).[15]

Our argument suggests that as Anglo enrollment in a school district declines, so will Anglo turnout in school board elections. Hispanics, therefore, might attain a voting majority in school board elections while remaining an overall minority in the school district. In Table 4–5 we attempt to estimate the point where an Hispanic voting majority occurs. By using the percentage Hispanic in the district to predict the percentage Hispanic in the student body, the regression coefficient and intercept show that student enrollment percentages run about 24 percent above population percentages. Solving this equation for a 50 percent majority in the student body (and thus the implied 50 percent voting majority) reveals that school districts with 38 percent Hispanic population have on the average 50 percent Hispanic enrollment.[16]

Table 4–5   The Relationship Between Hispanic Students
and Hispanic Population

Dependent Variable = Percent Hispanic Students

Independent Variable	Slope	t-score
Hispanic Population*	1.20	35.25

Intercept	3.97
r^2	.90
F	1242.74
N	138

*estimated Population Percent that Produces a Majority = 38

To investigate the impact of electoral structure on Hispanic minorities, the five-variable regression equation from Table 4–3 was reestimated for only those districts with less than 38 percent Hispanic population. Table 4–6 shows that the impact of at-large elections is much more severe when Hispanics are clearly a minority than when they have the potential to become an electoral majority. In at-large elections, Hispanics are able to attain only 46 percent of the representation predicted based on their population. This 46 percent compares unfavorably with the 88 percent representation Hispanics attain in ward systems and the 78 percent they attain in appointive systems.[17] The detrimental impacts of at-large elections on Hispanics are especially clear in school districts where Hispanics are a numerical minority of the voting electorate.

Table 4–6   Hispanic School Board Representation: Districts
with an Hispanic Voting Minority

Dependent Variable = Percent Hispanic School Board Seats

Independent Variables	Slope	t-score
Ward * (Hispanic Population)	.88	5.86
Appointed * (Hispanic Population)	.78	2.95
At-Large * (Hispanic Population)	.46	4.01
Hispanic High School Education	.13	1.55
Percent Anglos Below Poverty	.42	1.20

R^2	.29
Adjusted R^2	.26
F	9.05
Intercept	-11.77
N	118

Representation of Mexican Americans, Puerto Ricans and Cubans

In chapter 2 we argued that Hispanics cannot be considered a single monolithic group and that the political experiences of Hispanics vary greatly. The nature of our data set allows us to examine the differences in political representation for three of the major Hispanic groups in the United States—Mexican Americans, Puerto Ricans, and Cuban Americans. The school districts in our study were divided into three groups, depending on which Hispanic group was the largest. Although the overwhelming majority of the school districts were characterized as Mexican-American, sufficient Cuban-American and Puerto Rican districts exist to make some preliminary observations.

Table 4–7 shows the school board representation in Mexican-American, Puerto Rican, and Cuban-American school districts. Mexican-American districts achieve the best school board representation, with 13.3 percent of the school board seats, while both Puerto Rican and Cuban-American districts attain 9.5 percent. Such raw figures are misleading, however, since the three groups vary a great deal in terms of numbers, resources, and types of community where they reside.

Table 4–7   **Representation Levels for Mexican-American, Puerto Rican, and Cuban-American School Districts**

	Districts that are Predominantly		
	Mexican-American	Puerto Rican	Cuban-American
School Board Representation	13.3%	9.5%	9.5%
Administrator Representation	13.8%	3.2%	7.4%
Teacher Representation	12.6%	5.6%	7.9%
Number of Districts	117	17	3

The first major factor that needs to be controlled in assessing the relative representation of the three Hispanic groups is population size. Similar to the method of assessing the impact of electoral structures, representation measures were determined by a regression with an interaction between Hispanic population and the type of district it is (i.e., Mexican-American, Puerto Rican, Cuban-American). In addition, two dummy variables are added to this equation to hold constant the impact of electoral structure.[18]

Table 4–8 reveals the representation coefficients for the three Hispanic subgroups. Predominantly Mexican-American school districts achieve a representation ratio of .87, compared to .75 for Puerto Rican districts and .70 for predominantly Cuban-American districts. (Note also the significant positive impact of ward elections). These representation figures, while more revealing than those in Table 4–7, still do not show the entire pattern. Since Hispanics residing in Cuban-American districts are better educated and likely to have more political resources than either Mexican Americans or Puerto Ricans, a true representation picture will only be discerned when appropriate controls are entered.[19]

Table 4–8   **Representation Levels for Mexican-American, Puerto Rican and Cuban-American Districts and Type of Selection Plan**

Dependent Variable = Percent Hispanic School Board Members

Independent Variable	Slope	t-score
Population * Mexican-American District	.87*	14.66
Population * Puerto Rican District	.75*	3.90
Population * Cuban-American District	.70*	1.99
Ward Elections	5.83*	2.30
Appointive Selection	7.93	1.57

$R^2 = .63$ Adjusted $R^2 = .61$ F = 43.68   N = 137
Intercept = -7.63

*p <.05

In Table 4–9, the representation slopes are reestimated with the addition of controls for Hispanic resources (high school graduation percentage) and Anglo poverty. The resulting regression coefficients are highly revealing. When controls for the greater resources of Cuban Americans are introduced, their representation ratio drops to .53, compared to ratios of .60 for Puerto Rican districts and .76 for Mexican-American districts. The access of Cuban Americans to school board representation, therefore, is well below expectations, given the higher level of resources available to them.[20] Mexican Americans are clearly the most successful group in mobilizing their numbers to produce representation, a result consistent with the literature on greater ethnic identification among Mexican Americans than among Cuban Americans. Puerto Ricans actually do better than Cuban Americans when their lower levels of income and education are considered.

Table 4–9   **School Board Representation for Mexican Americans,
Puerto Ricans, and Cuban Americans**

Dependent Variable = Percent Hispanic School Board Members

Independent Variables	Slope	t-score
Population * Mexican-American District	.76*	8.82
Population * Puerto Rican District	.60*	2.58
Population * Cuban-American District	.53	1.52
Hispanic Education	.25*	2.41
Percent Anglos Below Poverty	.81*	2.60
Ward Elections	6.19*	2.41
Appointment Selection	6.91	1.40

R^2	.65
Adjusted R^2	.63
F	34.27
N	137
Intercept	-24.87

*p <.05

Rainbow Coalitions or Anglo Cooptation

In their analysis of minority political incorporation in ten Northern California cities, Browning, Marshall, and Tabb (1984) argue
that Hispanic incorporation [representation] is best achieved by
coalitions with blacks and liberal whites. Their findings call for a
cooperative strategy among minority groups. Analyses of several
major cities using the Browning, Marshall, and Tabb approach,
however, have failed to find cooperative rainbow coalitions in
Miami, Boston, and other large cities (Travis 1986; Warren, Stack,
and Corbett 1986). Early public opinion surveys of Los Angeles
and San Antonio, in fact, find three-fourths of Hispanics rejecting
political coalitions with blacks (Grebler, Moore, and Guzman 1970,
569). Our theoretical approach also calls into question the promise
of rainbow coalitions. The power thesis of intergroup relations
holds that groups compete and that conflict is a function of social
distance between groups. This thesis implies that Anglo politicians
will seek to prevent a rainbow coalition that would displace them
from political power. The power thesis predicts that they would be
most likely to seek a coalition with the group or groups that most
resemble themselves. If the dominant Anglo group is forced to
chose between Hispanic and black groups for coalition purposes,
the power thesis suggests that, all things being equal, they will

seek a coalition with Hispanics. Because Hispanics, especially middle-class Hispanics, are more likely to "pass" as Anglo, they share more similarities with the Anglo majority than blacks do.

Some case study support exists for the power thesis rather than the rainbow coalition hypothesis. In Miami, Cuban Americans have established political control that is essentially conservative and supportive of Anglo economic institutions while blacks remain unrepresented (Warren, Stark, and Corbett 1986). The election of Hispanic mayors in both San Antonio and Denver[21] resulted in moderate mayors that were supportive of Anglo business interests.[22] While Hispanics were part of Harold Washington's coalition in Chicago (Santillan 1988a: 112), most Hispanics left that coalition to support Richard Daley after Washington's death.

Distinguishing between the rainbow incorporation thesis and the power thesis empirically is somewhat difficult. The power thesis holds that, as black voters increase their position in the electorate, Anglos would be more supportive of Hispanic candidates and Hispanics would gain additional representation. Similarly, the rainbow incorporation thesis holds that, as black voters increase, the potential of rainbow coalitions increase and the correlation of black population with Hispanic representation should be positive.

The critical test for choosing between the rainbow incorporation thesis and the power thesis is what happens to black representation as Hispanic numbers increase. The power thesis holds that an increase in Hispanic population would be unlikely to increase Anglo votes for blacks because blacks are less similar to Anglos than Hispanics are. The relationship between black population and Hispanic representation in this case should be negative. The rainbow coalition thesis, on the other hand, contends that as Hispanic population increases, the potential for a rainbow coalition increases. The correlation between Hispanic population and black representation, therefore, should be positive.

Tables 4–10 and 4–11 show two different models of black and Hispanic representation, using different measures for the impact of electoral structure. The top regression in both tables reveals that the correlation between black population and Hispanic representation is positive, exactly as both theses predict. The bottom tables reveal that Hispanic population is negatively related to black representation. This finding is consistent with the power thesis and inconsistent with the rainbow coalition.

Table 4–10   **Racial Group Competition for School Board Seats**

Hispanic School Board Members

Independent Variables	Slope
Percent Hispanic Population	.829*
Hispanic High School Education, Percentage	.310*
Percent Anglos Below Poverty	.646*
Ward Elections for the School Board	7.167*
Appointed Selection for School Board	1.549
Percent Black Population	.184#

$R^2 = .66$ Adjusted $R^2 = .65$ $F = 42.07$ $N = 136$
Intercept = -29.83

Black School Board Members

Independent Variables	Slope
Percent Hispanic Population	-.123#
Black High School Education, Percentage	.077
Percent Anglos Below Poverty	.503*
Ward Elections for School Board	1.298
Appointed Selection for School Board	-3.978
Percent Black Population	1.005*

$R^2 = .65$ Adjusted $R^2 = .64$ $F = 40.19$ $N = 136$
Intercept = -7.07

*p <.05
#p<.1

Although the results of Tables 4–10 and 4–11 directly challenge the rainbow incorporation thesis, more studies are needed before a definitive conclusion is possible. The tables provide one additional bit of information that reflects on the issue. Previous research has shown that appointive school board systems are based on a "fair share" allocation to groups that supported the winning coalition (Robinson, England, and Meier 1985). If Anglos are likely to form coalitions with Hispanics in preference to blacks, we would expect to see appointive selection processes produce higher Hispanic representation but lower black representation. The regressions shown in Table 4–10 show exactly this result. Appointive systems increase Hispanic representation and decrease black representation.[23] The power thesis again gains support.[24]

Table 4–11   A Second View of Intergroup Competition for
School Board Seats

Hispanic School Board Members

Independent Variables	Slope
Ward Election * Hispanic Population Percentage	1.014*
Appointed * Hispanic Population Percentage	.673*
At-Large Elections * Hispanic Population Percentage	.730*
Hispanic High School Education Percentage	.282*
Percent Anglos Below Poverty	.710*
Percent Black Population	.166#

$R^2 = .67$ Adjusted $R^2 = .65$ $F = 43.47$ $N = 136$
Intercept = -26.45

Black School Board Members

Independent Variables	Slope
Ward Election * Black Population Percentage	1.086*
Appointed * Black Population Percentage	.694*
At-Large Elections * Black Population Percentage	1.023*
Black High School Education Percentage	.070
Percent Anglos Below Poverty	.535*
Percent Hispanic Population	-.129*

$R^2 = .66$ Adjusted $R^2 = .64$ $F = 41.96$ $N = 136$
Intercept = -6.62

*p <.05
#p <.1

The Representation of Hispanic Administrators

The policy-making literature frequently demonstrates that administrators exercise discretion just as elected officials do (Rourke 1984). Because bureaucratic discretion exists, the representativeness of bureaucracy becomes an important political question (Mosher 1968). Since education is a policy area where administrative officials have been highly successful in defining a set of decisions as their own professional prerogative (Tucker and Zeigler 1980) and since school boards are rarely full-time positions, bureaucratic discretion among school administrators is perhaps even greater than discretion in other bureaucracies. As a result of the linkage between discretion and representation, representation in educational bureaucracies should be a major focus of study.

Although only one study has examined the Hispanic representativeness of school administrators, the literature on representative bureaucracy is extensive. Much of this literature measures racial (mostly blacks) or other demographic representation. The literature concerning Hispanics is much smaller. In a series of articles, Lee Sigelman and his colleagues have documented the representation of Hispanics in state and local governments. Cayer and Sigelman found a representation ratio of .86 for Hispanic males and .42 for Hispanic females for all state and local governments (1980, p. 445). Hispanic employment, however, is not uniformly distributed across levels of government; as one would expect, Hispanics are concentrated at lower levels of the bureaucracy. For 1980, Dometrius and Sigelman calculated Hispanic representation ratios of .65 for all employees, .48 for technical and professional employees, and .37 for managers (1984, p. 244).[25]

For employment at state government levels only, Dometrius discovered Hispanic representation ratios of .47 for all employees, .28 for second-line officials, and .15 for top leaders in 1978 (1984, p. 129). Using a sample of twenty-five Texas cities, Hall and Saltzstein found a representation ratio of .59 for all employees (1977, p. 866). Welch, Karnig, and Eribes show only a slight underrepresentation of Hispanics in city government (1983, p. 666), but they use a different measure of representation which is difficult to compare to the representation ratio. Finally, Dye and Renick report data that produces the following ratios: .31 for administrators, .42 for professionals and protective workers, .69 for office workers, and 1.51 for service workers (mostly maintenance) (1981). In sum, past studies of representative bureaucracy reveal Hispanics to be underrepresented in government employment except at the lowest levels of the bureaucracy (see also Mladenka 1989b).

Data reported by the U.S. Bureau of the Census (1989) permit us to update the representation ratios reported by others. Table 4–12 shows the Hispanic representation ratios of city and state governments combined, and Table 4–13 shows the representation ratios for the federal government. In both cases the familiar pattern of underrepresentation appears, and most Hispanics are concentrated at the bottom of the bureaucratic hierarchy.

Table 4–14 shows the 1986 Hispanic representation ratios for the set of school districts in this study. The Hispanic administrators' ratio of .39, showing 61 percent underrepresentation, is consistent with the previous figures on bureaucratic representation. In comparison, this representation ratio is only about one-half that for black school administrators for a comparable set of school districts (Meier, Stewart, and England 1989, 73). One reason why black representation is significantly higher for school administrative positions is related to segregation. Because several states maintained segregated school systems for blacks, many blacks held teaching and administrative positions in all-black schools. Black institutions of higher education such as Fisk, Morehouse, and Howard provided training for future teachers and other professionals. Despite the segregation of Hispanics in the southwest, no Hispanic institutions of higher education were established. So while segregation provided some avenues of upward mobility for blacks, it did not provide them for Hispanics.

Table 4–12   Representation Levels of Hispanics: State and
Local Government Employment

Type of Position	Representation Ratio
Administrators/Officials	.35
Professionals	.47
Technicians	.62
Protective Services	.65
Paraprofessionals	.64
Clerical	.84
Skilled Craft	.81
Service/Maintenance	1.08

Source: U.S. Bureau of the Census, 1989: p. 294; and authors' calculations.

Table 4–13   Hispanic Representation in
Federal Government Employment

Level	Representation Ratio
Wage Board	.88
GS 1–4	.69
GS 5–8	.57
GS 9–12	.46
GS 13–15	.25
Executives	.17
All Federal Employees	.58

Source: U.S. Bureau of the Census, 1989: p. 321; and authors' calculations.

The process by which Hispanic administrators are hired is linked to politics in the school district. According to our theory in chapter 1, Hispanic access to administrative positions generally follows a pattern similar to Hispanic access to school board seats, with a few modest differences. Hispanic administrators should be a function of Hispanic resources (education and population) and

Anglo poverty. Since selection plans for the school should not directly affect the selection of administrators, that variable is omitted. In its place, the percentage of Hispanic school board members is used.

Table 4–14   Hispanic and Anglo Teacher and Administrator Ratios

| Year | Hispanics | | Anglos | |
	Mean	Standard Deviation	Mean	Standard Deviation
TEACHERS				
1968	.20	.19	1.55	1.32
1969	.18	.17	1.76	1.54
1970	.21	.18	1.66	1.47
1971	.22	.18	1.76	1.61
1972	.24	.17	1.76	1.77
1986	.38	.23	2.36	2.07
ADMINISTRATORS				
1986	.39	.32	2.51	3.68

The relationship of minority elected officials to the subsequent access of minorities to government jobs has been demonstrated in the research literature. Much of this work, however, focuses solely on blacks (Eisinger 1982a, 390). Dye and Renick, who examine Hispanics, conclude: "The single most important determinant of Hispanic employment in cities is Hispanic representation on city councils" (1981, p. 483). Although political representation appears to be more important for upper-level administrative jobs than for lower-level ones, the relationship remains significant even with controls for Hispanic population, city size, per capita income, and median education (p. 484). Polinard, Wrinkle, and Longoria in their study of Texas districts find school board representation positively correlated with Mexican-American school administrators (1988, p. 12).

Our four-variable model of bureaucratic representation predicts reasonably well for Hispanic school administrators, accounting for three-fifths of the variance (Table 4–15). Unfortunately, only two variables, Hispanic population and school board membership, are statistically significant.[26] The regression coefficients reveal that Hispanics attain 59 percent of the representation among school district administrators that one would expect, given their population (the intercept is negligible, so no threshold exists). In addition, for each percentage point increase in Hispanic school board representation, Hispanic administrative representation increases by .16 percentage points. Another way to express the political linkage is that the addition of one Hispanic representative to a five-person school board translates into a 3.2 percentage point increase in Hispanic administrators, all other things being equal. Political representation is related to bureaucratic representation.

Table 4–15   Determinants of Hispanic Administrative Representation

Dependent Variable = Percent Hispanic Administrators

Independent Variables	Full Model	Reduced Model
Hispanic Population Percentage	.52*	.59*
Hispanic School Board Members	.13#	.16*
Hispanic Education	.09	— a
Percent Anglos Below Poverty	.59	— a
Intercept	-10.16	-1.71
R²	.61	.59
Adjusted R²	.59	.59
F	49.04	94.13
N	133	133

ᵃEquation reestimated omitting this variable.
*p <.05
#p <.1

Representative bureaucracy varies across the various Hispanic communities. As Table 4–7 showed, school districts that were predominantly Mexican-American had proportionally as many administrators as school board members (13.8 percent versus 13.3 percent). Cuban-American districts did relatively less well, with only 7.4 percent administrators (compared to 9.5 percent board members); and Puerto Rican districts fared least well with only 3.2 percent administrators (versus 9.5 percent board members).

The differences in administrative representation are clearly presented by the four-variable model of representation in Table 4–16. The reduced model shows that Hispanics in predominantly Mexican-American districts have 62 percent of the bureaucratic representation that their numbers would suggest; Puerto Rican districts have only 11 percent, and Cuban-American districts 35 percent. Representation on the school board remains a significant factor in this regression, showing that school board members coexist in districts with higher Hispanic representation in the school bureaucracy.[27]

Table 4-16   **Determinants of Administrative Representation for Mexican-American, Puerto Rican and Cuban-American Districts**

Dependent Variable = Percent Hispanic Administrators

Independent Variables	Full Model	Reduced Model
Population * Mexican-American District	.47*	.62*
Population * Puerto Rican District	-.22	.11
Population * Cuban-American District	.22	.35
Hispanic School Board Members	.10	.14*
Percent Anglos Below Poverty	.95*	— a
Hispanic Education	.05	— a
Intercept	-9.17	-.97
R²	.66	.63
Adjusted R²	.65	.62
F	41.16	54.13
N	133	133

ᵃEquation reestimated omitting this variable.

*p <.05

#p <.1

Hispanic Teachers

Because higher-level administrators are more likely to make policy decisions, representative bureaucracy has generally been concerned with the upper reaches of the bureaucracy. The representativeness of "street-level bureaucrats" (Lipsky 1980), however, is also important. No organization can operate without vesting some discretion in the individuals who interact with clientele. Teachers, the equivalent of implementation bureaucrats in a school system, use discretion when they apply guidelines issued by administrators or policies passed by the school board. Someone must decide if a particular policy is applicable in a given situation, and that person is usually a teacher. In addition, contact between lower-level administrators and clients is often facilitated if administrators are representative of the clients. Just as black teachers have a greater understanding of the problems and needs of black students (Silver 1973), we would expect Hispanic teachers to be more receptive to the special needs of Hispanic students (So 1987a; see also Smith and June 1982, 232). Finally, a representative bureaucracy at lower levels implies an openness of government to all individuals. Hispanic teachers can serve as role models to Hispanic students and illustrate the potential of succeeding in the education system (Thomas and Brown 1982, 168).

As noted above, Hispanics are not well represented in state and local bureaucracies; the exception is lower-level positions. Only among service workers did Dye and Renick (1981) find that Hispanics reached or exceeded parity in public-sector jobs. For teachers, a pattern of underrepresentation continues. Garcia and Espinosa presented data that reveal a representation ratio of only .21 for all California schools (1977, p. 220). In a more comprehensive study of Hispanic teachers, Fraga, Meier, and England, studying thirty-five large city school districts, calculated a representation slope of .27 (1986, p. 860). Hispanics held only about one quarter of the teaching slots that one would expect, given their population.[28]

Hispanic representation among teachers has improved greatly since the 1971 data used in the Fraga, Meier, and England study. Table 4–14 showed that the teacher representation ratio increased from .20 in 1968 to .38 in 1986. Although this growth is impressive given the dramatic increase in the number of Hispanic students, the representation ratio still lags far behind parity.

A more informative look at Hispanic teachers is revealed in Table 4–17, the multivariate analysis of Hispanic teacher representation. Using the model explaining Hispanic administrators, but adding the proportion of Hispanic administrators as an independent variable, Table 4–17 predicts the proportion of Hispanic teachers. Three hypothesized forces are significant—Hispanic population, Hispanic administrators, and Anglo poverty; and the model predicts fairly well (86 percent). Of these variables, Hispanic population is the least influential. The role of Hispanic administrators is aptly demonstrated by the regression coefficient that predicts a one percentage point increase in Hispanic administrators is associated with a .53 percentage point increase in Hispanic teachers. (This finding is consistent with Polinard, Wrinkle, and Longoria 1988, 13). The power thesis also comes into play. In districts with a large number of poor Anglos, Hispanic teachers are much more likely to be hired for teaching positions.[29]

The absence of a role for Hispanic school board members in attracting Hispanic teachers contradicts the findings of Fraga, Meier, and England (1986). In that research, Hispanic school board members were significantly associated with more Hispanic teachers. That research, however, did not have access to a measure of Hispanic administrators, the addition of which eliminates any direct impact for school board members. The impact of Hispanic school board members on teacher hiring, therefore, operates indirectly through increases in Hispanic administrators. That is, Hispanic school board members have a positive impact on the number of Hispanic teachers by affecting the number of Hispanic administrators.

Table 4–17   **Determinants of Hispanic Teacher Representation**

Dependent Variable = Percent Hispanic Teachers

Independent Variables	Full Model	Reduced Model
Hispanic Population	.15*	.12*
Hispanic School Board Members	-.05	— a
Hispanic School Administrators	.54*	.53*
Hispanic Education	.02	— a
Percent Anglos Below Poverty	.51*	.47*
Intercept	-4.40	-2.79
R²	.86	.86
Adjusted R²	.86	.86
F	154.30	256.99
N	130	130

ªEquation reestimated omitting this variable.
*p <.05
#p <.1

The ability of Hispanic teachers to gain school district employment also varies across the subgroups of Hispanics. Once again, Mexican-American districts have the best record with 12.6 percent of the teaching slots, while Cuban-American districts have 7.9 percent and Puerto Rican districts lag with 5.6 percent (see Table 4–7). To link these differences to previously established differences in administrative representation, the determinants of teacher representation were reestimated with controls for the predominant Hispanic group.

Table 4–18 demonstrates again the vital role of Hispanic administrators. When Hispanic subgroup is controlled, a one percentage point increase in Hispanic administrators increases the percentage of Hispanic teachers by almost .6 percentage points. Rather than faring as poorly as the raw figures suggest, Puerto Rican and Cuban-American districts do slightly better than Mexican-American districts when the level of Hispanic administrators is considered. The lower Hispanic teacher representation in Puerto Rican and Cuban-American districts is quite clearly related to lower levels of administrative representation. Neither Anglo poverty nor Hispanic education affects this relationship.[30]

Table 4–18   Determinants of Teacher Representation for Mexican-American, Puerto Rican and Cuban-American Districts

Dependent Variable = Percent Hispanic Teachers

Independent Variables	Full Model	Reduced Model
Population * Mexican-American District	.12*	.18*
Population * Puerto Rican District	.06	.26*
Population * Cuban-American District	.19	.25#
Hispanic Administrators	.52*	.58*
Anglos Below Poverty	.52*	— a
Hispanic Education	.01	— a
Intercept	-3.48	-.01
R^2	.86	.84
Adjusted R^2	.85	.84
F	126.47	169.58
N	130	130

[a]Equation reestimated omitting this variable.

*p $<.05$

#p $<.1$

Recruiting Hispanic Teachers

The large change in Hispanic teacher representation stands in stark contrast to the relative stability of black teacher representation over this time period. While the Hispanic representation ratio has doubled, the black ratio remained constant. The growth in Hispanic teacher representation suggests that examining the patterns of growth would be fruitful since it might provide some clue as to how to increase Hispanic teacher representation further.

Three factors immediately suggest themselves as variables to examine. First, much of the current political debate centers on the low pay in the teaching profession, thus implying that higher salaries will attract more individuals to teaching. Across districts, this assertion implies that districts with greater resources will be able to attract teachers from districts with fewer resources. Two measures of resources are used; the first is fairly direct: the median family income in the school district—which should be directly related to the district's tax base. The second measure, district size as measured by student enrollment, should be related to promotion opportunities for teachers.

Second, teachers may be enticed to transfer to a school district for social mobility reasons. A district with an Hispanic middle class should be more attractive to teaching professionals than one without such a middle class. The size of the Hispanic middle class is operationalized as the percent of the Hispanic population over age twenty-five with college degrees.[31]

Third, attracting Hispanic teachers might be a function of prior Hispanic representation, particularly Hispanic representation on the school board and among school administrators. The regression model in Table 4–19 uses these five variables to predict the change in the percentage of Hispanic teachers (the variable is the percentage Hispanic teachers in 1986 minus the percentage of Hispanic teachers in 1968). It shows that the attractiveness of the district is not a factor in increasing the percentage of Hispanic teachers; neither district size nor median income is related to Hispanic teacher change.

Table 4–19   Determinants of Changes in Hispanic Teachers

Dependent Variable = (Hispanic Teachers 1986 – Hispanic Teachers 1968)

Independent Variables	Full Model	Reduced Model
Hispanic Administrators	.47*	.47*
Hispanic School Board Members	-.07*	-.07*
Hispanic College Educated	-.30*	-.30*
District Size	-.00	— a
District Median Income	-.00	— a
R^2	.63	.63
Adjusted R^2	.62	.62
F	41.27	70.37
N	126	127

[a]Equations reestimated omitting this variable.
*$p < .05$
#$p < .1$

Once again, the dominant influence on attracting teachers over time is the same as the dominant influence in explaining representation: Hispanic administrators. Each percentage point increase in Hispanic administrators is associated with a .47 percentage point increase in Hispanic teachers between 1968 and 1986. This impact is twice the size of the impact of black administrators on recruiting black teachers (Meier, Stewart, and England 1989, 77).

Surprising in the analysis are the two negative relationships for Hispanic school board members and college education. The college education relationship shows that Hispanic teachers do not fare well in school districts with large Hispanic middle classes; this underscores the previous finding concerning Hispanic teachers being located in schools districts with larger proportions of Anglo poverty. The school boards relationship defies explanation.

The Impact of Immigration on Representation

Our assessment of Hispanic representation has not considered the impact of one crucial factor. Because Hispanics are continuing to immigrate either legally or illegally to the United States, many Hispanics are not citizens and, therefore, cannot vote. To investigate the impact of immigration on Hispanic representation, this section replicates some of the findings in this chapter and includes an immigration measure. We expect that immigration will be negatively correlated with Hispanic representation. As a measure of immigration, we will use the percentage of the local population who were born in either South or Central America.

Table 4–20 predicts Hispanic school board representation as a function of Hispanic resources (population and education), electoral structure, Anglo poverty, and immigration. Population is made to interact with structure. The immigration figure is highly significant, adding 9 percent explained variation to the model. An increase of one percentage point in Hispanic foreign-born population is associated with a 1.4 percentage point decline in school board representation.

Controlling for immigration has an interesting affect on the population coefficients. A one percentage point increase in Hispanic population is associated with a 1.265 percentage point increase in Hispanic representation in ward systems, 1.406 percentage points in appointive systems, and 1.005 percentage points in at-large systems. The respective coefficients, without controls for immigration, are .96 for wards, .88 for appointed systems, and .68 for at-large systems. Hispanics are better represented when immigration is considered because the immigration variable makes an adjustment for citizenship. One surprising finding is that appointive systems actually produce better relative representation than either wards or at-large systems. This may reflect the location of the appointive systems since these are in larger eastern cities that are more likely to have large numbers of immigrants. At-large elections still produce the least representation for Hispanics.

Table 4–20   Immigration and Hispanic School Board Representation

Dependent Variable = Percent Hispanics on School Board

Independent Variables	Slope	t-score
Ward Elections * Hispanic Population	1.265	11.67
Appointed * Hispanic Population	1.406	4.80
At-Large Elections * Hispanic Population	1.005	10.82
Hispanic High School Education	.202	2.31
Percent Anglos Below Poverty	.478	1.78
Percent Foreign-Born Hispanics	-1.410	5.89
R^2	.73	
Adjusted R^2	.72	
F	57.84	
N	137	
Intercept	-18.16	

Immigration is likely to affect Cuban Americans who are more recent immigrants to a greater extent than it affects either Mexican Americans or Puerto Ricans. Table 4–21 replicates Table 4–8 and includes the immigration variable. Immigration clearly depresses Cuban-American representation the most (the regression coefficient increases from .70 to 1.918, more than doubling). Mexican Americans, with the fewest foreign-born, are least affected by immigration (the coefficient increases from .87 to 1.194), with Puerto Ricans experiencing a similar modest impact (an increase from .75 to 1.081).

Table 4–21 underscores the impressive nature of Cuban-American political gains. When the recency of their immigration is considered, they achieve significantly higher levels of representation than other groups of Hispanics. Clearly the middle-class nature of the Cuban community allows Cubans to overcome many of the normal handicaps of immigration and gain political power faster than either Mexican Americans or Puerto Ricans. As more Cuban Americans become citizens, we can expect even greater Hispanic representation in these school districts.

The immigration status of Hispanics is also relevant to our discussion of rainbow coalitions. If Hispanics are recent immigrants, their economic and political position will more resemble that of blacks. Ethnic identification in the United States often is delayed for a period of time by an Americanization process until individuals become citizens. If this is the case, we would expect that immigration would be positively associated with black representation on school boards. Since Hispanic non-citizens could not form coalition partnerships with Anglos, blacks should benefit if more Hispanics are recent arrivals.

Table 4–21 Immigration and Representation in Different Hispanic Communities

Dependent Variable = Percent Hispanic on School Board

Independent Variable	Slope	t-score
Mexican District * Hispanic Population	1.194	17.00
Cuban District * Hispanic Population	1.918	5.40
Puerto Rican District * Hispanic Population	1.081	6.22
Ward Elections	5.454	2.49
Appointed Selection	10.527	2.39
Percent Foreign-Born Hispanic	-1.734	6.70
R^2	.72	
Adjusted R^2	.71	
F	56.08	
N	137	
Intercept	-6.89	

Table 4–22 replicates the bottom portion of Table 4–10; it predicts black school board representation as a function of black population, black political resources, electoral structure, Hispanic population, and Hispanic immigration. Our expectations are confirmed. Hispanic immigration is positively and significantly associated with black school board representation. In addition, Hispanic population has a larger and more significant negative impact on black representation. These findings suggest that black-Hispanic coalitions are less likely as the Hispanic community becomes more stable (i.e., experiences less immigration). Since Hispanic representation is depressed by recent immigration, these findings suggest that Hispanics will not only gain additional representation as their immigration becomes more distant, but also will be less likely to coalesce with blacks in a rainbow coalition.

Immigration might also affect Hispanic representation at bureaucratic levels. Table 4–23 includes immigration in a replication of our model of Hispanic administrative representation as a function of Hispanic population, school board representation, education, and

Anglo poverty. While immigration has a negative effect on Hispanic administrative representation, the impact is barely significant and adds almost nothing to the level of explained variation.

Table 4–22   The Impact of Hispanic Immigration
on Black Representation

Dependent Variable = Percent Black School Board Members

Independent Variables	Slope	t-score
Percent Hispanic Population	-.211	2.68
Percent Black High School Graduates	.067	1.10
Percent Anglos in Poverty	.574	2.65
Ward Elections	1.235	.71
Appointed Selection	-4.619	1.29
Percent Black Population	.987	12.82
Percent Foreign-Born Hispanic	.370	1.95
R^2	.66	
Adjusted R^2	.64	
F	35.74	
N	136	
Intercept	-6.74	

Table 4–23   The Impact of Immigration on
Administrative Representation

Dependent Variable = Percent Hispanic Administrators

Independent Variables	Slope	t-score
Percent Hispanic Population	.675	5.39
School Board Representation	.054	.64
Percent Hispanic High School Graduates	.093	1.08
Percent Anglos Below Poverty	.529	1.87
Percent Foreign-Born Hispanic	-.475	1.81
R^2	.62	
Adjusted R^2	.60	
F	40.59	
N	133	
Intercept	-9.79	

Table 4–24 provides an analysis of Hispanic teacher representation that includes immigration. In this case, immigration not only does not add any additional explanation (see Table 4–17), but it is positively associated with teacher representation. That is, as immigration increases, the proportion of Hispanic teachers increases. Tables 4–23 and 4–24 along with the results of the pre-

vious tables, suggests that immigration is a major factor affecting political representation of Hispanics on school boards. It does not appear to be a major direct influence on representation among administrators or among teachers. This finding makes some sense. Citizenship is required for voting, so many immigrants are not able to vote. Citizenship, however, is not required to work for a school as either a teacher or an administrator if education and other requirements are met by the individual.

Table 4–24   The Impact of Immigration on
                    Hispanic Teacher Representation

Dependent Variable = Percent Hispanic Teachers

Independent Variable	Slope	t-score
Percent Hispanic Population	.068	1.28
Percent Hispanic Administrators	.547	12.86
Percent Hispanic High School Graduates	.017	.42
Percent Anglos Below Poverty	.512	3.79
Percent Foreign-Born Hispanic	.193	1.71
R^2	.86	
Adjusted R^2	.86	
F	156.04	
N	130	
Intercept	-4.15	

This brief examination of immigration and its relationship to Hispanic representation should be viewed as only the first look at what is a complex phenomenon. Little theory exists in political science to guide an examination of immigration and the political process. What is clear from this preliminary look, however, is that immigration is an important factor in explaining Hispanic representation and must be considered in future analyses.

Conclusion

This chapter examined Hispanic representation for large urban school districts. Hispanics approach representational equity on school boards, but fall far short in terms of school administrators and teachers. More informative is the politics of representational equity for Hispanics. Access to school board seats for Hispanics is a function of Hispanic political resources (population and education), the electoral structure of the district, and higher levels of poverty among Anglos. At-large elections, particularly in those districts with an Hispanic voting minority, have a detrimental effect on Hispanic representation. Hispanic representation is also increased by a large black population. The analysis reveals that black-Hispanic coalitions are unlikely. As blacks become more numerous, Anglos become more supportive of Hispanics.

Administrative representation, in turn, was a function of resources (Hispanic population) and access to political positions (i.e., the school board). Hispanic teacher representation was associated with Hispanic resources (population), bureaucratic representation, and social class (large Anglo poverty). Growth in Hispanic teachers occurred most often in districts with Hispanic administrators.

This study is the first to contrast the political representation of Mexican Americans, Puerto Ricans, and Cuban Americans. When appropriate controls are introduced, Mexican Americans are best able to attain school board representation, while Puerto Rican and Cuban-American districts lag behind. Similarly, while all Hispanics do less well in administrative representation, Mexican Americans can point to moderate successes, while Cuban Americans and especially Puerto Ricans can point to few. Differences in administrator representation become the major explanation of intra-Hispanic differences in teacher representation. One explanation offered for this difference is the greater minority identification and the greater political development of the Mexican-American communities.

Many of the findings presented were also affected by the recent immigration of Hispanics to the United States. Recent immigration greatly depressed school board representation. At the same time, immigration had only a modest impact on administrator and teacher representation. Immigration and the resulting lower levels of citizenship, therefore, affects political representation, but only indirectly (through political representation) affects bureaucratic representation.

The core linkage of Hispanic representation is fairly simple. To get elected, Hispanics must have both citizens and an educated population to produce both candidates and voters. Their electoral prospects are best in districts with little recent immigration that uses ward elections and with an Anglo population that resides in poverty and a sizable black population so that upwardly mobile Hispanics are more likely to appeal to Anglo voters than are blacks or lower-class Anglos. Representation on the school board, in turn, has a major impact (along with population) on administrative representation. Administrative representation then becomes the best method of generating greater teacher representation.

With the pattern of representation established, the linkages between politics and bureaucracy becomes clear. Representation in one political institution is often helpful in gaining representation in other political institutions. What is done with this representation? Does it matter if a school district elects Hispanic board members, hires more Hispanic administrators, and recruits more Hispanic teachers? These questions are the subject of chapter 5.

Notes

1. Eulau et al.'s work also specified a third role, a politico who takes a position somewhat in between a delegate and a trustee. On the utility of these roles see Hedlund and Friesema 1972 and Friesema and Hedlund 1974.

2. One could tie electoral sanctions to bureaucrats if the government operated under a patronage system. In such a system, an electoral defeat would remove both the elected official and the bureaucrat. Alternatively, if elected officials had significant ways to reward or punish bureaucrats, the electoral threat could then be extended to the bureaucracy. The concept of *overhead democracy* (Redford 1969) is one such proposal to get greater bureaucratic responsiveness to the wishes of elected officials.

3. They also estimated a representation ratio of .34 for these cities in 1973 based on a secondary analysis of other data. The only other study to examine Hispanic representation on school boards is MacManus, who estimated that Hispanics were underrepresented by 2.8 percent (1978, p. 157). Since MacManus used a different measure of representation (the percentage difference) and since all 243 central cities with 50,000 population were included—even those with few Hispanics—others have discounted these findings (see Davidson and Korbel 1981).

4. Because blacks are more segregated in cities than are Hispanics (Lopez 1981, 54), the impact of at-large elections on blacks should be greater than it is for Hispanics. Fraga, Meier, and England reach this conclusion for school board elections (1986, p. 859).

5. See Davidson and Korbel (1981) for a review to 1981 and

a discussion of the exceptions. For those studies after 1981, see Meier, Stewart, and England (1989, p. 64).

6. Karnig and Welch, in contrast, found no relationship between district elections and Hispanic representation (1979, p. 475). Brouthers and McClure, using a set of cities in the southwest, argue that at-large elections actually help Hispanics gain representation (1984, p. 269).

7. A better way to examine this finding would be to present the representation indices for cities with various types of selection plans. No one to date has done this with the 243-case urban data set.

8. This is not a true interaction since the model assumes an interaction rather than tests for it. See Fraga, Meier, England (1986, footnote 6) for a more elaborate critique.

9. Table 4–2 assumes that the threshold is the same for each of the electoral systems. By allowing the intercepts as well as the slopes to vary, thresholds for each selection plan can be estimated. This regression estimates a threshold of 5.7 percent and a representation index of 1.06 for wards with an at-large threshold of 6.5 percent and an index of .81.

10. Most of the literature on black resources finds a significant relationship.

11. There are some exceptions. Montebello, California; Baldwin Park, California; El Monte, California; and Kingsville, Texas, have underrepresented Hispanics and at-large elections. El Paso, Texas, underrepresents Hispanics with ward elections. Without some further information as to the nature of school board politics in these districts, any explanation of this absence of a pattern in these districts would be pure speculation.

12. Sande Milton's (1983) assessment of turnout in school board elections argues that turnout is much higher than these numbers. Milton's analysis focuses on Florida elections, which are partisan and held on the same day as other partisan elections. In addition, she measures turnout by using rolloff percentages rather than total voting percentages. These differences make her figures less likely to be generalized than those of Taebel, Minar, or Crow.

13. One illustration of the increase in turnout as a result of Hispanic candidates is Shockley's (1974) case study of Crystal City,

Texas. When Hispanic candidates challenged the Anglo majority and when the La Raza Unida candidates made their initial challenge, turnout for city council and school board elections was greater than the turnout for the preceding presidential election.

14. We distinguish between school board elections and elections on school bond issues or education budget referendum. The literature on school bond issue elections (Cataldo and Holm 1983) finds that having children in school is a predictor of favorable voting, but not a strong predictor. A school bond issue election, by definition, is more salient than a school board election since many voters have an interest in low taxes. In addition, these studies try to predict actual vote rather than just turnout, the concern of our argument. School board elections should not attract such voters, making children in school a major determinant of turnout.

15. Most other voters either were employees of the school district or friends of one of the candidates running for the school board.

16. We may underestimate the break-even point since the size of Hispanic families is larger than the size of Anglo families. To make such a correction, one would have to include not only family size for Anglos and Hispanics, but also for blacks.

17. The lower level of explained variation is worthy of note. Hispanic population is not as good a predictor of election results when Hispanics are a minority. A similar regression for blacks explains 44 percent of the variation. We might speculate that this reflects variation in Hispanic mobilization, including variation in the percent of Hispanics who are citizens or are otherwise eligible to vote.

18. The use of a dummy variable for ward elections and another for appointive selections is more revealing than also having these variables interact with population as the earlier analysis did. When these variables also interact with population and are used as independent variables in the regression in Table 4-8, collinearity is so great that the regression coefficients become uninterpretable.

19. See Table 4–21 for the dramatic impact that recent immigration has on these coefficients.

20. This does not account for the lower level of citizenship

and the more recent immigration of most Cuban Americans. See Table 4–21 below.

21. Peña does well in black districts of Denver (Hero 1987), but the question remains concerning how responsive his policies have been to the black community.

22. Social class also plays a role here. In the Crystal City, Texas, case Anglos sought a coalition with middle-class Mexican Americans in opposition to more radical candidates from the Mexican-American working class (see Shockley 1974).

23. An interesting question is whether or not this relationship holds when blacks have greater numbers than they have in the cities in this study. In Meier and England's (1984) study of school board elections with large, heavily black cities, appointive election systems aided blacks. What we may be seeing here is what happens when the Hispanic and black population are relatively balanced rather than what happens when one or the other is the only large minority group.

24. The relationship of Hispanic representation to black representation raises an interesting question. The differences among Mexican Americans, Cuban Americans, and Puerto Ricans are often stressed in the literature. Some authors even attribute the lack of political impact of the Puerto Rican community to the large number of other Hispanics who reside in the same communities. Cuban Americans in Miami were part of a coalition that elected a Puerto Rican mayor but then abandoned that coalition when a Cuban-American candidate ran. The empirical question is what is the impact of the heterogeneity of the Hispanic population on their ability to gain school board representation. To determine this, a measure of Hispanic homogeneity was calculated. This measure is essentially the percentages of the Cuban Americans, Mexican Americans, Puerto Ricans, and other Hispanics squared and then summed. To standardize this measure, it was divided through by ten thousand (the measure is identical to the Herfindahl index used to measure monopoly power). The resulting index can then be used to discount the voting strength of the Hispanic population by multiplying the Hispanic population percentage by this number. If heterogeneity hurts Hispanic representation, we would expect the slope for population to increase and the level of prediction for the equation to increase. The results are shown in Table 4–25.

Table 4–25   Does Heterogeneity Reduce Hispanic Representation?

Dependent Variable = Hispanic School Board Percentage

Independent Variables	Slope	With Heterogeneity
Hispanic Population	.77*	.84*
Hispanic Education	.26*	.31*
White Poverty	.75*	.78*
Ward Elections	6.57*	6.27*
Appointed Boards	5.86	7.38
R^2	.65	.62
F	48.10	42.58
N	137	137

*$p < .05$

The results of this analysis show a slight increase in the size of the regression coefficient, but the level of prediction actually drops. From these equations it appears as the heterogeneity of the Hispanic population does not act to reduce representation to a significant degree.

25. Dometrius and Sigelman actually calculated separate ratios for Hispanic males and Hispanic females. We combined the raw data that they presented to calculate these ratios.

26. Examining Dye and Renick's tables reveals that either city council representation or Hispanic population is significant, but no other variables are. Our findings, therefore, are highly consistent with those of Dye and Renick (see also Mladenka 1989b).

27. The significant relationship for Anglo poverty is an artifact. Anglo poverty and Hispanic school board representation are highly collinear. Inclusion of one in the regression will almost always render the other insignificant. The theoretical importance of representation suggests that it, rather than Anglo poverty, should be given precedence.

28. Polinard, Wrinkle, and Longoria examine Hispanic teachers in Texas schools but present no information on the representation ratio (1988, p. 12).

29. One might speculate if this relationship is a result of discrimination rather than the power thesis. Discrimination is possible in that the districts with wealthy Anglo populations do not hire Hispanic teachers, saving these more lucrative positions for Anglo teachers. Large Hispanic representation in these districts, there-

fore, might simply show that Hispanic teachers can only get jobs in districts with less wealth.

30. Again, collinearity affects this model. In particular, Anglo poverty and Hispanic representation on the school board are collinear.

31. This might also be a labor-force variable since teachers must have college degrees. Districts with a better-educated Hispanic population are likely to have a larger labor pool from which to hire Hispanic teachers.

Chapter 5

The Impact of Hispanic Representation on Second-Generation Educational Discrimination

The previous chapter revealed a generally low level of Hispanic representation in the educational policy process. The central question concerning this analysis, however, is this: Does the representation of Hispanics among school board members, educational administrators, and teachers affect Hispanic students' access to equal educational opportunities? In theoretical terms, we are interested in whether or not passive representation translates into active representation. Our theory of political representation and public policy in chapter 1 suggests that academic grouping, discipline, and educational attainment are crucial areas for investigating the role of Hispanic representation.

This chapter presents an analysis of educational policy in four stages. First, several tables examine Hispanic students' access to equal educational opportunity by examining representation ratios for academic grouping, discipline, and educational attainment. Second, we argue that the patterns represent discrimination against Hispanic students, a form of discrimination usually titled "second-generation educational discrimination." Third, the measures of second-generation discrimination will be analyzed within our political theory of educational policy. Discrimination will be linked to Hispanic representation, Hispanic resources, Anglo poverty, black student enrollments, and district size. Finally, we will seek to rule out other causes of restricted access to educational opportunities, such as resources, language, and immigration patterns.

The Differential Impact of Educational Policies

Hispanic students who attend schools with Anglo students can be segregated or resegregated by limiting contact between Hispanic and Anglo students, and in the process restricting Hispanic students' access to education. In chapter 1 we argued that resegregation can be accomplished by a variety of means, including academic grouping and discipline. No single study can examine all the nuances of resegregation with a multischool sample. Our study is limited by the data collected by the federal Office for Civil Rights (OCR). OCR's data-collection requests vary from year to year. Some data are gathered for several years and then dropped from the survey without explanation. Other data requests are added as new federal programs such as Title IX focus on different aspects of discrimination. Finally, some data are never gathered.

Data limitations restrict our analysis to three educational policies—academic grouping, discipline, and educational attainment. Academic grouping includes placement in classes for the educable mentally retarded (EMR), the trainable mentally retarded (TMR), the gifted, and the limited English-proficient (bilingual classes).[1] Discipline measures include corporal punishment, suspensions, and expulsions. Educational attainment is defined as not dropping out of school and graduating from high school.

Because our data are limited by OCR surveys, some aspects of resegregation cannot be studied at all. First, OCR does not collect data on curriculum tracking, except for data focusing on sexual distributions in industrial arts, physical education classes, and athletic participation.[2] For an ideal study, data on college bound tracks, vocational tracks, and intermediate tracks would be available. Second, how teachers encourage or discourage individual students is not available. A school need not totally isolate a student to deprive him or her of access to educational opportunity. Discouragement by teachers or administrators does not appear in our categories as discipline or academic grouping, but it might be equally effective. Third, OCR collects no information on how well students perform in class, other than if they graduate from high school. Objective test scores, of course, have numerous problems of bias and interpretation, but access to consistent scores across a set of school districts would reveal a great deal about the access of individual students to education (see chapter 6).

Finally, we need to note that OCR requests information from a sample of school districts, not from the entire population of school districts. Data on school districts, particularly smaller school districts, are gathered only intermittently. Since some of our districts have as few as five thousand students, in many cases we do not have data for each district for every year.

Academic Grouping

1. EMR Classes. Classes for the educable mentally retarded are a common form of special education. Nationwide, the 1986 OCR survey found about one percent of all students were assigned to EMR classes. Of the various special education classes, including classes for trainable mentally retarded, specific learning disability classes, and severely emotionally disturbed classes, EMR classes have the greatest potential for discrimination. EMR classes are based on a general problem definition and, thus, have the fewest restrictions in terms of placement.

To determine the degree of differential assignment to EMR classes (and for other policies), a representational index is constructed. The index assumes that Hispanic students should be assigned to various classes or punished in approximately the same proportion as their student numbers. For EMR classes, the index is calculated by first dividing the number of Hispanic students in EMR classes by the total number of Hispanic students. This quotient is then divided by the quotient of the total number of students in EMR classes divided by the total number of students in the school system. This ratio is often called the *odds index* because it provides the relative odds of an Hispanic student being assigned to an EMR class.[3]

To illustrate, assume a school district has one hundred students, and twenty of these are Hispanic. This district has an EMR class of six students; two EMR students are Hispanic. Calculations reveal that 10 percent of the Hispanic students are in the EMR class, compared to 6 percent of all students. The EMR representation ratio for this district would be 10 percent divided by 6 percent, or 1.67. This section of chapter 5 is concerned only with the differential assignment of students to classes; it does not argue that such assignments are the result of discrimination. That argument is presented later in the chapter.

The representation index for EMR class assignments has the same properties that it had for political representation. If Hispanics are assigned to EMR classes in the same proportion that they constitute in the student body, the representation ratio will be 1.0. Ratios above 1.0 indicate proportionately more Hispanics are in EMR classes, and ratios below 1.0 indicate proportionately fewer Hispanics are in EMR classes. An index of 1.20, for example, indicates that Hispanics are 20 percent more likely to be assigned to an EMR class than are students in general.

The Hispanic EMR ratios are listed in Table 5-1. The findings are expected and consistent with the past literature. Although Hispanic EMR ratios by themselves do not appear to show disproportionate assignment, they do when compared to Anglo ratios. Hispanics are overrepresented in EMR classes anywhere from 24 to 4 percent (depending on the year), and in all cases Hispanic ratios are significantly higher than Anglo ratios for the same year. In comparison, however, one should note that Meier, Stewart, and England found black EMR ratios in excess of 1.95 for a similar sample of districts (1989, p. 82).

Table 5-1   Placement in Classes For the Educable Mentally Retarded:
                   Policy Ratios for Hispanics and Anglos

	Hispanics		Anglos	
Year	Mean	Standard Deviation	Mean	Standard Deviation
1973	1.24*	.53	.72	.22
1974	1.20*	.56	.71	.27
1976	1.19*	.54	.73	.25
1978	1.13*	.47	.69	.25
1980	1.13*	.57	.73	.30
1982	1.04*	.43	.77	.31
1984	1.04*	.43	.69	.25
1986	1.13*	.66	.73	1.13

*ratios different at p <.05

Examining the means for EMR classes does not reveal the significant variation in EMR ratios for districts. In 1986, for example, the Hispanic EMR ratio ranged from a high of 6.29 to a low of .12. In many districts, EMR ratios exceed the national mean by significant amounts; this variation is examined later in this chapter.

The final observation about Table 5-1 concerns the trend. Placement of blacks in EMR classes has been a concern of OCR since 1973; at one time OCR specified that an EMR placement ratio of 1.2 should trigger a program review (Bullock 1976). Placement of Hispanics in EMR classes has not received as much attention from OCR, but logically the same concerns should apply. A slight trend over time indicates that disproportionate Hispanic enrollments were decreasing until 1984. If the 1986 mean represents an anomaly rather than a change in policies, then the generally stable pattern of Anglo EMR enrollments suggests that proportionate equality in EMR classes will be achieved by the turn of the century—a promising but not particularly encouraging trend.

If the 1986 mean represents a real increase, then proportionate equality may never be reached.

2. TMR Classes. A trainable mentally retarded class is a more severe designation than an EMR class.[4] The average school district in OCR's sample had a 1986 TMR enrollment of .26 percent of the student body, or approximately one-fourth the size of the EMR enrollment. Given the smaller classes and the greater burden of proof to assign a student to a TMR class, we would expect that the differential assignment of Hispanics to TMR classes would not be as great as the differential assignment of Hispanics to EMR classes.[5]

Table 5-2, however, does not reveal consistently lower Hispanic assignments; the internal dynamic of assignments is more subtle. Hispanic TMR assignment ratios declined from 1.13 in 1973 to 1.0 in 1978 (actually lower than the Anglo ratio). In 1980 and subsequent years, the decline reversed itself rising to 1.23 by 1984.[6] The ratio dropped in 1986 but remained significantly higher than the Anglo ratio. In 1984, the Hispanic TMR ratio exceeded not only the Anglo TMR ratio, but also the Hispanic EMR ratio.[7]

Table 5-2	Placement in Classes for the Trainable Mentally Retarded: Policy Ratios for Hispanics and Anglos			
	Hispanics		Anglos	
Year	Mean	Standard Deviation	Mean	Standard Deviation
1973	1.13*	.47	.91	.21
1974	1.14*	.54	.92	.28
1976	1.17*	.57	.93	.33
1978	1.00	.37	1.02	.71
1980	1.05	.33	1.04	.52
1982	1.14*	.19	.99	.32
1984	1.23*	.97	.99	.32
1986	1.08*	.45	.92	.37

*ratios different at p <.05

3. Gifted Classes. Gifted classes are normally the highest-quality education that a school district offers to its students. Gifted classes may provide for college preparation in all areas or may be specialized by science, language, performing arts, or other areas. In some school districts these classes are isolated in separate schools to serve as magnets that attract a diverse student body; in other districts they are special, restricted classes within a school.

According to Table 5-3, Hispanics have only limited access to gifted classes. The Hispanic ratio hovers around .5, suggesting a 50 percent underrepresentation of Hispanics; Anglos, in contrast, have proportionately three times as many seats in gifted classes. The Anglo ratio appears to be increasing slightly over time, while the Hispanic ratio is relatively stable. This pattern suggests that ethnic disparities in gifted class enrollments are increasing, not decreasing.[8]

Table 5-3   Placement in Gifted Classes:
Policy Ratios for Hispanics and Anglos

	Hispanics		Anglos	
Year	Mean	Standard Deviation	Mean	Standard Deviation
1976	.50*	.36	1.35	.68
1978	.53*	.37	1.46	.64
1980	.48*	.23	1.54	.63
1982	.43*	.22	1.56	.52
1984	.50*	.22	1.56	.53
1986	.52*	.27	1.77	1.29

*ratios different at $p < .05$

Bilingual Education

As noted in previous chapters, bilingual education, at least as currently operated, has resegregative properties. OCR requires that school district not only report the number of students who are in bilingual programs, but also the number of students who are in need of bilingual instruction. The latter figure is highly suspect since every school district in our sample reported fewer students in need of bilingual education than students enrolled in bilingual education.

Although bilingual education classes enroll Asians, American Indians, Anglos, and blacks, as well as Hispanics, 1986 OCR figures reveal that bilingual education is primarily an Hispanic program. Almost three-fourths of all students in bilingual education are Hispanic; and over one-fourth of all Hispanic students are placed in bilingual education programs.

The massive Hispanic bilingual ratios in Table 5-4, therefore, should come as no surprise. Hispanics in 1986 were three and one-half times more likely than the average student to be placed in a bilingual class. The odds that an Hispanic student in a bilingual class will sit next to an Anglo student are extremely rare. For 1986, the Anglo bilingual ratio was only .11.[9] This difference is, of course, statistically significant.

Table 5–4 **Bilingual Education Policy Ratios for Hispanics and Anglos**

| | Hispanics | | Anglos | |
Year	Mean	Standard Deviation	Mean	Standard Deviation
1976	6.01	6.21	.07	.16
1978	6.40	6.25	.09	.21
1980	4.59	4.20	.10	.28
1982	4.48	3.52	.13	.24
1984	3.25	2.68	.09	.21
1986	3.45	2.71	.11	.21

Note: All differences between Hispanics and Anglos are significant at .0001.

Table 5–4 also shows a significant trend. The disparities of Hispanic enrollment in bilingual education classes are decreasing over time. In 1976, for example, the Hispanic bilingual ratio was more than 6.0; by 1984 this ratio had dropped to 3.25, with a slight increase to 3.45 in 1986. Although current data do not show the reason, an examination of bilingual enrollments reveals that increasing Asian enrollments is the reason for the decline. In 1976, a non-Spanish bilingual class was fairly rare; in 1986 such classes were more common.

A second way to look at bilingual class enrollments is to examine the proportion of Hispanic students that are assigned to bilingual classes. For the districts in the survey, bilingual assignments constitute significantly fewer students than the 25 percent assigned nationwide.[10] Hispanic assignments to bilingual classes have grown from 11.4 percent of all Hispanic students in 1976 to 18.2 percent in 1986 (see Table 5–5).

Discipline

Just as most academic grouping is not reported to OCR, much discipline also evades its notice.[11] Perhaps the most frequent form of discipline is a verbal reprimand or being sent to see the principal. These minor forms of discipline, as well as detention or required work time, are not reported to OCR. OCR only collects information on corporal punishment, suspensions, and expulsions.

Table 5-5   **Percentage of Hispanic Students that Are
Enrolled in Bilingual Education Programs**

Year	Mean	Deviation	Low	High	N
1976	11.4	10.4	0	47.6	144
1978	13.5	10.6	0	46.1	124
1980	18.3	12.8	0	67.7	129
1982	18.3	11.8	0	46.0	87
1984	18.7	14.3	0	66.8	108
1986	18.2	13.0	.5	69.3	113

1. Corporal Punishment. In theory, corporal punishment is the least severe of the disciplinary actions reported to OCR. Even so, corporal punishment is the most controversial. Parents have filed lawsuits against schools to prevent corporal punishment of their children. Legislative and school board debates of corporal punishment's merits are rarely dispassionate. Even though nine states[12] have banned the use of corporal punishment in schools, current estimates are that 1.5 million students receive corporal punishment every year (Baker et al. 1987, 61).

Hispanic and Anglo corporal punishment ratios in Table 5-6 show that differences between Anglos and Hispanics have disappeared. From 1976 through 1980, Hispanics were significantly more likely to be punished than Anglo students, although the relative differences were not large. Starting in 1982 and continuing in 1984, corporal punishment rates for Hispanics and Anglos are roughly equal.[13]

Table 5-6   **The Application of Corporal Punishment:
Policy Ratios for Hispanics and Anglos**

	Hispanics		Anglos	
Year	Mean	Standard Deviation	Mean	Standard Deviation
1976	1.04*	.61	.90	.35
1978	1.10*	.55	.93	.29
1980	1.10*	.55	.93	.29
1982	.96	.27	.93	.51
1984	.95	.41	.92	.50
1986	1.00	.31	.92	.44

*ratios different at p <.05

2. Suspensions. Suspension ratios for Hispanics do not follow the same downward trend apparent in the corporal punishment ratios. Table 5-7 shows that Hispanic ratios remain around parity or slightly above except for 1973, the first year with reported data. Anglo ratios are also remarkably stable, clustering around .85. The differences between the Hispanic and the Anglo ratios are statistically significant. One should not downplay the small but significant differences between Hispanics and Anglos. Because suspensions are twice as frequent as corporal punishment and affect over six percent of the student population annually, they can have an major impact on a student's access to education.

Table 5–7   Suspensions: Policy Ratios for Hispanics and Anglos

| Year | Hispanics | | Anglos | |
	Mean	Standard Deviation	Mean	Standard Deviation
1973	.99*	.41	.86	.34
1974	1.01*	.37	.85	.25
1976	1.05*	.45	.82	.27
1978	1.05*	.41	.86	.28
1980	1.10*	.35	.88	.28
1982	1.01*	.31	.86	.24
1984	1.04*	.32	.84	.24
1986	1.10*	.35	.85	.24

*ratios different at p <.05

3. Expulsions. Of the three available discipline measures, expulsions are clearly the most important. School administrators are hesitant to expel students because this permanently separates a student from the school system. Nationally, school districts have ten suspensions for every expulsion.

The Office for Civil Rights gathered data on expulsions from 1971 (the first measure of racial disparities gathered other than for teachers) to 1980. In 1982, requests for expulsions data disappeared without explanation from the OCR survey. Expulsions data are perhaps the least reliable of the discipline measures, however, because many school districts failed to report expulsion data to OCR.[14] Despite the data problems, we feel expulsions are the crucial disciplinary measure.

Table 5–8 shows significant racial disparities in expulsions. Hispanic expulsion rates fluctuate greatly, ranging from a low of 1.20 in 1971 to a high of 2.05 in 1973. Large standard deviations suggest that Hispanic expulsion rates vary greatly across districts. Anglo expulsion rates are more stable and average about one-half to one-fourth the size of the Hispanic ratios. In every year, the difference between the Hispanic and the Anglo ratios was statistically significant. The substantial overtime variation in Hispanic expulsions does not follow any discernible trend.

Table 5–8   Expulsions: Policy Ratios for Hispanics and Anglos

| | Hispanics | | Anglos | |
| | | Standard | | Standard |
Year	Mean	Deviation	Mean	Deviation
1971	1.20*	.87	.75	.77
1972	1.24*	1.12	.64	.58
1973	2.05*	3.05	.57	.53
1974	1.65*	2.03	.78	1.22
1976	1.49*	1.38	.64	.57
1978	1.72*	1.66	.52	.47
1980	1.43*	1.01	.73	.78

*ratios different at $p < .05$

Educational Attainment

Of all the indicators of equal educational access, the most important are the indicators of educational attainment. An Hispanic student who graduates from high school has probably received a lower-quality education than has an Anglo student, but at least that Hispanic student has a credential needed to go on to college or to apply for many jobs. As noted in chapter 1, an Hispanic's return on investment for a year of education is approximately the same as the return on education for an Anglo. OCR gathered data on high school graduation rates in every biennial survey from 1976 to 1986; dropout rates were collected only in 1976.

1. Graduation Rates. High graduation rates are affected by other racial disparities in educational access. If an Hispanic student is discouraged from attending school through greater discipline or bored with school because he or she has been tracked, then the probability of remaining in school and graduating declines. Even so, high school graduation rates are policy outcomes rather than policy outputs. They are not a direct result of actions taken by teachers or administrators, but rather actions of teachers and administrators affect policy outputs (i.e., discipline, tracking, grouping), which in turn affect policy outcomes (i.e., graduation). Because graduation rates are affected by a variety of forces that are outside the school system's control, they are only an indirect indicator of educational equity.

As expected, Hispanic high school graduation ratios trail those for Anglos (Table 5–9). Hispanic high school graduation rates are only about three-fourths the size that one would expect, given their student numbers. Anglo graduation rates are 20 percent and more above expected percentages. Differences are statistically significant in all cases. Neither an upward nor a downward trend is apparent in the Hispanic graduation rate.

Table 5–9   High School Graduates and Dropouts: Policy Ratios for Hispanics and Anglos

High School Graduates

| | Hispanics | | Anglos | |
Year	Mean	Standard Deviation	Mean	Standard Deviation
1976	.73*	.32	1.17	.37
1978	.71*	.24	1.22	.28
1980	.73*	.23	1.23	.26
1982	.69*	.19	1.23	.28
1984	.79*	.16	1.25	.31
1986	.78*	.17	1.19	.31

Dropouts

| | Hispanics | | Anglos | |
Year	Mean	Standard Deviation	Standard Mean	Deviation
1976	1.27*	.52	.95	.31

*ratios different at p <.05

2. Dropouts. OCR gathered data on dropouts for only a single year, 1976. As a result, any analysis can only be speculative. In 1976 the Hispanic dropout ratio of 1.27 was significantly higher than the Anglo dropout ratio of .95. The data on graduates suggests that these figures have changed little in the past ten years.

Education in Different Hispanic Communities

Obscured in the previous analysis is the variation in academic grouping, discipline, and educational attainment for Mexican Americans, Cuban Americans, and Puerto Ricans. Given the different educational histories of each group, we would expect that current educational policies would vary. Perhaps most significant would be placements in bilingual education. Puerto Rican students are more likely to be temporary residents of the United States with expectations of returning to the island when economic conditions change. Similarly, Cuban Americans are more recent and less voluntary immigrants to the United States. The timing of immigration and future plans should affect language skills, and thus assignment to bilingual classes.

Table 5–10 shows an interesting pattern of bilingual class ratios. Cuban-American districts generally have the highest bilingual class ratios, but the ratios for these districts dropped sharply from 11.77 in 1976 to 5.95 in 1986. Mexican-American districts have the lowest level of bilingual ratios; they have also declined in recent years, but not as sharply as they have for Cuban Americans. Puerto Rican students fall in a middle group, with assignment ratios between those for Cuban Americans and those for Mexican Americans.

Table 5–10	Bilingual Class Ratios for Districts that Are Primarily Mexican-American, Puerto Rican, and Cuban-American		
Year	Mexican-American	Puerto Rican	Cuban-American
1976	5.70	8.50	11.77
1978	6.06	8.70	10.76
1980	4.27	7.03	8.86
1982	4.00	5.54	7.54
1984	2.94	4.65	6.94
1986	3.14	4.99	5.95

The remaining policy ratios for Mexican-American, Puerto Rican and Cuban-American districts are shown in Table 5–11. Each of these figures is the mean ratio of the associated districts based on all the years that district reported data from 1971 to 1984. These averaged means remove some of the biases of reporting errors and allow a consistent pattern to be observed for both single districts and for all districts.

The different educational patterns are clearly apparent. Academic grouping into lower-ability group classes is a phenomenon that affects Mexican-American students more than either Puerto Rican or Cuban-American students. Cuban-American academic grouping ratios, in fact, are fairly close to the ratios for Anglo students nationwide. Despite the variation in lower academic grouping assignments, none of the Hispanic groups gets much access to gifted classes, generally attaining policy ratios of .5 or less.

Discipline patterns are the most unique. Cuban Americans do not suffer great disparities in discipline. Their policy ratios are .9 for suspensions, .75 for corporal punishment and an exceptionally low .43 for expulsions. The Cuban-American ratios compare favorably to the national ratios for Anglos. Mexican Americans in all cases have significantly higher discipline ratios than do Cuban Americans. In all three forms of punishment, Mexican Americans equal or exceed ratios of 1.0. Puerto Ricans have the most interesting pattern. Despite having ratios of less than one for corporal punishment and suspensions, Puerto Ricans are 43 percent overrepresented among the expelled.

Table 5–11	Mean Policy Ratios for Districts Predominantly Mexican-American, Puerto Rican, and Cuban-American		
Policy Ratio	Mexican Americans	Cubans	Puerto Ricans
EMR Classes	1.19*	.75*	1.05
TMR Classes	1.10	.98	.97#
Gifted Classes	.47	.40	.51
Suspensions	1.07*	.80	.77*
Corporal Punishment	1.01*	.74	.87
Expulsions	1.39*	.43#	1.43
Dropouts	1.31*	1.01	1.12#
High School Graduates	.74#	1.02*	.59*
Bilingual Classes	4.75	9.17	7.04

*$p < .05$
#$p < .1$

Note: Significance in column 1 compares Mexican Americans to Cuban Americans, in column 2 compares Cuban Americans to Puerto Ricans, and in column 3 Puerto Ricans to Mexican Americans.

The different patterns of discipline and academic grouping translate into different patterns of educational attainment. Mexican Americans have the highest dropout ratios and low graduation ratios. While the Puerto Rican dropout ratio is not as high as the Mexican-American ratio, their high school graduation ratio is the lowest of the three groups. Cuban Americans, on the other hand, do not fit the pattern. Their dropout rate is the same as other students attending their schools, and their graduation rate is actually two percentage points higher.

Three distinct educational patterns emerge. The education experiences for Mexican Americans follow the classic pattern found for black students. Mexican Americans are disproportionately assigned to lower academic groups and kept out of higher academic groups. They are punished more frequently and are less likely to finish high school. The pattern for Puerto Ricans is different. Puerto Ricans are not disproportionately grouped in lower academic group classes and are not disproportionately punished or suspended. They do not get access to gifted classes, however, and are expelled in greater numbers. The end result is similar to that for Mexican Americans—high dropout rates and low high school graduation rates. Only Cuban Americans avoid the general pattern. While Cuban Americans also do not get access to gifted classes, they are not assigned disproportionately to lower academic group classes, they are not excessively punished, and they finish high school more often than their classmates.

The patterns of access to educational opportunity reflect, in part, the social class differences among the Hispanic communities. Cuban-American educational patterns mirror the advantages of middle-class status except for access to gifted classes. Mexican-American patterns and, to a lesser extent Puerto Rican patterns, are also consistent with their lower-socioeconomic class status.

Differential Assignments as Discrimination

Although differences in treatment of Anglo and Hispanic students have been amply demonstrated by the first nine tables in this chapter, the question of discrimination has not yet been fully addressed. Academic grouping and discipline are part of virtually every U.S. school system and predate efforts to integrate Hispanic students into the Anglo school system.[15] Such practices exist even in schools that have only Anglo students. Other than racial or class discrimination, two justifications for academic grouping and discipline have been specified (Eyler, Cook, and Ward 1983, 127). First, academic grouping and discipline can reflect professional norms concerning how school systems should operate. Only when students are grouped by ability, the argument goes, can the brightest students be challenged to learn and the slower students given the special help that they need. Despite the absence of empirical support for this position (see chapter 1), advocates use it to argue that "resegregation is necessary in order for each child to attain the highest level of achievement" (p. 127). Similarly, discipline is part of the school administrator's duty to maintain a school environment where learning is possible. If certain students are disciplined in greater numbers, this may reflect that group's greater disciplinary problems.

The second possible reason for disproportionate academic grouping and disciplinary actions relates to incentives. School officials are subject to a wide variety of pressures. The federal government requires bilingual education, special education, and some programs for the economically or educationally disadvantaged. Both the federal government and state governments offer the school district incentives to establish such programs by providing additional funds. Yet implementing such programs results in some resegregation, as students (many of them Hispanic) are pulled out of regular classes to meet federal or state mandates.

Even though actions consistent with both the professional norms and the financial incentives explanation of grouping still result in some resegregation of school systems, the intent is to assist disadvantaged students rather than to hinder them. The assertion of discrimination implies that a school district is, in fact, hindering the student's education by using such practices. Terming such practices *discrimination,* however, does not necessarily mean that they were done intentionally. Teachers, administrators, and school board members might well have been pursuing normal educational practices or conflicting mandates and inadvertently discriminated against Hispanic students. When discriminatory practices are part of the norms and institutional structure of the organization, decision-makers may be unaware of any discriminatory impact (Feagin and Feagin 1986, 31).

Whether or not such practices were implemented with the intent of discrimination, this section argues that evidence consistent with discrimination exists. This evidence is inconsistent with the assertion that academic grouping and discipline are simply good educational practices. The proof is indirect, but the evidence is there.

The Consistency of Results

The representation ratios show a pattern of consistency that is inconsistent with the argument that academic grouping and discipline are merely good educational practices. If racial or class discrimination were an underlying cause of the actions studied in this chapter, we would expect Hispanic students to be underrepresented in those policies that reflect positive benefits (gifted classes and graduation) and overrepresented in policies that reflect negatively on a student (EMR classes, TMR classes, corporal punishment, suspensions, expulsions, and dropouts). The relative costs and benefits of assignment to a bilingual class are open to dispute, so these classes will not be part of this analysis.

Tables 5–1 to 5–3 and 5–6 to 5–9 compared Hispanic and Anglo students on eight different policy ratios for as many as eight different years. There were fifty comparisons. In every case where the policy was a positive benefit, Hispanic students were underrepresented compared to Anglo students. In every case but two (in one of those cases the groups were equal) where the policy was a negative reflection on the student, Hispanic students were overrepresented compared to Anglo students. In forty-five of the fifty cases, the differences between Hispanic students and Anglo students were statistically significant. Such consistency does not prove that the policies were discriminatory, but given such a rare pattern, one should be skeptical about claims that academic grouping and discipline are merely good educational practices.

The Intercorrelations

If the policy ratios investigated represent nothing more than good educational practices or conflicting mandates, many of the policies should be unrelated to each other. To be sure, corporal punishment and suspensions should be related; and a clear relationship exists between dropouts and graduates. No apparent reason exists, however, why placement of Hispanics in EMR classes should be related to corporal punishment of Hispanic students. Similarly, the absence of Hispanics in gifted classes should be totally unrelated to the expulsion of Hispanics from the school system.

If the policy measures reflect some measure of racial or class discrimination, a predictable pattern of intercorrelations should result. All indicators that reflect positively on the student (gifted classes, graduates) should be positively related to each other, and all indicators that reflect negatively on students (EMR, TMR, punishment, suspensions, expulsions, dropouts) should also be positively related to each other. In addition, correlations between positive actions and negative actions should be negative.

Table 5–12 shows the pooled intercorrelation table for the policy ratios. The structure of the data set permits us to examine interrelationships of all indicators for the years 1971 to 1986. Of the twenty-eight correlations (excluding those for bilingual education) that appear in Table 5–12, twenty-three are consistent with a hypothesis of discrimination; seventeen of those are statistically significant. Of the five correlations inconsistent with discrimination, only one (the .12 correlation between suspensions and graduates) is statistically significant. The probability that twenty-three of twenty-eight relationships would be in a predicted direction if the pattern were actually random is .0004.[16]

Table 5–12   Policy Ratio Intercorrelations: Pooled Data Set

	EMR	TMR	Suspend	Expel	Punish	Dropout	Gifted	Graduates
TMR Classes	.21*	—	—	—	—	—	—	—
Suspensions	.36*	.14*	—	—	—	—	—	—
Expulsions	.23*	.07	.38*	—	—	—	—	—
Punishment	.37*	.08	.37*	.25*	—	—	—	—
Dropouts	.30*	.21*	.38*	.38*	.21*	—	—	—
Gifted	-.11*	.06	-.08	-.14	-.13*	-.19	—	—
Graduates	-.05	.05	.12*	.06	-.18*	.09	.17*	—
Bilingual	-.10	-.04	-.13	.09	.06	-.23*	-.30*	-.34*

*p <.05

Some of the individual correlations in Table 5–12 merit brief discussion for illustrative purposes. The strong correlations between EMR placement and all three disciplinary measures, for example, is difficult to explain without reference to racial or class discrimination. After all, if an EMR placement helps a student, then the student should learn more and be less likely to be a disciplinary problem. The strong relationship between dropouts and EMR placements and the three discipline measures is exactly as predicted if discipline and academic grouping encourage students to drop out of school.

The bilingual correlations require a separate discussion. If bilingual programs are operated as separate segregated programs, them we would expect bilingual programs to have a negative impact on student performance. A mixed and insignificant pattern exists, except for gifted programs and graduates.[17] In both cases, significant negative relationships exist. Schools with large bilingual class ratios have proportionately fewer Hispanics in gifted classes and eventually produce fewer Hispanic graduates. The results suggest that bilingual class ratios should be included in any analysis of how the policy ratios cluster.

Clustering of Measures

A more comprehensive way of viewing the interrelationships of the policy indicators is via factor analysis. Rather than examining the factor structure for each individual year, only the factor structure for 1986 and the over-time district means are presented. The over-time district means measure requires some elaboration. Since the OCR survey is not sent to every school district every year, some districts report figures for some of our years and not for others. This means that analysis based on individual years has a different set of districts for each year. To provide generalizations across all districts and to smooth out any reporting errors, for each district a mean policy ratio was calculated for each policy indicator based on the number of OCR surveys the district received. This over-time mean policy ratio is presented in Table 5–13 for the nine policy measures. The over-time means not only show the pattern of disproportionate Hispanic assignments, but they also show the large range of policy variation across districts.

Table 5–13   School District Means for Averaged Policy Ratios

Hispanic Ratio for	Mean	Deviation	Low	High
EMR Class Placement	1.16	.43	.33	2.75
TMR Class Placement	1.08	.40	.23	2.71
Gifted Class Placement	.48	.22	.07	1.20
Corporal Punishment	.99	.47	.17	3.64
Suspensions	1.03	.31	.38	2.47
Expulsions	1.36	1.33	.03	10.56
Dropouts	1.27	.52	.20	4.42
High School Graduates	.73	.20	.25	1.42
Bilingual Classes	5.01	4.56	.41	31.08

Factor Analysis

If the measures of academic grouping, discipline, and educational attainment have a common core that can be termed second-generation discrimination, factor analysis is an appropriate technique to extract that common core. For black students, the measures of academic grouping, discipline, and educational attainment cluster exactly as predicted. A factor analysis for blacks reveals loadings consistent with the predicted clustering for the correlations (see Meier, Stewart, and England 1989, 92). Since the pattern of actions relative to Hispanics differs greatly from the patterns of actions relative to blacks, we should not be surprised if the factor analysis reveals a more complex picture for Hispanics.

Table 5–14 shows the 1986 factor loadings for a two-factor solution. Column one shows that the first factor has three strong loadings for EMR classes, corporal punishment, and suspensions, plus a moderate loading for TMR classes. This factor illustrates again the common linkage between lower-ability grouping and discipline. This dimension of resegregation could be termed *punishment*. The second factor has strong negative loadings for gifted classes and high school graduates, and a strong positive loading for bilingual classes. This factor, by reversing the signs, can be termed *educational attainment.*

Table 5–14	Factor Analysis of Measures: 1986	
Measure	Factor 1	Factor 2
EMR Classes	*.87*	.14
TMR Classes	*.55*	-.02
Graduates	.14	-*.73*
Corporal Punishment	*.74*	.02
Suspensions	*.77*	-.01
Gifted Classes	-.18	-*.81*
Bilingual Education	.06	*.73*
Eigenvalue	2.32	1.67
Percent of the Variance	33	24

Note: Italicized values indicate variables loading on the designated factor.

Two aspects of this factor analysis merit a further note. First, large bilingual class loadings are associated with a lack of future educational attainment for Hispanics. Such a finding is consistent with the use of bilingual classes as an Hispanic track rather than a program that builds skills needed to succeed in school.[18] Second, TMR ratios load only modestly. Throughout this analysis we have argued that discrimination is more difficult in TMR assignments than in EMR assignments. The weaker loading may reflect this difficulty.

The factor analysis for the mean policy measures is shown in Table 5–15. Two significant factors result from the analysis. Although this pattern is somewhat different from that in 1986 (as it should be, given that measures of dropouts and expulsions are included), the general thrust of the clustering is similar. The first factor is clearly a punishment factor with positive loadings for EMR classes, TMR classes, corporal punishment, suspensions, expulsions, and dropouts. The second factor is an educational attainment factor with positive loadings for graduation rates and gifted classes, and a negative loading for bilingual classes. The policy means factor analysis, therefore, suggests that second-generation discrimination techniques have two dimensions for Hispanics; one is punishment to discourage the student, and the other is denial of access to quality education.

Table 5–15   Factor Analysis of Mean Policy Ratios

Indicator	Factor 1	Factor 2
EMR Classes	*.77*	-.26
TMR Classes	*.41*	.17
High School Graduates	.07	*.76*
Corporal Punishment	*.72*	-.30
Suspensions	*.85*	.17
Bilingual Classes	-.07	*-.74*
Expulsions	*.65*	.19
Gifted Classes	-.13	*.65*
Dropouts	*.53*	-.31
Eigenvalue	2.78	1.83
Percentage of the Variance	31	20

Note: Italicized values indicate variables loading on the designated factor.

The patterns in Table 5–15 are worth discussing. The common loading of punishment factors with lower academic groups confirms that large Hispanic EMR and TMR class ratios exist in the same districts that disproportionately punish Hispanic children. This suggests that special education classes might be used to punish children. Similarly, the loading of bilingual education on educational achievement is cause for concern. Even though this relationship exists at the aggregate level, it implies that the segregation of Hispanic students in bilingual classes has an eventual negative effect on their future educational performance. If bilingual classes were integrated (as advocates of bilingual-bicultural education suggest), we would not expect to find this relationship.

Clustering: A Summary

The results of the clustering analysis reveal a pattern different from that for black students, but still a pattern consistent with the notion of second-generation discrimination. With black students, the clustering of discriminatory measures was so consistent that no conclusion other than second-generation discrimination was possible. With Hispanic students, this was not the case. The preponderance of the evidence is consistent with the notion of second-generation discrimination, but exceptions to the pattern exist. At times Hispanics were not treated as badly as second-generation discrimination would imply; at other times relationships that should have been significant were not.

Despite the lack of perfect consistency, however, the weight of the analysis still suggests that a pattern of second-generation educational discrimination exists. That the pattern is not as consistent as the pattern for black students makes some sense. Desegregation was a policy targeted at white schools for the benefit of black students. Except in the southwest, and then only late in the desegregation process, Hispanics were not part of the movement to desegregate schools. Where alternative methods of limiting the contact between Anglos and Hispanics were needed, the Hispanic community offered a readily available mechanism, bilingual education. The massive size of the bilingual education program (averaging five times the size of EMR programs and twenty times the size of TMR programs) may well make the use of other methods of academic grouping less crucial.

The Size of Impact

One often-raised counterargument is that EMR classes and TMR classes are relatively small programs and are not sufficiently large by themselves to resegregate a school system (see Wainscott and Woodard 1988). This counterargument can be dismissed for two reasons. First, it misinterprets our argument. We do not contend that we have measured all the forms of academic grouping and discipline that can be used for discriminatory purposes. Because OCR collects data only on EMR, TMR, and gifted programs, we cannot examine any of the forms of curriculum tracking (e.g., vocational versus college prep tracks) or other forms of academic grouping. In addition, numerous forms of discipline other than corporal punishment, suspensions, and expulsions exist. The data presented only reveal the tip of the iceberg.

Second, the counterargument is wrong even for these measures. Using the 1986 OCR survey, we measured the percentage of Hispanic students that were assigned to EMR classes, TMR classes, bilingual classes, or were disciplined. For our school districts in the 1986 OCR survey, the average district had 27.8 percent of its Hispanic students affected by one of these actions. This mean obscured significant variation across school districts. These programs affected 77 percent of all Hispanic students in Los Angeles, California, and 63 percent of all Hispanic students in Holyoke, Massachusetts.[19] If vocational tracking is also used in these and other districts, patterns close to complete resegregation would be possible.

The Politics of Second-Generation Discrimination

Our political theory of second-generation discrimination, presented in chapter 1, argues that five forces affect second-generation

discrimination against Hispanic students. First, political representation of Hispanics should mitigate the amount of second-generation discrimination. Generally, studies of second-generation discrimination have focused on the impact of teachers rather than
school board members or administrators in limiting discrimination against students (Meier, Stewart, and England 1989). These
studies examined black students, however, and the level of black
teacher representation is significantly higher than the level of Hispanic teacher representation in comparably sized schools. Effective policy advocacy with so few representatives, we feel, requires
representation both among teachers and on the school board (see
Karnig and McClain 1988).

The need for teacher representation rests on the crucial role
that teachers play in the education of children. The teacher makes
the initial assessment of a student's ability and is likely the first
person to interact with the student in terms of discipline. School
board members, in turn, are a source of support for Hispanic
teachers and serve as shields to deflect political pressures away
from teaching professionals. In addition, they can advocate policy
changes that restrict the use of second-generation discrimination.

The actual representation measure, therefore, is somewhat
complex. The percentage of Hispanic teachers is multiplied by the
percentage of Hispanics on the school board. To adjust this measure back to a percentile figure, the square root is taken of this
product. The result is an Hispanic representation percentage that
requires representation both on the school board and among
teachers.[20]

Second, Hispanic resources should limit the amount of second-
generation discrimination against Hispanic students. In communities with a politically active Hispanic population, Hispanics can
exert pressures on the school district and voice their objections to
certain policies. Two measures of Hispanic resources are used.
The first is the percentage of Hispanics over age twenty-five who
have graduated from high school. The second is the ratio of Hispanic median family income to Anglo median family income (com-
puted as a percentage). The latter is an attempt to measure the
level of Hispanic resources relative to Anglo resources.

Third, social class should affect second-generation discrimination. We have argued that the power thesis of Giles, Evans, and
Feagin applies to second-generation discrimination. In this view,
discrimination against Hispanic students is a function of both race
and social class. In districts with large populations of lower-class

Anglos, similar discriminatory actions will be taken against lower-class Anglos. The result will be that, in districts with large lower-class Anglo populations, discrimination against Hispanic students will be mitigated. The specific indicator is the percentage of the Anglo population with an income below the poverty level.

Fourth, black enrollments must be considered. In a discriminatory school district Hispanics have an advantage over blacks. A middle-class Hispanic can more easily "pass" as Anglo than can a black student. Just as Hispanics can avoid some second-generation discrimination when such measures are targeted at poor Anglos, they can also avoid discrimination when blacks are targeted. Black assignments to special education classes, therefore, will leave fewer assignments that can be made to Hispanic students. This racial-competition hypothesis will be operationalized as the representation ratio of black students for the policy in question. When the measure under consideration is assignment to EMR classes, for example, the independent variable will be the black EMR assignment ratio.

Fifth, school district size should be negatively related to second-generation discrimination. The larger a school district is, the more likely that the school district is to be professionalized. Greater levels of professionalization should result in greater awareness of the problems of Hispanic students and greater recognition that something like second-generation discrimination is possible. The indicator of district size is the total school enrollment (in thousands).

The dependent variables are the nine policy indicators in Table 5–13, with one small alteration. An examination of the distribution of these variables revealed that several were skewed somewhat by extreme values. Extreme values can distort a regression by giving too much weight to a deviant case. To avoid this problem, a log transformation of each indicator was used—similar to Finn's (1982) approach to this problem. The log transformation changes the interpretation of the results somewhat in that regression slopes now refer to percentage changes in the dependent variable rather than one-unit changes (Tufte 1974, 113–28).[21]

EMR Classes

The political model of Hispanic assignments to EMR classes works well, explaining 67 percent of the variation in Hispanic EMR ratios. EMR policies are a function of three variables—relative Hispanic resources, Hispanic representation, and black placements. Districts where the Hispanic population has a higher income relative to Anglos assign proportionately fewer Hispanics to EMR classes. Similarly, districts that achieve higher levels of Hispanic political representation also reduce Hispanic assignments to EMR classes. Finally, greater assignment of blacks to EMR classes reduces the assignment of Hispanics. None of the other relationships are statistically significant.

Table 5–16   The Policy Impact of Hispanic Representation on Placement in EMR Classes: Multivariate Model

Dependent Variable = Hispanic EMR Ratio

Independent Variables	Slope	Slope
Hispanic Education	.073	———— a
Percent Anglos Below Poverty	-.083	———— a
Hispanic/Anglo Income Ratio	-.642*	-.575*
Hispanic Representation	-.062	-.112*
Blacks in EMR Classes	-.489*	-.509*
District Size in Thousands	-1.751	———— a
R^2	.68	.68
Adjusted R^2	.67	.67
F	44.40	88.02
N	131	131

*$p < .05$
[a]Equation reestimated omitting this variable.

Hispanic EMR assignments, therefore, are a function of three different forces. First, the black EMR relationship suggests that school officials make tradeoffs between Hispanics and blacks when placing students in EMR classes. A one percent increase in the black EMR ratio reduces the Hispanic EMR ratio by .509 percent. The least favorable interpretation of this relationship is that Hispanics are able to avoid some discrimination when blacks, the more visible target for discrimination, are present. The most favorable interpretation is that when blacks with greater needs for EMR classes are present, Hispanic students do not receive as many EMR assignments. Either interpretation suggests discrimination.

Second, the Hispanic community has a role. The resources of the Hispanic community, measured as the Hispanic-Anglo income ratio, provide a climate that reduces the amount of differential EMR assignments. While we have interpreted this as a political resource, one might also interpret it as a social-class variable. As Hispanic social-class status approaches that of Anglos, differential assignment of Hispanic students to EMR classes declines.[22] Third, Hispanic representation provides a crucial role in reducing EMR assignments for Hispanic students. When districts have Hispanic representation, both on the school board and among the teachers, proportionally fewer Hispanics are assigned to EMR classes. A one percentage point increase in representation reduces the EMR ratio by .11 percent.

TMR Classes

Because TMR classes are significantly smaller than EMR classes and require a higher burden of proof to place a student in them, we expect our political theory of second-generation discrimination to work less well for TMR classes. These expectations are met by the results in Table 5–17. The six-variable model explains only 13 percent of the variation, and only two independent variables are statistically significant. In this case, as black enrollments increase proportionately in TMR classes, Hispanic enrollments decline. Similarly, an increase in Hispanic representation is associated with a decline in TMR assignments. The relationships for TMR classes, however, are modest at best.

Table 5–17   **Impact of Hispanic Representation on Placement of Hispanic Students in TMR Classes**

Dependent Variable = Hispanic TMR Ratio

Independent Variables	Slope	Slope
Hispanic Education	.059	———— a
Percent Anglos Below Poverty	.066	———— a
Hispanic/Anglo Income Ratio	-.042	———— a
Hispanic Representation	-.071	-.073#
Blacks in TMR Classes	-1.940*	-2.041*
District Size in Thousands	-.584	———— a
R^2	.18	.17
Adjusted R^2	.13	.16
F	3.61	10.95
N	109	109

*p < .05
#p < .1
aEquation reestimated omitting this variable.

Gifted Classes

Gifted classes are the school district's best education. Students taking such classes are exposed to the best teachers in the district and interact with other students in an enriched environment. The political model (see Table 5–18) for gifted classes performs moderately well, explaining 45 percent of the variance in the reduced model.

Table 5–18   **The Impact of Hispanic Representation on Placement of Hispanics in Gifted Classes**

Dependent Variable = Hispanic Gifted Ratio

Independent Variables	Slope	Slope
Hispanic Education	-.014	——— a
Percent Anglos Below Poverty	.369	——— a
Hispanic/Anglo Income Ratio	.807*	.757*
Hispanic Representation	.310*	.430*
Blacks in Gifted Programs	.382*	.402*
District Size in Thousands	1.165	——— a
R²	.47	.46
Adjusted R²	.44	.45
F	17.69	35.18
N	126	126

*p <.05
#p <.1
aEquation reestimated omitting this variable.

Three variables have a significant impact on the Hispanic gifted class ratio—the Hispanic-Anglo income ratio, blacks in gifted programs, and Hispanic representation. The power thesis is supported; for each additional one percentage point increase in the Hispanic-Anglo income ratio, the Hispanic gifted class ratio increases by .757 percent. Similarly, an increase in black students in gifted classes is associated with proportionate increases in Hispanic student access. The single most significant impact, however, is for Hispanic representation. An increase of one percentage point in the Hispanic representation score results in a .43 percent increase in the Hispanic gifted class ratio. In short, Hispanic representation improves Hispanic student access to quality education.

Bilingual Classes

Examining the bilingual class ratio involves altering the political model somewhat. Since few blacks are enrolled in bilingual classes, the black policy ratio is omitted from the analysis. The remaining five variables (see Table 5–19) are able to account for 47 percent of the variation in Hispanic bilingual ratios, but only two of the variables are statistically significant.

Table 5–19   **The Impact of Hispanic Representation on Placement of Hispanic Students in Bilingual Classes**

Dependent Variable = Hispanic Bilingual Class Ratio

Independent Variables	Slope	Slope
Hispanic Education	-.102	———— a
Percent Anglos Below Poverty	-1.431*	-1.295*
Hispanic/Anglo Income Ratio	.055	———— a
Hispanic Representation	-.792*	-.799*
District Size in Thousands	-.001	———— a
R^2	.49	.49
Adjusted R^2	.47	.48
F	23.86	60.72
N	131	131

*p <.05
aEquation reestimated omitting this variable.

An increase of one percentage point in the number of Anglos residing in poverty results in a 1.295 percent decrease in the Hispanic bilingual ratio. In other words, in districts with a large poor Anglo class, Hispanic enrollments in bilingual classes decrease. A similar relationship exists for Hispanic representation. For each one percentage point increase in Hispanic representation, the Hispanic bilingual ratio *decreases* by .799 percent.

These two relationships merit some comment. Political representation and social class push the bilingual policy ratio in the same direction. We find negative relationships between Hispanic social class and representation and the size of bilingual education programs. If bilingual programs do not provide for integrated, multicultural education but rather are little more than an Hispanic track, then one would expect that policy-makers would recognize this and limit Hispanic enrollments in bilingual programs. This interpretation is consistent with a negative relationship between Hispanic representation and bilingual education and for the negative relationship between social class and bilingual education.

Corporal Punishment

The political model of corporal punishment fares moderately well, able to explain 42 percent of the variance in Hispanic corporal punishment ratios (see Table 5–20). The Hispanic corporal punishment ratio is unaffected by Hispanic resources, social class, or district size. Only Hispanic representation and the black corporal punishment ratio are significantly related to the Hispanic corporal punishment ratio.

Table 5–20   **The Impact of Hispanic Representation on the Use of Corporal Punishment Against Hispanics**

Dependent Variable = Hispanic Corporal Punishment Ratio

Independent Variable	Slope	Slope
Hispanic Education	.093	——— a
Percent Anglos Below Poverty	.039	——— a
Hispanic/Anglo Income Ratio	-.138	——— a
Hispanic Representation	-.075#	-.111*
Corporal Punishment of Blacks	-.342*	-.348*
District Size in Thousands	-1.802	——— a
R^2	.46	.43
Adjusted R^2	.42	.42
F	13.00	37.26
N	100	100

*p <.05
#p < .1
aEquation reestimated omitting this variable.

Although the lack of relationship between many political factors and corporal punishment might suggest that corporal punishment is not being used for discriminatory purposes, the relationship with black corporal punishment is disconcerting. No logical reason exists why the Hispanic punishment ratio should be negatively related to the black punishment ratio. Punishment is not a scarce commodity (that is, it does not consume resources as EMR classes do); therefore, there should be no need to trade off punishment of one minority for the punishment of another. In addition, a one percentage point increase in Hispanic representation is associated with a .111 percent decline in the corporal punishment ratio. Before concluding that school districts are somehow manipulating discipline to play one minority off against another, the relationship for suspensions and expulsions should be examined.

Suspensions

The political model predicts suspensions moderately well (54 percent), but again the social-class variables are not the major factors (see Table 5–21). Hispanic resources and social class are unrelated to the Hispanic suspensions ratio. Only Hispanic representation, district size, and the black suspensions ratio are significantly related to Hispanic suspensions.

Table 5–21   The Impact of Hispanic Representation on Suspensions

Dependent Variable = Hispanic Suspension Ratio

Independent Variables	Slope	Slope
Hispanic Education	.050	——— a
Percent Anglos Below Poverty	-.036	——— a
Hispanic/Anglo Income Ratio	-.139	——— a
Hispanic Representation	-.098#	-.137*
Suspensions for Blacks	-.333*	-.331*
District Size in Thousands	-4.852*	-4.302*
R^2	.56	.55
Adjusted R^2	.54	.53
F	25.92	50.79
N	131	131

*p <.05
#p < .1
aEquation reestimated omitting this variable.

The district size variable is in the predicted direction, with larger districts having more equitable suspension activities. A one percentage point increase in Hispanic representation is associated with a .137 percent decline in the suspension ratio. Again, the black suspension ratio has the troublesome negative relationship indicating that, as the black suspension ratio increases, the relative level of suspensions among Hispanics decreases. The tradeoff hypothesis concerning discipline gains additional credence.

Expulsions

The good level of prediction for disciplinary actions using the political model continues to hold for expulsions (see Table 5–22). None of the social-class variables is significant, including Hispanic resources, Anglo poverty, or district size. Only two variables—Hispanic representation and the black expulsion ratio—are able to account for 58 percent of the variation in Hispanic expulsion ratios.

As predicted, districts with better Hispanic representation have proportionately fewer Hispanic students expelled. Again, as the expulsion ratio for blacks increases, the expulsion ratio for Hispanics declines. For all three forms of discipline, therefore, the actions taken against blacks are intertwined with the actions taken against Hispanics.

Table 5–22   The Impact of Hispanic Representation on the Expulsion of Hispanic Students

Dependent Variable = Hispanic Expulsion Ratio

Independent Variable	Slope	Slope
Hispanic Education	.367	——— a
Percent Anglos Below Poverty	.239	——— a
Hispanic/Anglo Income Ratio	-.260	——— a
Hispanic Representation	-.359*	-.410*
Expulsions of Blacks	-.596*	-.580*
District Size in Thousands	1.985	——— a
R^2	.61	.59
Adjusted R^2	.58	.58
F	23.04	65.65
N	95	95

*p <.05
#p <.1
[a]Equation reestimated omitting this variable.

The consistent linkage between discipline of black students and discipline of Hispanic students strongly implies that race is a consideration in dispensing discipline. If level of disruption were the driving force, then one would expect to see both Hispanic and black ratios increase so that there would be a positive relationship between the two (assuming that Anglo disciplinary actions remain constant). If unacceptable behavior increased across all racial groups, including Anglos, then the correlation between black and Hispanic disciplinary ratios would be essentially zero. The pattern that Hispanics receive more corporal punishment, more suspensions, and more expulsions when blacks receive less, and vice versa, implies that administrators compensate for disciplining one group by lessening discipline of the other group. Only an effort to play off blacks against Hispanics could predict such a pattern.

Such a pattern cannot but be at least as disturbing as a pattern that was explained by the social-class factors in the political model. In fact, since black political and social class forces explain black disciplinary ratios fairly well (see Meier, Stewart, and England 1989), the implication is that black political clout can reduce the amount of second-generation disciplinary discrimination against blacks. When such a reduction is attained, however, Hispanics then become the focus of discriminatory disciplinary practices. Lacking the same level of political resources as the black community, therefore, Hispanics lose access to educational opportunities just as blacks gain them.

Dropout Rates

Dropout rates form a pattern of relationships similar to the disciplinary patterns (see Table 5–23). Hispanic resources, Anglo poverty, and district size are unrelated to Hispanic dropout rates. Blacks in the school system and Hispanic representation are able to explain 24 percent of the variation in Hispanic dropout rates. Both variables have negative coefficients, suggesting that Hispanics do relatively better in districts with greater Hispanic representation and larger black populations.[23] Again, the negative relationship for blacks raises the question of tradeoffs in discrimination against blacks and Hispanics. Since dropout data were collected for only one year, however, speculation should be restricted.

Table 5–23   The Impact of Hispanic Representation on Hispanic Dropout Rates

Dependent Variable = Hispanic Dropout Ratio

Independent Variables	Slope	Slope
Hispanic Education	-.095	———— a
Percent Anglos Below Poverty	-.403*	———— a
Hispanic/Anglo Income Ratio	-.041	———— a
Hispanic Representation	-.081#	-.197*
Blacks in the School System	-.279*	-.276*
District Size in Thousands	.288	———— a
R^2	.28	.25
Adjusted R^2	.24	.24
F	6.99	18.77
N	115	115

*p < .05
#p < .1
aEquation reestimated omitting this variable.

Graduation Rates

An intermediate product of the educational process should be the production of high school graduates; the end product being students with academic and vocational skills. The political model of Hispanic high school graduation rates continues its good performance, explaining 42 percent of the variance (see Table 5–24). A one percentage point increase in Hispanic education produces a .438 percent increase in Hispanic graduation rates. A one percentage point increase in Anglo poverty is associated with a .61 percent increase in the Hispanic graduation ratio. Similarly, a one percentage point increase in Hispanic representation produces a corresponding increase of .121 percent in Hispanic graduation rates. District size, in turn, appears to reduce the likelihood of Hispanic students graduating from high school.

Table 5–24   **The Impact of Hispanic Representation on Hispanic Graduation Rates**

Dependent Variable = Hispanic Graduation Ratio

Independent Variables	Slope	Slope
Hispanic Education	.363*	.438*
Percent Anglos Below Poverty	.637*	.610*
Hispanic/Anglo Income Ratio	.224	——— a
Hispanic Representation	.067#	.121*
Blacks in School System	-.009	——— a
District Size in Thousands	-1.692*	-2.891*
R^2	.47	.44
Adjusted R^2	.45	.42
F	17.03	22.62
N	120	120

*$p < .05$
#$p < .1$
[a]Equation reestimated omitting this variable.

Policy Impact: A Summary

The political model of second-generation discrimination reveals a pattern that varies across the forms of discrimination. Perhaps the most consistent force is one that cannot be directly influenced by the Hispanic political community—black students. The findings for black students are consistent with the power thesis of discrimination. In school districts with more blacks, discriminatory actions are taken first against black students, thus easing some of the pressure on Hispanic students. Large black enrollments in EMR and TMR classes reduce the size of Hispanic enrollments greatly.

Similarly, large black enrollments in gifted classes increase Hispanic enrollments. Punishment actions reveal a similar pattern; in districts that punish a disproportionately large number of black students, Hispanic students receive less disproportionate punishment. This relationship holds for corporal punishment, suspensions, and expulsions.

Although the size of the black student body is outside the control of the Hispanic community, Hispanic representation is not. Hispanic representation reduces the amount of second-generation discrimination in all nine areas. First, greater Hispanic representation is associated with proportionately fewer Hispanic students placed in EMR and TMR classes. Second, it is positively correlated with enrollments in gifted programs. Third, it is negatively correlated with enrollments in bilingual programs. All four of these indicators represent academic grouping; Hispanic representation is also negatively related to disparities in discipline. Finally, Hispanic representation is positively associated with educational outputs; well-represented districts graduate proportionately more students from high school. Hispanic representation is rarely the most important factor in combating second-generation discrimination (as it is for blacks), but it always is a significant one.

The political resources of the Hispanic community have only a modest impact on second-generation discrimination. Hispanic income levels are negatively associated with Hispanic EMR assignments and positively associated with gifted class placements. Hispanic education levels are positively correlated with graduation rates. Finally, Anglo poverty is negatively related to bilingual education and positively related to Hispanic high school graduation rates. Social class, therefore, while not as significant as political representation and race, plays an important role in limiting Hispanic student access to equal educational opportunities.

District size, representing level of professionalization and visibility to antidiscrimination agencies, has a significant impact with only two of the nine measures. Large school districts suspended Hispanic students in proportionately smaller numbers than did smaller districts. In addition, large districts were less likely to have Hispanics graduate from high school.

The political model of second-generation discrimination, particularly that part with representation and political resources, does not predict as well for Hispanics as it does for blacks (Meier, Stewart, and England 1989). This relatively lower impact can be explained. Hispanic representation trails far behind that of blacks in similar cities. Hispanics have only about one-third as many teachers and significantly fewer political representatives. Similarly, Hispanic political resources are also lower than those for blacks. Hispanic education and income levels still trail those of blacks. Political models of Hispanic discrimination do not predict as well as black models, therefore, because Hispanics do not have the same political clout that blacks do.

Other Explanations of Educational Inequity

Before concluding that political representation, race, and social class are the predominant causes of Hispanic inequities in access to education, three other possible causes should be discussed. Hispanics might be denied access to education because they are segregated in school districts with few resources, because they have difficulties with the English language, or because they are recent immigrants and therefore have all the problems associated with recent arrivals in this country. This section will examine briefly each of these possible determinants of Hispanic access to equal educational opportunities.

School District Resources

School districts with fewer resources will have fewer resources devoted to gifted classes and other quality education programs. Resource constraints could limit access by all students to quality education, and because Hispanics tend to live in poorer school districts, they will also have only limited access. Our measure of educational resources is the school district's 1985–86 operating budget per student. This measure has a mean of $3,414 and a standard deviation of $607.

To determine if educational resources have an impact on Hispanic student access to equal educational opportunities, the school budget measure was added to the regression equations that appeared in Tables 5–16 through 5–24. Rather than repeat these nine tables in their entirely, Table 5–25 shows the amount of variation that the original equation explained (the R^2 and F value), the slope of educational budget variable, a t-score to determine if the slope is significant, and the amount of variation that the original equation plus the educational budget can explain.

Table 5–25   The Impact of Resources on Policy Ratios:
                    Impact of Education Budget

| | Control | | | | | |
Dependent Variable	R^2	F	Slope	t-score	R^2	F
EMR Classes	.68	88.02	.051	.42	.68	61.63
TMR Classes	.17	10.92	-.097	.73	.18	7.44
Gifted Classes	.46	35.18	-.160	1.71	.47	26.41
Bilingual Classes	.49	60.72	.126	1.43	.49	40.28
Corporal Punishment	.43	37.26	-.252	1.41	.45	25.75
Suspensions	.56	50.79	-.282	2.49*	.57	41.22
Expulsions	.59	65.65	.261	.87	.59	43.91
Dropouts	.25	18.77	-.088	.54	.25	12.53
Graduates	.44	22.62	.087	.84	.44	18.19

*$p < .05$
Notes: Slopes are multiplied by 100.
Control Equations are those in tables 5–16 through 5–24.

The results of Table 5–25 show that educational resources have little impact on the access of Hispanic students to equal educational opportunities. In eight of the nine equations, the slope for educational resources is not statistically significant. For the Hispanic suspensions ratio, a statistically significant relationship exists. The slope is negative, suggesting that school districts with greater resources will suspend proportionately fewer Hispanic students. While this finding is consistent with the resources hypothesis, the more probable conclusion, based on the entire table, is that educational resources have little relationship to Hispanic student access to educational opportunities.[24]

Language Problems

The patterns of second-generation educational discrimination found might also be related to student difficulties mastering English. As chapter 2 noted, many Hispanic persons speak Spanish as their primary language in the home. Language difficulties have been associated with inappropriate assignment of students to lower-ability groups and have been used as the basis for discipline (see chapter 3). To determine whether or not the patterns that we found here might be attributable to language difficulties, we repeated our analysis of second-generation educational discrimination using the Census Bureau's data for the percentage of Hispanics in a school district whose primary language at home was Spanish.[25]

Table 5–26 shows the impact of Spanish language on second-generation discrimination, controlling for the political factors discussed above. Only three of the relationships attain statistical significance: those for EMR classes, gifted classes, and bilingual classes. Contrary to expectations, a one percentage point increase in Spanish language is associated with a .116 percent *decline* in the Hispanic EMR ratio. Similarly, a one percentage point increase in Spanish language is correlated with a .159 percent *gain* in Hispanic gifted class assignments and a .613 percent *decline* in bilingual class ratios.

Table 5–26   **The Impact of Language on Policy Ratios**

Independent Variable = Percent Speaking Spanish at Home

Dependent Variable	R^2	F	Slope	t-score	R^2	F
		Control				
EMR Classes	.68	88.02	-.116	2.35*	.69	69.06
TMR Classes	.17	10.92	.065	1.06	.18	7.68
Gifted Classes	.46	35.18	.159	1.80#	.48	27.67
Bilingual Classes	.49	60.72	-.613	4.85*	.57	55.46
Corporal Punishment	.43	37.26	-.070	1.37	.45	25.69
Suspensions	.56	50.79	-.056	1.34	.56	38.78
Expulsions	.59	65.65	-.061	.61	.59	43.60
Dropouts	.25	18.77	-.093	1.63	.25	13.59
Graduates	.44	22.62	-.001	.02	.44	17.94

*$p < .05$
#$p < .10$
Note: Control Equations are those in tables 5–16 through 5–24.

All three findings are contrary to expectations. Rather than a contributing factor toward increased second-generation discrimination, Spanish-language use appears to reduce second-generation discrimination in EMR, gifted, and bilingual assignments. In the case of bilingual education ratios, the increase in explained variation is substantial. The findings of Table 5–26 clearly imply that the results of this chapter cannot be attributed solely to language difficulties on the part of Hispanic students. If anything, bilingualism appears to be a modest advantage for some Hispanic students when measures of ability grouping are considered.

Immigration

One final alternative explanation for the patterns found in this chapter is immigration. Because Hispanics are recent and continuing immigrants, they are likely to have problems adjusting to the educational system. School systems have long used their sorting abilities to deny educational opportunities to immigrant children (see Tyack 1974). The impact of immigration on second-generation discrimination can be investigated.

Acquiring immigration figures for Hispanics is difficult for a variety of reasons. Illegal immigration figures are simply not available. Legal immigration figures are of limited utility because Puerto Ricans are U.S. citizens and, therefore, do not qualify as immigrants. To circumvent this problem, for each school district an immigration figure was calculated as the percentage of Hispanic residents who were foreign-born (born in Latin or Central America only) plus one half the Hispanic residents who are of Puerto Rican ancestry. The 50 percent figure for Puerto Ricans is fairly close to the percentage of mainland Puerto Ricans who were born on the island (see chapter 2).

Table 5–27 shows the impact of immigration on second-generation discrimination, controlling for the political, racial, and social class variables in Tables 5–16 through 5–24. Immigration does not appear to have any impact on either ability grouping or educational attainment. It does have a significant impact on corporal punishment and suspensions, but the impact is negative. A one percentage point increase in Hispanic immigration is associated with a .121 percent decline in Hispanic corporal punishment ratios and a .153 percent decline in suspension ratios.[26] In other words, immigration is associated with less discipline rather than more discipline. While this is an intriguing finding, it directly contradicts the thesis that patterns of second-generation educational discrimination reflect immigration.

Table 5–27   The Impact of Immigration on Policy Ratios

Independent Variable = Percent of Hispanics Who Are Immigrants

Dependent Variable	R^2	F	Slope	t-score	R^2	F
			Control			
EMR Classes	.68	88.02	-.008	.21	.68	65.53
TMR Classes	.17	10.92	-.005	.11	.17	7.23
Gifted Classes	.46	35.18	-.041	1.61	.47	26.34
Bilingual Classes	.49	60.72	-.020	.23	.49	40.20
Corporal Punishment	.43	37.26	-.121	2.38*	.47	27.93
Suspensions	.56	50.79	-.153	4.48*	.61	48.85
Expulsions	.59	65.65	-.084	.98	.59	44.07
Dropouts	.25	18.77	-.075	1.57	.27	13.50
Graduates	.44	22.62	-.013	.37	.44	17.99

*p <.05

Note: Control Equations are those in tables 5–16 through 5–24

Conclusion

This chapter examined the linkage between Hispanic representation and educational policies that affect Hispanic students. Information on academic grouping, discipline, and educational attainment was presented for a set of urban American school districts. Compared to Anglo students, Hispanic students are overrepresented in classes for the educable mentally retarded, in classes for the trainable mentally retarded, and in bilingual classes. Hispanic students are underrepresented in classes for the gifted and talented.

Disciplinary practices show a similar pattern, though not as extreme. Compared to Anglos, Hispanic students are not subject to more corporal punishment, but they are subject to more suspensions and expulsions. Given these Hispanic-Anglo differences, that Hispanics have lower high school graduation rates should come as no surprise.

Following the presentation of ethnic differences in academic grouping, discipline, and educational attainment, an argument was presented that these patterns are consistent with the notion of second-generation educational discrimination. In virtually all cases, Hispanics were overrepresented in situations with negative connotations and underrepresented in situations with positive connotations. Intercorrelations between the policies also revealed a pattern consistent with the idea of discrimination. A factor analysis revealed two dimensions. The first included lower-level academic grouping and discipline, suggesting that grouping is used to handle disciplinary problems. The second dimension consisted of high graduation rates, high gifted class enrollments, and low bilingual class enrollments. The second dimension links bilingual education to efforts to limit Hispanic access to equal education opportunities.

The final portion of this chapter examined academic grouping, punishment, and educational attainment with a political theory of education presented in chapter 1. Two findings in this analysis are particularly important. First, as black placements increase in any category, Hispanic placements decline. This pattern is consistent with theories of group conflict that argue Hispanics will fare better in multiracial situations because Anglos are more concerned with contacts with blacks than with Hispanics. Second, Hispanic representation is associated with greater access to equal education. The process of second-generation discrimination, therefore, can be countered by political action designed to increase the number of Hispanics in policy-making positions. These relationships were not influenced by school district resources, language difficulties, or recent immigration.

Notes

1. OCR also collects data on placement in classes for specific learning disabilities (LD) and classes for the seriously emotionally disturbed (SEMD). A preliminary examination of these classes for both blacks and Hispanics revealed that racial disparities were not as large as they are for EMR, TMR, and gifted classes. We believe that the relative racial equity in SEMD results because these classes are smaller and a greater burden of proof is placed on the educator who wishes to place a student in such classes. Classes for the specific learning disabled, while large, require a more precise diagnosis than do EMR classes, which again makes discrimination more difficult. This finding is contrary to that of Tucker (1980), who argues racial disparities exist for LD classes. In 1986 we found an LD ratio of 1.04 for black students and .96 for Hispanic students.

2. Data on industrial arts programs would be a valuable measure of tracking if OCR collected such data by ethnicity of student. Unfortunately OCR only requires school districts to report such data according to sex.

3. Our measure is similar to Finn's *logged odds index* (1982, p. 330), but with two slight differences. Finn uses the white student population as the base for comparison rather than the total student population. Using only white students creates some problems in studying Hispanics because many of the school districts also contain black students. In addition, Finn uses a log transformation of his index. We use a similar transformation where the index is used in regression equations, but do not use it in the descriptive tables because the index is more interpretable than the logged index.

4. Definitions of TMR and EMR classes and who is eligible to be placed in such classes vary from state to state and from school district to school district (see Heller, Holtzman, and Messick 1982, 24).

5. This is the pattern for black students (see Meier, Stewart, and England 1989, 82).

6. Black TMR ratios follow a similar pattern but do not decline as much or subsequently rise as much. In 1984, the black TMR ratio was 1.29 (Meier, Stewart, and England 1989, 82).

7. Heller, Holtzman, and Messick (1982) argue that this pattern would occur if school districts relied heavily on IQ tests for assignments. Because IQ tests are culturally biased, particularly at the extremes, the ratio of Hispanic to Anglo students is greater the lower one descends on the IQ scale. Using such scores for TMR assignments, therefore, would result in higher Hispanic TMR ratios than EMR ratios. The recency of this development, given the general bias in IQ tests, is cause for concern.

8. Black gifted class ratios are generally slightly lower than Hispanic ratios, but not strikingly so (see Meier, Stewart, and England 1989, 82).

9. In this case, the term Anglo might be a misnomer. White students in a bilingual class are unlikely to be the long-time Anglo residents who make up most of the student body. They are likely to be recent immigrants, except in those rare school districts that make an effort to balance their bilingual class compositions.

10. This difference results from a statistical artifact. The Los Angeles school district enrolls 67 percent of its Hispanic students in bilingual classes. When total numbers nationwide are used to calculate enrollments, the 25 percent figure results. When the percentage enrollment in bilingual classes is averaged, the 18 percent figure results. The later method reduces significantly the impact of Los Angeles and other large districts.

11. Tropea presents evidence that appears to show that the number of suspensions is underreported by a factor of ten or more. The problem may be in what school districts define as a formal suspension (1987b, p. 349).

12. These states are California, Hawaii, Maine, Massachusetts, New Hampshire, New Jersey, New York, Rhode Island, and Vermont.

13. Black corporal punishment ratios reported by Meier, Stewart, and England (1989, p. 85) hover around 1.8 for 1976 through 1984.

14. It is possible, but not likely, that some school districts did not expel any students and, therefore, did not report any data to

OCR. We feel this is unlikely because districts often skipped one year and reported data (enumerating too many cases for it to temporarily have dropped to zero) in subsequent years. In addition, in a school district of five thousand students, one would expect at least a few students to be expelled.

15. Whether academic grouping and discipline predate discrimination is another question. Academic grouping techniques were developed at about the same time that school populations became more diverse with the advent of universal education. Hispanics at this time did not have access to Anglo institutions of education. The social-class biases in early academic grouping practices imply that Hispanics will be subjected to the same treatment for the same reasons.

16. The probability is determined using the binomial probability distribution with twenty-eight trials, twenty-three or more successes, and an initial random probability of .5.

17. The correlation for dropouts can safely be ignored since it is based on only a single year.

18. Another possibility is that this relationship might represent a failure to build language skills needed to graduate from high school.

19. When the figures for bilingual education are deleted from the analysis, only 9.6 percent of Hispanic students are affected, although the high is 33.4 percent. This is a fairly low level compared to the 30.8 percent of black students who are affected by OCR-reported ability grouping and discipline measures. It illustrates how bilingual education can be used in place of other methods of resegregation.

20. We prefer this measure for both theoretical reasons and practical reasons. The practical reasons are that Hispanic teachers and Hispanic board members have less impact on public policy when used separately or in combination without this interaction effect. Theoretically, the measure is attractive since it directly links both forms of representation.

21. An examination of the ordinary least squares regressions reveals that the errors for the regressions are heteroscedastic. As a result, ordinary least squares estimates for these equations are not robust (Berry and Feldman 1985, 77). To overcome these

problems and provide estimates that are more robust, we used interative weighted least squares (Rubin 1983; Krasker 1988). Specifically we use the sine estimates approach of David Andrews which generates coefficients that are "resistant to gross deviations of a small number of points and relative efficient over a broad range of disruptions" (1974, p. 523). When the data meet the error assumptions of ordinary least squares, this technique produces estimates that are similar to least squares estimates.

22. Because we have measured Hispanic income as a percentage of Anglo income, a one percentage point increase in this ratio is associated with a .575 percent decline in EMR assignments.

23. Hispanic representation and Anglo poverty suffer from collinearity problems in this regression. As a result, Anglo poverty is significant in the full equation but not in the reduced equation.

24. This finding calls into question some of the research done on school funding equity. Because we have indicators of only some measures of second-generation discrimination, we do not feel safe in concluding that resources have no role in affecting second-generation discrimination. Our findings are only suggestive; however, they do imply that discriminatory practices exist independently of the budget problems of a school district.

25. As noted earlier in this chapter, we are skeptical that the language assessments of the schools are unbiased. Because the Census Bureau does not have a stake in how many individuals speak Spanish, we feel their figures are more accurate.

26. These findings remain when other measures of immigration are used. We tried simply the percent Hispanic foreign-born (thus omitting Puerto Ricans) and the percent Hispanic foreign-born plus the percent Puerto Rican (thus overemphasizing Puerto Ricans) and got virtually the same results.

Chapter 6

The Consequences of
Second-Generation Discrimination

In chapter 5 we argued that academic grouping, discipline, and educational attainment have a common core that can be termed second-generation educational discrimination. Bilingual education, although not normally perceived in these terms, was also related to discriminatory educational patterns. Second-generation discrimination against Hispanics was then related to social class, race, political resources, and the political process. That portions of academic grouping, discipline, and educational attainment are related to discrimination and that political pressure can be used to mitigate this discrimination is not in doubt. These findings are not affected by school district resources, student language problems, or the extent of recent immigration.

Left for analysis are the ramifications of our findings in chapter 5. What are the interrelationships and consequences of an educational system that uses second-generation discrimination? In this chapter we first examine the interrelationships between the various indicators of second-generation discrimination. Second, second-generation discrimination is linked to desegregation. Third, the relationship between second-generation discrimination and the phenomenon of declining white enrollments is examined. Fourth, we examine the relationship between second-generation discrimination and student classroom performance.

Patterns of Second-Generation Discrimination

If academic grouping and discipline form a pattern of second-generation discrimination, then individual acts of discrimination are not discrete events. They form a pattern of actions that limit the equal access of Hispanic students to the best education available in the school district. Discrimination in academic grouping can produce inequities in discipline, and both can affect the ability of Hispanics to graduate from high school (see Velez 1989, 121). The theoretical interrelationships of the second-generation discrimination measures are shown in Figure 6–1. Our data set provides a unique opportunity to examine these linkages.

The model in Figure 6–1 should not be interpreted as a rigid deterministic model. We are not arguing, for example, that the only determinant of disproportionate Hispanic placements in TMR classes is the placement of Hispanics in EMR classes. A wide variety of factors affect TMR placement, including but not limited to the characteristics of the student, the characteristics of the teacher, funds for TMR classes, procedures used to classify students, and emphasis on special education in the school district. Our interest is not to explain fully Hispanic TMR enrollments, but rather to postulate a theoretical model of relationships that would exist if discrimination against Hispanic students underlies these actions. The theoretical model is then compared to the data to see if they are consistent with each other. If the results are inconsistent with the model, then we reject discrimination as a determinant. If the results are consistent, then the hypothesis of discrimination gains credibility.

Figure 6–1   A Model of Second-Generation Discrimination

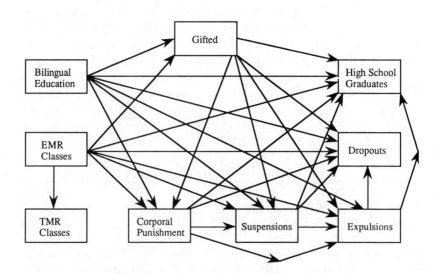

TMR Classes

The second-generation discrimination model suggests that placement of Hispanics in TMR classes is a function of placement in EMR classes. If EMR classes are used to separate Hispanic students from Anglo students, then a large number of Hispanic students will be referred to EMR classes. Enrollment pressures on EMR classes require a response because school districts do not have unlimited resources for this single type of class. One way to ease some of the crowding in EMR classes is to shift some EMR students to TMR classes.[1] If ethnicity or class is a consideration in initial assignments to EMR classes, then ethnicity or class is quite likely a reason to assign students to TMR classes, either initially or as the result of enrollment pressures. Such a pattern was found for black students (see Meier, Stewart, and England 1989, 110).

Table 6–1 shows the relationship between EMR classes and TMR classes from 1976 through 1986.[2] The table also shows the relationship for the pooled data set containing all reported data from 1976 though 1986 as a single relationship. Although Hispanic EMR assignments are related to Hispanic TMR assignments, the relationship is weak and changing over time. In 1976, the relationship for Hispanics is strongest, when a one percent increase in the EMR ratio is associated with a .36 percent increase in the TMR ratio and 14 percent of the variation is explained.[3] After 1976 the strength of the relationship declines, and the size of the regression coefficient does also. By 1984 this relationship no longer exists, and the slope, while not significant, is negative.

Table 6–1   **TMR Class Assignments as a Function of EMR Classes**

Dependent Variable = Hispanic TMR Ratio

Year	Independent Variable EMR	R^2	F	n
1976	.36*	.14	15.46	97
1978	.29*	.08	8.43	99
1980	.21*	.08	7.67	85
1982	.28*	.06	3.75	63
1984	-.12	.01	1.04	74
1986	.11	.02	1.42	81
Pooled	.19*	.04	21.05	497

*p <.05

Note: Pooled estimate includes years 1976, 1978, 1980, 1982, 1984, and 1986.

The relationships in Table 6–1 form a pattern that was initially consistent with second-generation discrimination, but no longer is. The decoupling of these classes may reflect the legal pressures on schools to make appropriate special education assignments (see, for example, Tucker 1980). We should be skeptical, however, of such an impact because the EMR-TMR relationship continues to hold for black students (see Meier, Stewart, and England 1989, 110).

Gifted Classes

In a world without discrimination, gifted classes could be viewed as the highest quality education a school district offers, and gifted placements would be based on nondiscriminatory evaluations of ability. In such a world, one would not expect that gifted class enrollments would be related to either EMR class enrollments or to bilingual education. In fact, if bilingual education were the effective educational mechanism that its proponents contend, we might even expect a positive relationship between bilingual education and gifted class enrollments. The second-generation discrimination model, however, predicts differently. It holds that Hispanic assignments to gifted classes will be negatively related to both the Hispanic EMR ratio and the Hispanic bilingual ratio.

The relationships between Hispanic EMR ratios, Hispanic bilingual ratios, and Hispanic gifted class ratios are shown in Table 6–2. An interesting pattern appears. In 1976 and 1978 there are no relationships, a finding inconsistent with the second-generation discrimination model.[4] From 1980 to 1986, however, the predicted negative relationships appear (as they also do in the pooled data set), and the predictive ability of the model improves. The relative impact of EMR and bilingual classes changes also. EMR classes become less important over time, and the impact of bilingual classes becomes more important. By 1986, bilingual classes have a strong negative relationship on Hispanic assignments to gifted classes, and EMR classes have a modest negative relationship.

The reasons for the change in relationships are unknown, but some speculation is possible. Bilingual education is highly valued by the Hispanic community and is a much larger program than EMR classes. A discriminatory school system might, therefore, have seen bilingual education as an easy way to create an Hispanic track and still retain support from the Hispanic community.

Because such options are not available for black students, the relationship between black EMR assignments and black gifted class enrollments remains, even when it disappears for Hispanic students. The emergence of a significant relationship between EMR and gifted classes in 1986, however, suggests that we should not be too quick to assume practices have changed.

Table 6–2   **Gifted Class Assignments as a Function of EMR Assignments and Bilingual Class Assignments**

Dependent Variable = Hispanic Gifted Class Ratio

Year	Independent Variables EMR	Bilingual	R^2	Adjusted R^2	F	N
1976	.06	-.16#	.05	.03	1.94	73
1978	-.08	-.09	.02	.00	.80	98
1980	-.39*	-.27*	.20	.19	13.39	110
1982	-.25	-.40*	.21	.19	9.76	75
1984	.01	-.29*	.20	.19	11.95	96
1986	-.17#	-.29*	.17	.15	10.40	105
Pooled	-.13*	-.22*	.10	.10	30.61	556

*p <.05
#p <.1

Note: Pooled estimate includes years 1976, 1978, 1980, 1982, 1984, and 1986.

Corporal Punishment

A theory of second-generation discrimination would hold that corporal punishment would be positively related with negative academic grouping. Such a relationship is found for black students in major urban school districts (Meier, Stewart, and England 1989, 112). Some recent historical analysis supports the second-generation linkage tested here. In Baltimore, Tropea found that the number of students assigned to special classes for disciplinary reasons dropped precipitously in 1922 while the enrollments in "subnormal" classes exploded. He concluded that the reason for assigning the students was changed but the same type of students were assigned (1987a, p. 44). With the introduction of psychological testing, the subnormal classes were redesignated as mentally handicapped. With continued growth in these classes, disciplinary referrals dropped to zero. In the Washington, D.C. school district, after federal courts forced the school district (for racial discrimination reasons) to eliminate referrals to the "basic track" for academic reasons, a proportionate increase in referrals for behavioral (i.e., discipline) reasons occurred (Tropea 1987b, 344). Lower-level academic groups and discipline, it seems, have had much in common for a long period of time.

Still, the linkage between negative ability grouping and punishment has not been examined for Hispanic students. The unique pattern of second-generation discrimination for Hispanic students suggests that punishment is less likely to be a factor in discrimination against Hispanics, that academic grouping is sufficient to discourage Hispanic students and keep them separate from Anglo students.

Table 6–3 shows the interrelationships between the Hispanic corporal punishment ratio and the Hispanic EMR and bilingual class ratios. A decidedly mixed pattern appears that in part confirms the general nature of second-generation discrimination, in part notes the unique aspects of second-generation regarding Hispanics, and in part implies the decoupling of discipline from academic grouping. EMR assignments generally have a strong positive relationship with corporal punishment ratios, except for 1984 when the size of the coefficient remains the same, but it is no longer significant.[5] Bilingual education forms an inconsistent relationship with corporal punishment; at times the relationship is weak and positive, and at other times there is no relationship at all.

Table 6–3   **Corporal Punishment as a Function of EMR Assignments and Bilingual Class Assignments**

Dependent Variable = Hispanic Corporal Punishment Ratio

| Year | Independent Variables | | R^2 | Adjusted R^2 | F | N |
	EMR Ratio	Bilingual				
1976	.20	-.04#	.11	.09	5.74	97
1978	.37*	.09*	.19	.17	9.74	86
1980	.49*	.09#	.25	.24	13.80	84
1982	.31*	.07	.17	.13	5.08	54
1984	.37	-.13	.06	.03	1.92	59
1986	.33*	.02	.19	.16	7.10	63
Pooled	.35*	.04#	.13	.13	33.75	442

*p <.05
#p <.1
Note: Pooled estimate includes years 1976, 1978, 1980, 1982, 1984, and 1986.

The relationship between academic grouping and corporal punishment may then be characterized as uncertain. We may be seeing the transformation of a weak relationship into one without much consequence at the same time that negative academic grouping is increasing its impact on gifted classes. This change would suggest that punishment is no longer a major factor in second-generation discrimination against Hispanics, that academic grouping may be sufficient (if relationships are found with educational attainment). Alternatively, the pattern might indicate that the academic grouping and punishment paths of second-generation discrimination against Hispanics have been separated, but that each continues to operate.

Suspensions

A second-generation discrimination theory of suspensions would link suspensions to both academic grouping and previous punishment. For black students, corporal punishment ratios, EMR ratios, and gifted class ratios were associated with greater suspension ratios (Meier, Stewart, and England 1989, 113). For Hispanics, only EMR class placements and corporal punishment affect suspensions (see Table 6–4). Unlike for corporal punishment, EMR assignments are a consistent factor in explaining Hispanic suspensions. A one percent increase in Hispanic EMR ratios translates into a .26 to .42 percent increase in Hispanic suspension ratios. Corporal punishment has a modest but positive relationship with suspensions.

Table 6–4	Supensions as a Function of EMR Assignments and Corporal Punishment					

Dependent Variable = Hispanic Suspension Ratio

	Independent Variables			Adjusted		
Year	EMR Ratio	Punishment	R^2	R^2	F	N
1976	.31*	.27*	.25	.25	17.42	100
1978	.37*	.02	.27	.25	15.83	90
1980	.28*	.14*	.34	.33	21.42	85
1982	.26*	.29*	.34	.31	12.90	54
1984	.42*	.16*	.37	.35	16.76	59
1986	.40*	.16	.41	.38	19.75	61
Pooled	.32*	.17*	.28	.27	84.41	447

*p <.05
#p <.1
Note: Pooled estimate includes years 1976, 1978, 1980, 1982, 1984, and 1986.

The results of Table 6–4 suggest that the separate academic grouping and discipline tracks of Table 6–3 might be overgeneralized. Negative academic grouping is strongly and consistently related to suspensions, a relationship stronger than that between corporal punishment and suspensions. Because many schools do not permit corporal punishment, the relationships for suspensions are more likely to reflect the disciplinary experiences of most Hispanic students.

Expulsions

In theory, expulsions might be a function of all the academic grouping and punishment measures that precede it. In practice, however, the effects of academic grouping and corporal punishment on expulsions are indirect. Their impact on expulsions is through their impact on suspensions. As shown in Table 6–5, the Hispanic suspensions ratio is the only significant influence on the Hispanic expulsions ratio, with strong positive relationships for every year with data. Such a direct and simple pattern does not dispute the second-generation theory of discrimination, however, if one looks at all previous relationships rather than just those in Table 6–5.

Table 6–5   **Expulsions as a Function of Suspensions**

Dependent Variable = Hispanic Expulsion Ratio

Year	Independent Variable Suspension Ratio	R^2	F	N
1976	.46*	.11	7.32	61
1978	.66*	.09	4.25	43
1980	.99*	.23	14.11	49
Pooled	.74*	.15	39.13	229

*p <.05
#p <.1
Note: Pooled estimate includes years 1973, 1974, 1976, 1978, and 1980.

Dropouts

Hispanic dropout ratios were measured only for 1976, so conclusions about the impact of other forces on dropouts will of necessity be tentative. For blacks, the dropout ratio was found to be associated with the expulsion ratio only (Meier, Stewart, and England 1989, 115). Recent work by Velez however, found a positive relationship between suspensions and dropouts for Hispanics (1989, p. 123). Velez also argues that enrollments in advanced or academic tracks, such as gifted classes, should reduce dropouts (p. 121). The pattern for Hispanics in our data is more interesting and more consistent with second-generation discrimination patterns than were the black student patterns. Table 6–6 illustrates that dropouts are positively related to Hispanic suspensions ratios and negatively related to Hispanic gifted class ratios. The twin forces of greater discipline and denial of access to quality education are apparent. A one percent increase in the suspensions ratio translates into a .55 percent increase in the dropout ratio. A one percent increase in the Hispanic gifted class ratio is associated with a .11 percent decrease in dropouts.

Table 6–6   **Determinants of the Hispanic Dropout Ratio**

Dependent Variable = Hispanic Dropout Ratio
Regression Coefficients Year = 1976

Independent Variables	Slope
Hispanic Suspension Ratio	.55*
Hispanic Gifted Ratio	-.11*
R^2	.25
Adjusted R^2	.24
F	19.42
N	119

*$p < .05$

High School Graduation

The final educational attainment measure is that for high school graduation. Even if an Hispanic student is able to graduate from high school, however, the educational opportunities afforded Hispanic students may still not be equal to those afforded Anglo students. Despite the limitation of the high school graduation rate as a measure of educational attainment, some interesting patterns are revealed. Table 6–7 shows the analysis of high school graduation ratios for 1976, the only year with complete data. The difficulty in interpreting this equation is immediately evident. Only twenty school districts remain in the analysis, and collinearity is high. The result are unstable regression coefficients and strong limits on generalizations.

Avoiding the problem of limited cases requires that more years be included in the analysis. The increase in years essentially means dropping the dropout and expulsion measures from the analysis.

Table 6–8 shows the end results of this extended analysis. Three measures affect the Hispanic high school graduation ratio. The Hispanic corporal punishment ratio is negatively and weakly related to graduation rates; only for the pooled data set is the relationship significant. Hispanic gifted class ratios are positively and significantly related to graduation rates, although the relationship is again modest. Finally, Hispanic bilingual class ratios are negatively associated with high school graduation; this relationship, while modest, is the most consistent of the relationships. Larger bilingual class ratios are associated with declines in high school graduation rates.

Table 6–7   Determinants of High School Graduates

Dependent Variable = Hispanic High School Graduate Ratio

Regression Coefficients Year = 1976

Independent Variables	Slope
Hispanic Dropout Ratio	-.52*
Hispanic Expulsion Ratio	-.04
Hispanic Suspension Ratio	.62*
Hispanic Punishment Ratio	.21*
Hispanic Gifted Ratio	.12#
Hispanic EMR Ratio	-.09#
R^2	.88
Adjusted R^2	.83
F	15.82
N	20

*p <.05
#p <.1

Table 6–8   The Impact of Corporal Punishment, Gifted Classes, and Bilingual Education on High School Graduates

Dependent Variable = Hispanic Graduates Ratio

Year	Independent Variables			R^2	Adjusted R^2	F	N
	Punish	Gifted	Bilingual				
1976	-.10	.07	-.04	.11	.05	1.76	45
1978	-.14	.05	-.18*	.24	.21	6.92	69
1980	-.06	.11#	-.12*	.20	.16	5.66	74
1982	-.02	.15*	-.12#	.22	.17	4.36	51
1984	.07	.12*	-.09*	.35	.31	9.08	54
1986	.01	.17*	-.07	.30	.27	8.73	64
Pooled	-.06#	.10*	-.13*	.23	.23	35.37	356

*p <.05
#p <.1

Note: Pooled estimate includes years 1976, 1978, 1980, 1982, 1984, and 1986.

The results of this analysis allow us to redraw Figure 6–1 showing the interrelationships between the various measures of second-generation discrimination. Figure 6–2 shows these relationships and provides a summary of the findings in this section. Hispanic high school graduation rates are negatively associated with corporal punishment and bilingual classes, and positively associated with gifted classes. Hispanic dropout rates are positively associated with suspensions and negatively associated with gifted class enrollments. Expulsions are a function of suspensions alone. Hispanic suspension ratios reflect positive relationships with EMR classes and corporal punishment. Hispanic corporal punishment ratios are positively associated with EMR class enrollments and bilingual class enrollments. Gifted class enrollments correlate negatively with EMR class enrollments and bilingual class assignments.

Figure 6–2   **An Empirical Model of Second-Generation Discrimination for Hispanic Students**

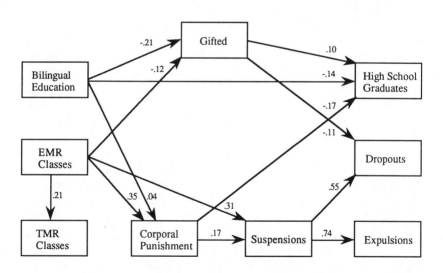

The pattern of relationships shows that second-generation discrimination against Hispanics follows a pattern different from discrimination against blacks. For blacks, the process starts with and is centered around assignments to EMR classes (see Meier, Stewart, and England 1989). For Hispanics, two starting points exist, EMR classes and bilingual education classes. The latter is most significant. As currently operated in many school districts, bilingual education classes serve a role similar to EMR classes—they separate Hispanics student from Anglo students. The separate education for Hispanics becomes unequal education. School districts with proportionately smaller bilingual programs produce greater access to equal educational opportunities for Hispanic students. Because bilingual education classes are so much larger than EMR classes, there is less need to use EMR classes for resegregative purposes.

Patterns of Discrimination in the Hispanic Communities

The patterns of second-generation discrimination shown in this chapter mask variations that exist among the different Hispanic communities. Given the different political and social resources and economic status of Mexican Americans, Cuban Americans, and Puerto Ricans, one would expect that the relationships might differ for each of these subgroups. To circumvent the problem with the limited number of cases available for analysis, only the pooled time series data set will be used. This data set provides a sufficient number of cases to permit at least some preliminary observations about second-generation discrimination for Mexican Americans, Cuban Americans, and Puerto Ricans. The research strategy is to replicate the results of Figure 6–2 for each subset of districts containing Mexican-American, Cuban-American, and Puerto Rican pluralities.

The model of second-generation discrimination for Mexican Americans is quite similar to that for all Hispanics (see Figure 6–3). This similarity is to be expected, given that the overwhelming majority of school districts in our sample are Mexican-American. In fact, only three differences between the results for all Hispanics and the results for Mexican Americans exist. For Mexican Americans, there are no relationships between EMR class assignments and gifted class assignments, between bilingual class enrollments and corporal punishment, and between corporal punishment and high school graduation rates. All other relationships continue to exist, even if the magnitude of the relationships changes somewhat. The pattern identified for second-generation discrimination, therefore, is primarily a pattern for Mexican-American school districts.

Figure 6–3   **An Empirical Model of Second-Generation Discrimination for Mexican-American Students**

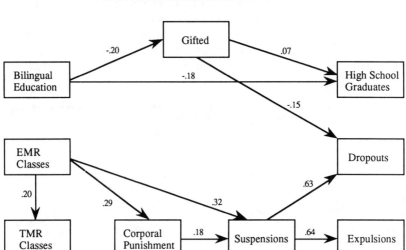

Puerto Rican school districts show a much different pattern from that in Mexican-American school districts (see Figure 6–4). The most striking aspect of Figure 6–4 is that the relationships for discipline drop out of the model, and the model becomes almost exclusively an academic grouping model. One explanation for this centers on corporal punishment. Few Puerto Rican school districts are in states that permit corporal punishment; as a result, the figures for corporal punishment are exceptionally weak.

Other relationships, however, become much stronger for Puerto Rican school districts. A one percent increase in Hispanic EMR assignments results in a full one percent decrease in Hispanic gifted class enrollments, and a one percent increase in bilingual class enrollments results in a .52 percent decrease in Hispanic gifted class enrollments. These coefficients are 25 times and 2.5 times larger, respectively, than the same coefficients for Mexican Americans. EMR classes, in fact, dominate the pattern of relationships, producing the only significant relationships with corporal punishment and suspensions. High school graduation rates are affected by both gifted classes and EMR classes.

The discrimination relationships for Cuban Americans follows a third pattern (see Figure 6–5). Virtually all the linkages found for Mexican Americans disappear for Cuban Americans. Only five significant relationships remain. A one percent increase in corporal punishment results in a 1.09 percent increase in suspensions, and a one percent increase in suspensions produces a .31 percent increase in dropouts (generally expected relationships). EMR classes have only one impact, but it is an extremely important one. A one percent increase in Hispanic EMR assignments is associated with a .48 percent decline in high school graduation rates.

Figure 6–4   An Empirical Model of Second-Generation Discrimination for Puerto Rican Students

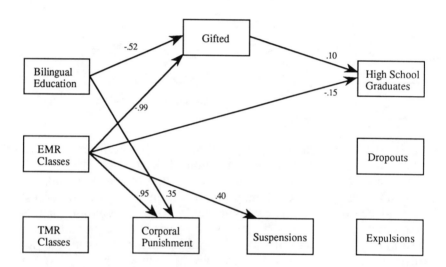

Bilingual education relationships, however, are where the Cuban-American model differs greatly from the others. A one percent increase in Hispanic bilingual class assignments results in a .25 percent *increase* in the Hispanic gifted class ratio. Furthermore, a one percent increase in the bilingual ratio produces a .14 percent *increase* in Hispanic high school graduation rates. For the first time, bilingual class assignments appear to produce positive impacts on Hispanic students.

Understanding why the bilingual class relationships are positive for Cuban Americans and negative for other Hispanics is reasonably straightforward. Cuban Americans, as has been widely documented, have distinct economic advantages over other Hispanics (see chapter 2). Combining their economic success with their geographic concentration, most Cuban Americans live in cities that are genuinely bilingual and bicultural. A proficiency in Spanish but lack thereof in English is no disadvantage in such cities; in Miami, the dominance of Hispanic business interests make it a distinct disadvantage not to speak Spanish. Bilingualism, in short, has economic advantages in cities populated by Cuban Americans. Such is not the case in other cities, even with Hispanic majorities. In addition, Cuban Americans are much more likely to be middle class and use this status to take advantage of opportunities in the school system. Social class, because it is also related to political power, might be the sole reason for the different Cuban-American pattern. Because Mexican Americans and Puerto Ricans have not achieved the same level of economic success, they have not been able to convert bilingualism into an educational advantage as Cuban Americans have.

Figure 6–5   An Empirical Model of Second-Generation Discrimination for Cuban-American Students

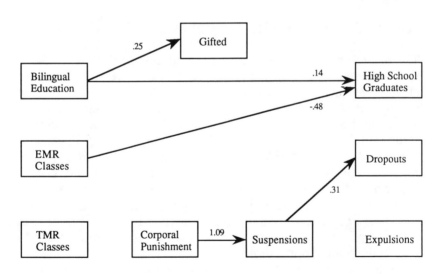

The separate analysis of Mexican-American, Puerto Rican, and Cuban-American school districts has been fruitful. Mexican Americans show the classic two-factor version of second-generation discrimination. Negative academic grouping and punishment are related, and both forces are related to dropping out of school. The second factor links bilingual education (a negative) with gifted class enrollments (a positive) and high school graduation rates.

Puerto Ricans see only one dimension of second-generation educational discrimination—academic grouping. Bilingual education classes and EMR classes place severe limits on getting into gifted classes. The limit on gifted enrollments plus the higher EMR enrollments produce the lower level of high school graduation rates. Academic grouping appears to work so successfully in discouraging Puerto Ricans in the school system that excessive discipline in not required.

Cuban Americans follow a unique pattern. For them, bilingual classes are turned into educational assets. Punishment remains a separate phenomenon that is unlinked to academic grouping. Bilingual classes improve educational performance, while EMR assignments severely limit it. Cuban Americans concerned with second-generation discrimination, therefore, need only focus on a single indicator—assignment to EMR classes. No other factor is a major limit on the access of Cuban Americans to equal educational opportunities.

Desegregation and Second-Generation Discrimination

The use of academic grouping and discipline to resegregate classrooms has generally been associated with desegregation. Actions such as second-generation discrimination became visible in the south after southern schools were forced to desegregate in the late 1960s and early 1970s (Rodgers and Bullock 1972; Children's Defense Fund 1974; Smith and Dziuban 1977; Eyler, Cook, and Ward 1983; Trent 1981). For blacks in the south, such a linkage makes some sense. Until schools are desegregated, ability grouping, curriculum tracking, and discipline can play no role in separating white students from black students because interracial contact does not exist. Only after desegregation does a school district need to rely on second-generation techniques to limit access to equal educational opportunities.

As we have argued, however, second-generation discrimination is not limited to black students; it also affects Hispanic students. Neither are such efforts limited to southern school districts that once maintained segregated school systems. Northern school district also used second-generation techniques to limit the contact between white students and black students.

The relationship between second-generation discrimination techniques and desegregation is even more complex for Hispanics. Until the Supreme Court in *Keyes v. Denver* (1973) required that Hispanics also be desegregated, Hispanics students were generally shut out of the desegregation process. Only for Hispanics residing in the southwest, and possibly Puerto Ricans in the northeast, have the courts offered their remedies (see chapter 3). De jure segregation of Hispanic students by 1973 had long since disappeared, but de facto segregation remained. Many Hispanics also reside in northern or western districts that did not experience the same pressure to desegregate, nor did they desegregate as completely.

Assessing the relationship between second-generation discrimination against Hispanics and desegregation is restricted by the availability of data. OCR did not begin to gather second-generation discrimination measures until after most southern (including southwestern) schools had been desegregated; a full set of measures was not collected until 1976. Before-and-after comparisons of academic grouping and discipline, therefore, are not possible. Any assessment of the linkage between desegregation and second-generation techniques, as a result, will be only indirect.

One partial test is available. Because the amount of contact (e.g., degree of segregation) between Hispanic and Anglo students varies from school district to school district, those districts that have greater segregation can be contrasted with those that have less. If desegregation is necessary to implement second-generation techniques, as others contend, then we would expect to see districts with greater desegregation practicing more second-generation discrimination (Finn 1982, 353).

The most common measure of segregation is called the dissimilarity index, which Taeuber and Taeuber (1965) created to measure residential segregation. When applied to school systems, the dissimilarity index measures the percentage of minority students that would have to be moved from one school to another so that each school in the district would have the same percentage of minority students as the entire district. An index of 100 means that no Hispanics attend school with Anglo students, while an index of 0 means that Hispanics are equally distributed in all schools within the district.

Table 6–9 shows the dissimilarity indices for the school districts in our study for 1968 and 1976. The 1968 mean suggests that 43.8 percent of Hispanic students would need to be moved to provide complete statistical equality for all schools. By 1976 this figure had dropped slightly to 38.5 percent. In comparison, Meier,

Stewart, and England found mean dissimilarity indices between blacks and Anglos of 73.2 in 1968 and 46.1 in 1976 (1989, p. 123). Hispanics, although they remain moderately segregated, were less segregated in 1968 than blacks were after the major school desegregation efforts of the late 1960s and early 1970s.[6] The change measure in Table 6–9 is simply the 1976 measure subtracted from the 1968 measure.

Table 6–9   **Level of Hispanic-Anglo School Segregation**

Year	Mean	Deviation	Low	High
1968	43.8	16.4	0.0	79.6
1976	38.5	16.0	0.0	77.6
Change 1968 to 1976	- 5.3	8.5	-31.82	14.4

Note: Values are Taeuber indices.

The lower level of Hispanic-Anglo segregation reflects the lower level of residential segregation for Hispanics. Lopez, in his study of residential patterns in fifty-eight southwestern cities, found a black-Anglo dissimilarity index of 70.7 percent and an Hispanic-Anglo dissimilarity index of 42.9 percent. The modest level of change (5.3 percentage points for Hispanics versus 27.1 for blacks) between 1968 and 1976 reflects the lack of attention paid to Hispanic segregation by courts.

The correlations between segregation and the measures of second-generation discrimination are shown in Table 6–10. The time-ordered hypothesis, which suggests that second-generation techniques replaces segregation, implies a negative relationship between segregation and those measures that reflect negatively on Hispanics. For graduation rates and gifted class assignments, the relationships should be positive. The measures of second-generation discrimination are the policy mean figures summed over the entire time period that data were gathered.

The correlations in Table 6–10 are exceedingly modest. The predicted relationships for academic grouping are found (negative for TMR and EMR, positive for gifted), but the correlations are extremely small and not significant. The bilingual measure, on the other hand, is positively correlated with segregation. The disciplinary measures all have the predicted negative relationship, and the correlations for expulsions and suspensions are significant. For educational attainment, the pattern is somewhat bizarre. A significant negative relationship, as predicted, results for the Hispanic dropout ratio, but the correlation for graduates is also significant and negative. The latter relationship, while modest, suggests that Hispanic graduation rates are higher in schools where Hispanics are relatively more segregated from Anglos.

Table 6–10   The Relationship Between Segregation and Second-Generation Educational Discrimination

Discrimination Measure	Segregation 1976
Hispanic EMR Ratio	-.06
Hispanic TMR Ratio	-.01
Hispanic Gifted Ratio	.14
Hispanic Bilingual Ratio	.18#
Hispanic Corporal Punishment Ratio	-.08
Hispanic Suspension Ratio	-.31*
Hispanic Expulsion Ratio	-.20#
Hispanic Dropout Ratio	-.18#
Hispanic Graduation Ratio	-.26*

*p <.05

#p <.1

The positive relationship between segregation and bilingual education merits comment. Hispanic groups have often accepted bilingual education in lieu of desegregation; in fact, some Hispanic educators oppose desegregation because it would limit the use of bilingual education (see Cafferty and Rivera-Martínez 1981, 115). The modest relationship shown here reflects the fruits of their efforts; bilingual education not only increases in more segregated schools, it reduces the level of intergroup contact. Overall, the results show modest support for the idea that second-generation discrimination is a substitute for segregation. The relationships are small, however, and should not distract us from the basic nature of second-generation discrimination. Academic grouping and discipline are used to discriminate against Hispanic students, regardless of the level of formal school desegregation.

Declining Anglo Enrollment

In the literature on black school desegregation, perhaps the most controversial issue is that of declining Anglo enrollment—or, as it is popularly known, "white flight." A frequently expressed fear is that desegregation causes whites to leave the school system so that only black students remain, thus frustrating the intent of desegregation. This fear has caused what Willie and Fultz call *goal displacement* (1984, p. 163). "A court order that gave local school authorities primary responsibility for developing plans *that protect the rights of blacks* was transformed into a primary responsibility to develop school desegregation plans *that are least offensive to whites*" (pp. 163–64).

In a recent analysis of second-generation discrimination, Meier, Stewart, and England argued that second-generation discrimination against black students was linked to white flight. They found evidence that white flight from desegregated schools was reduced in those school districts that had significant amounts of second-generation educational discrimination against black students (1989, p. 131). Such findings imply that second-generation educational discrimination is a technique that is used to make a school system more attractive to whites and to retain their enrollments and support.

Although white flight has not been fully discussed in districts with large Hispanic populations, the same concerns exist. School administrators need political support to fund and maintain their school system. Support among Anglo parents, reflected by continued Anglo enrollment, would be especially prized. This section examines the interrelationship between Anglo enrollment declines and second-generation discrimination against Hispanic students. The working hypothesis is that greater second-generation discrimination will be associated with lower levels of Anglo enrollment decline.

Previous Research on Anglo Enrollment Declines

The literature on white flight has been dominated by a discussion of white enrollment declines in response to desegregation of black students (see Armor 1978). Because no discussion of white enrollment decline relative to Hispanic desegregation exists, the literature in regard to blacks will be used to suggest ways to assess the same phenomenon for districts with large Hispanic enrollments. The purpose of this review is to build a model of Anglo enrollment decline so that measures of second-generation discrimination can be added to that model. Essentially, the model will attempt to control for as many factors that affect Anglo enrollments as possible to make sure any relationships found for academic grouping or discipline are not spurious.

The issue of white flight was first publicized by James Coleman (see Coleman, Kelly, and Moore 1975; Coleman 1976; 1981). He argued that a substantial desegregation effort (that is, a reduction in the dissimilarity index of 20 or more) would result in a 6 percent loss of white enrollment during the year of implementation in districts with 25 percent or more black students. A 6 percent enrollment drop would be double the rate expected in such districts (see England and Morgan 1986).

Coleman's findings were disputed by a variety of studies (e.g., Farley 1975; Pettigrew and Green 1976; Armor 1978). The white flight debate degenerated into a series of charges and countercharges, with individuals labeled everything from "racist" to "incompetent." Eventually a consensus emerged that supported some of Coleman's original claims (Farley, Richards, and Wurdock 1980). In districts with 35 percent or more black students, the implementation of desegregation plans resulted in a white enrollment loss of 8 to 10 percentage points (Giles 1978). The extent of the loss was affected by the amount and distance of busing, the form of desegregation plan, the extent of publicity, and several other factors (see England and Morgan 1986; Wilson 1985; Welch 1987).

Modeling Anglo Enrollment Decline

Our intent is not to participate in the debate over the influences of white enrollment decline, rather we are interested in this debate only to the extent that it identifies factors for which we must control when looking at the relationship between second-generation discrimination and Anglo enrollments. The model we use is not intended to resolve any debates. We seek as complete a model as possible to avoid the omission of any relevant factors.

Franklin Wilson, in his study of white enrollment decline, argues that "the policy implications of the impact of school desegregation can best be addressed by focusing on the long-term effects rather than on any implementation year effects that may be compensated for later" (1985, p. 138). Anglo enrollments fluctuate greatly; short-term declines are often countered by long-term impacts in the opposite direction (Wilson 1985; England and Morgan 1986). Accordingly, we will model Anglo enrollment declines using the time period 1968–86 rather than on an annual basis. Although most literature relies on an annual change analysis, such short-term impacts can be misleading when longer term impacts are assessed.

The model uses Anglo student enrollment in 1968 to predict

Anglo student enrollment in 1986. Both variables are subjected to a log transformation to eliminate problems of heteroscedasticity and extreme values. This initial model is consistent with the consensus approach used to model white enrollment decline (see Wilson 1985; Welch 1987).

That Anglo enrollment has declined in our districts is beyond dispute. The average Anglo enrollment in these districts dropped from 26,476 in 1968 to 18,390 in 1986 or 30.5 percent. Not all of this decline can be linked to desegregation. Anglo enrollments in central city school districts would have declined without any desegregation efforts because these enrollments reflect declining birth rates, migration patterns from cities to suburbs, economic forces, crime patterns, and countless other factors.

To the basic model of Anglo enrollment, we will add several additional variables. If these variables have negative coefficients in the resulting regression, then they are associated with increased rates of Anglo enrollment decline. Positive slopes indicate that the variables attenuate the rate of white enrollment decline.

The first variable added to the equation is desegregation, measured as the change in the Taeuber dissimilarity index from 1968 to 1976.[7] In research on blacks, Giles (1975) found a tipping point of 35 percent black enrollment; in districts with more than 35 percent black students, desegregation results in white outmigration (see also Wilson 1985). To measure this conditional impact for Hispanic students, we created a dummy variable for those districts with more than 35 percent Hispanic enrollment. We used both this variable and a second variable, the interaction between desegregation (change in the Taeuber index from 1968 to 1976) and Hispanic enrollment (or the amount of desegregation multiplied by the Hispanic enrollment dummy variable). Such a procedure is consistent with previous work in this area (see Wilson 1985).

White withdrawal from a school system, according to Giles and Gatlin (1980), is a function of both attitudes toward desegregation and the ability to act. We cannot, with our current data set, measure Anglo attitudes toward either desegregation or toward Hispanics. We can, however, measure the ability of Anglos to leave the public school system. Anglo students who leave urban public schools, the research suggests, do not usually transfer to suburban schools (England and Morgan 1986). Escaping students are more likely to enroll in private schools. The opportunity to enroll in a private school is significantly limited by the availability of private schools. In a city without a developed private school system, an Anglo student may have no choice other than to remain in public schools. To tap this dimension, the percentage of school-age children enrolled in private schools in 1980 will be used.[8]

Having private schools is not a sufficient condition for leaving a public school system. Private schools charge tuition, and many individuals who would like to attend private school cannot because they lack the financial resources. A second measure of Anglo capacity to leave the public school system, therefore, is the Anglo median income in the district.

Social-class aversion, or what Giles and Evans call the power thesis, also plays a role (Giles and Evans 1985; 1986; Feagin 1980). The power thesis holds that intergroup hostility is a function of differences in both race and class. Some Anglo students, according to this theory, seek to leave the public school system, not because desegregation exposes them to Hispanic students, but because it exposes them to lower-class Hispanic students. To tap this social-class aversion view of desegregation, the percentage of Hispanics with a high school education will be used to indicate Hispanic social class. A second comparative indicator of social class will be the ratio of median Hispanic income to median Anglo income in the district.

Table 6–11   **A Model of Anglo Enrollment Decline**

Dependent Variable = Log (Anglo Enrollment 1986)

Independent Variable	Slope	Slope
Log Anglo Enrollment 1968	.99*	.95*
Private School Enrollment	-3.21*	-3.12*
Percent Hispanic Students	-.0033*	-.0043*
Desegregation* Hispanic Students	.00	_____ a
Anglo Median Income	-.00	_____ a
Hispanic Education	.00	_____ a
Hispanic-Anglo Income Ratio	-.01	_____ a
Segregation	.00	_____ a
Segregation Change	-.00	_____ a
R²	.89	.87
Adjusted R²	.88	.87
F	76.21	299.42
N	95	135

*p <.05
[a]Equation reestimated omitting this variable.

The Anglo enrollment decline regression is shown in Table 6–11. Since Hispanic desegregation has not been as visible or as comprehensive as black desegregation, we should not be surprised that many of the hypothesized relationships do not hold. In fact, only three of the factors discussed above have a significant impact on Anglo enrollment. Anglo enrollment is a function of previous Anglo enrollment, the availability of private schools, and the size of the Hispanic student body. A one percent increase in private school enrollment results in a 3.12 percent decline in Anglo public school enrollment, and a one percentage point increase in Hispanic enrollment is associated with a .0043 percent decline in Anglo enrollment. The overall equation predicts fairly well, explaining 87 percent of the variation in Anglo enrollments.

Academic Grouping, Discipline, and Anglo Enrollment

If academic grouping and discipline can be used as techniques to limit Anglo enrollment decline, then we would expect positive relationships between actions that adversely affect Hispanic students and overall Anglo enrollments. The measures of academic grouping and discipline are the multiple year averages reported in Table 5–13 because we are concerned with long-term rather than short-term impacts. These measures are subjected to a log transformation to eliminate problems with heteroscedasticity.

The regression coefficients for the second-generation discrimination measures are listed in Table 6–12. Each slope is the partial regression coefficient calculated after controls for previous Anglo enrollment, percentage of Hispanic students, and private school enrollment percentages. For academic grouping, all the relationships are in the correct direction. EMR, TMR, and bilingual classes are positively associated with greater Anglo enrollments. Hispanic enrollment in gifted classes is associated with declines in Anglo enrollment. Only the EMR coefficient is statistically significant, but the pattern is consistent, if not always significant.

For discipline, the pattern is the same. For suspensions, corporal punishment, and expulsions, higher Hispanic ratios are associated with greater Anglo enrollments. For both corporal punishment and suspensions, more Hispanic punishment is significantly related to greater Anglo enrollments. The significant positive relationship between Hispanic dropouts and Anglo enrollments is expected, but that for Hispanic high school graduates is not.

Table 6–12   **The Impact of Second-Generation Discrimination on Anglo Enrollment Decline***

Second-Generation Variable	Slope	t-score	R²
EMR Classes	.39	3.28	.82
TMR Classes	.01	.09	.81
Gifted Classes	-.12	1.39	.82
Bilingual Education**	.01	.42	.96
Corporal Punishment	.31	3.29	.86
Suspensions	.63	4.59	.83
Expulsions	.01	.13	.79
Dropouts	.30	1.98	.79
Graduates	.30	2.05	.81

*controls for previous Anglo enrollment, Hispanic student percentage, and private school enrollment percentage

**enrollment change from 1976 to 1986 only

Finding a relationship between academic grouping and discipline and Anglo enrollments suggests even stronger evidence concerning the discriminatory uses of academic grouping and discipline. The pattern found is consistent with a strategy on the part of school officials to ease the impact of desegregation on Anglo students. By separating Anglo students from Hispanics via academic grouping and by disciplining Hispanic students more, an environment is created that is more attractive to Anglo students. In this way, the intent of efforts to integrate schools is subverted into a policy that allows Anglo students to benefit from public education yet interact little with minority students.

Second-Generation Discrimination and Educational Performance

Our concerns with second-generation educational discrimination have focused on measures of equity: Do Hispanic students have access to the same educational opportunities as other students in the district? While we feel that unequal access to educational opportunities is by nature inferior education, the question of educational quality was not addressed. Clearly one might wonder if second-generation discrimination is directly tied to performance in the classroom. One might also ask if an Hispanic student who attends a "good" school that is segregated via academic grouping and discipline might not be better off than a Hispanic student who attends a "poor" school with relatively equal access to opportunities. Because Hispanic students are concentrated in major inner-city school districts, the suggestion that Hispanics are often sent to lower-quality schools is tenable.

To examine the linkage between quality education and second-generation discrimination would be a major research undertaking that would require completely new data for a wide variety of school districts. Efforts to measure the quality of education provided by school districts are still in their infancy. As a result, a national analysis similar to our second-generation educational discrimination study is many years in the future.

A tentative look at the linkage between second-generation discrimination and educational performance is possible, however, in those states that have a uniform assessment of educational performance. The state of Florida, for example, requires educational testing for all school districts and publishes district-by-district figures. Because many Florida school districts enroll substantial numbers of Hispanics, some preliminary analysis of quality versus access is possible.

Florida requires that, every year, standardized tests of performance be administered to students in grades three, five, eight, and ten (with two tests of tenth-grade students). Minimum competency levels are set, and the state publishes figures that report the percentage of students who meet or exceed the minimum competency levels for each school district. Table 6–13 shows the percentages of Hispanic and Anglo students who met minimum competency levels in 1985. Since not all sixty-seven Florida school districts have appreciable numbers of Hispanic students, the results of Table 6–13 are based on only fifty-four of the school districts.

Table 6–13	Measures of Student Performance: Percentage of Students Passing Competency Tests*			
	Hispanic		Anglo	
Grade Level	Mean	Deviation	Mean	Deviation
Third-Grade Exam	88.0	7.0	94.0	1.8
Fifth-Grade Exam	85.2	9.2	89.2	4.0
Eighth-Grade Exam	85.1	8.0	89.2	3.3
Tenth-Grade Exam I	86.1	8.9	92.6	1.8
Tenth-Grade Exam II	85.3	11.9	92.9	3.3

*Florida School Districts

Hispanic students perform fairly well on the Florida competency test; no less than 85 percent of Hispanic students pass the exam, regardless of level of schooling. Hispanic performance, however, lags behind that of Anglos, who score between 4 and 7 percentage points higher, depending on which test is considered. The percentage of Hispanic students who pass the Florida minimum competency tests will be our measure of educational performance. While this is only a partial measure, it will provide some indication of the proportion of Hispanic students who are able to perform above a certain level.

Florida school districts also provide data on second-generation discrimination measures, including EMR classes, gifted classes, bilingual classes, corporal punishment, suspensions, expulsions, and dropouts. Second-generation ratios were calculated for each of these measures. Table 6–14 shows the simple correlations between the second-generation discrimination measures and the Hispanic performance measures.

Table 6–14   Correlations Between Second-Generation Discrimination and Performance on Competency Exams: Florida

Access Measures	Third	Fifth	Exam Grade Level Eighth	Tenth I	Tenth II
EMR Classes	-.44*	-.24	.14	-.08	-.03
Gifted Classes	.37*	.07	.49*	-.03	-.01
Bilingual Classes	.01	.46*	.46*	.10	.35*
Corporal Punishment	.04	-.32*	-.01	.16	.02
Suspensions	-.15	-.27#	-.31*	.19	-.10
Expulsions	.18	.40	.11	.28	.36
Dropouts	-.37*	-.35*	-.35*	-.21	-.14

*p <.05
#p <.10

Because this effort is fairly preliminary, our attention will be limited to only significant relationships. If Hispanic students have their classroom performance limited by second-generation discrimination, we would expect that negative actions (EMR, bilingual, corporal punishment, suspensions, expulsions, and dropouts) would be negatively related to performance, while gifted classes would be positively related. If Hispanic students perform better in districts that limit their access to educational opportunities, then we would expect the correlations to be positive for the negative actions and negative for gifted classes.

For academic grouping, some evidence supports the position that second-generation discrimination hurts overall performance of Hispanic students. For EMR classes, only one relationship is significant, a negative correlation with third-grade exam performance. For gifted classes, we find positive correlations with third-grade and eighth-grade performance.

Other ability grouping relationships support the opposite conclusion. Bilingual education ratios are positively associated with performance on the exam for fifth-, eighth-, and tenth-grade students. Before concluding the ability grouping data is mixed, one additional factor should be considered. The positive bilingual relationship should be interpreted in light of other findings presented in this chapter. The Florida school districts are primarily Cuban-American or other Hispanic districts, rather than Puerto Rican and Mexican-American districts. As Figure 6–4 reveals, Cuban Americans are able to translate bilingual classes into positive benefits. The positive relationships found here are consistent with this finding.

For discipline, very few districts expelled any Hispanic students. As a result, none of the expulsion correlations are significant. The corporal punishment ratio is negatively related to fifth-grade exam performance, and the suspension ratio is negatively correlated with both fifth-grade and eighth-grade exam performance. Finally, dropout ratios are negatively related to exam performance for third-, fifth-, and eighth-grade students.

To make sure that the correlations in Table 6–14 are not simply a reflection of the quality of the school district, the results were rerun, controlling for the percentage of all students in the school district who pass the competency tests. The results in Table 6–15 are perhaps a better test of whether or not Hispanic students can do better in nondiscriminatory districts, even if the quality of education is not as high. Ability grouping and discipline measures appear to have a major impact on student performance at the lower grade levels. For the third-grade exam, significant negative partial correlations exist for EMR assignments, suspensions, and dropouts, with a positive relationship for gifted classes.

Second-generation discrimination's impact on performance holds for both the fifth- and eighth-grade exams also. For the fifth-grade exam, significant negative relationships exist for corporal punishment, suspensions, and dropouts, with a positive relationship for bilingual education. For the eighth-grade exam, there are positive relationships for gifted and bilingual classes, and negative relationships for suspensions and dropouts. Perhaps the most striking finding is that there are no relationships between second-generation discrimination and performance on the high school exams. One possible explanation for this lack of impact is our lack of tracking measures, which generally impact only at higher grade levels. While the evidence presented in Tables 6–14 and 6–15 is not overwhelming, it does suggest that school districts that have higher levels of second-generation discrimination are also districts where Hispanic students perform less well.

Table 6–15   **The Impact of Second-Generation Discrimination on Student Performance, Controlling for District Quality**

Access Measures	Third	Fifth	Exam Grade Level Eighth	Tenth I	Tenth II
EMR Classes	-.43*	-.24	.10	-.08	-.06
Gifted Classes	.57*	.15	.63*	.02	.01
Bilingual Classes	-.06	.45*	.40*	-.08	.24
Corporal Punishment	-.02	-.46*	.01	.18	.10
Suspensions	-.32*	-.40*	-.32*	.19	-.08
Expulsions	-.43	.07	.05	-.17	.44
Dropouts	-.44*	-.30#	-.29#	-.18	-.11

*p <.05
#p <.10

The second question that these data allow us to address is whether Hispanic students perform better in high-quality schools that have some second-generation discrimination or in lower-quality schools that have little second-generation discrimination. To answer this question, we divided the fifty-four school districts into two groups, based on all students' scores on the exams. Those school districts that were in the top half of all school districts were designated "good" schools, and those in the bottom half were designated "poor" schools. For our measures of second-generation discrimination, we performed the same classification. Schools with high EMR ratios (and other measures of discrimination) were classified as low-equity, while schools with low EMR scores to classified as high-equity.

For each test and each measure of second-generation educational discrimination, we compared the good schools that were low-equity to the poor schools that were high-equity. The mean percentage of Hispanic students passing each exam was taken as the measure of Hispanic student performance. Because the percentage of Hispanic students passing the exam in lower-quality/high-equity schools was subtracted from the percentage for high-quality/low-equity schools, negative scores will indicate that equity has a greater impact on student performance than does quality. Positive scores will indicate that attending good schools is more important than attending equitable schools.

The results of this analysis appear in Table 6–16. Discounting the results for bilingual education, twenty-one of the thirty comparisons support the position that access to educational opportunities are more important than the quality of the school that Hispanics attend. Such a pattern would occur on a random basis only two times out of one hundred. Only for the fifth-grade exam do the quality schools outperform the equity schools consistently. For the third-, eighth-, and both tenth-grade exams, equity schools generally outperform the quality schools.

Table 6–16	Difference in Test Performance Comparing Low Quality/High Equity versus High Quality/Low Equity*				
Equity Measure	Third	Fifth	Eighth	Tenth I	Tenth II
EMR Classes	- .4	6.1	-3.6	-3.4	6.6
Gifted Classes	4.5	-5.5	1.8	3.6	-1.5
Bilingual Classes	3.1	7.7	.1	-8.2	-4.6
Corporal Punishment	-1.0	4.2	-2.1	-4.0	.1
Suspensions	-4.8	2.6	-6.2	-4.4	-1.8
Expulsions	1.1	- .6	-8.6	-8.1	-11.4
Dropouts	- .2	4.3	-1.6	-4.1	-9.7

*Data: 54 Florida School Districts

The results of Table 6–16 are only a preliminary look at the question of equity versus quality. Several qualifications are in order. First, none of the differences are statistically significant. Second, performance on a standardized test is only one indicator of quality of education, and a controversial one at that. This test deals with a minimum level of competency, so it does not reveal how well the better students are performing. Third, all the school are located in Florida, which limits our ability to generalize about the relative tradeoff between quality and equity. The results of this analysis, therefore, should be treated as suggestive until further research is conducted.

Conclusion

This chapter examined four questions regarding second-generation discrimination against Hispanic students. First, the interrelationships between various forms of second-generation discrimination was probed. Hispanic high school graduation rates were affected by disproportionate corporal punishment, Hispanic access to gifted classes, and the size of bilingual education classes. Hispanic dropout ratios were a function of Hispanic suspension and gifted class ratios. Hispanic expulsion ratios were determined by Hispanic suspension ratios; suspension ratios in turn were influenced by EMR and corporal punishment ratios. Corporal punishment rates and gifted class ratios were affected by both EMR ratios and bilingual class ratios. Hispanic TMR ratios were influenced only by Hispanic EMR ratios. The identification of the interrelationships of second-generation discrimination reveals how individual policies form a pattern of discrimination. Especially important in this regard was the negative impact of EMR assignments and the use of bilingual classes.

The pattern of relationships differed greatly in the different Hispanic communities. For Mexican Americans, the two-factor pattern of negative ability grouping and punishment as one dimension, and bilingual classes, gifted classes, and high school graduation as the other, held. For Puerto Ricans, punishment virtually disappeared; discrimination was almost solely a function of ability grouping. For Cuban Americans, bilingual classes are translated into a positive benefit and are able to counter some of the impact of EMR assignments on high school graduation rates.

Second, the relationship between desegregation and second-generation discrimination was examined. Evidence was discovered that was consistent with the notion that second-generation discrimination techniques are a substitute for segregation. The modest size of these relationships, however, indicates that second-generation discrimination exists regardless of the level of formal desegregation.

Third, second-generation discrimination was linked to Anglo flight. Because actions that affected Hispanic students negatively reduced Anglo student loss, and actions that affected Hispanic students positively increased Anglo student loss, the question of intent must be raised. Such a relationship is consistent with the idea that second-generation discrimination is intentional rather than merely the result of institutional discrimination. School district officials need to maintain political support from Anglo parents, particularly support in terms of continued enrollment. The relationships found are consistent with the hypothesis that school district officials seek to make the system as compatible as possible to Anglo students, even if the actions result in discrimination against Hispanic students.

Finally, we made a tentative effort to relate second-generation discrimination to the performance of Hispanic students on standardized tests. Our analysis in this effort was limited to fifty-four Florida school districts. We found that second-generation discrimination negatively affected Hispanic student performance at lower grade levels. This relationship held even under controls for the overall quality of the school district. While the relationship was more suggestive than definitive, it supports our contention that second-generation discrimination reduces the quality of education that minority students receive. To determine if Hispanic students would perform better in quality schools even if segregated (via second-generation discrimination) or in unsegregated schools with lower quality, Florida districts were classified as either segregated or not and as either quality or not. Hispanic students in unsegregated but lower-quality schools generally performed better than Hispanic students in high-quality but segregated schools.

Notes

1. A student who actually belongs in an EMR class, for example, might be assigned to a TMR class because enrollment pressures on the EMR class require some students to be moved.

2. In all cases the log transformation of the ratios is used. This procedure results in a more explicable interpretation of the coefficients and is consistent with the analysis in the previous chapters. It is also consistent with the work of Finn (1982).

3. For blacks, the proportion of explained variation is usually double this level and only once drops as low as the Hispanic high point of 14 percent. The relationship between TMR and EMR classes is simply much stronger for blacks than for Hispanics.

4. We believe that this lack of relationship for 1976 and 1978 is, in part, a function of the OCR survey form. In 1976 OCR requested information on gifted classes only if they were part of special education. While this terminology may be clear to certain educators experienced in special education, it is not clear to everyone. Judging from the results of the 1976 survey, many smaller districts were confused by this request. Only after the request was changed to seek gifted class enrollments with no mention of special education do the data appear more reliable.

5. The lack of relationship for 1984 might be due to sampling error. Samples vary a fair amount from year to year; smaller school district are especially likely to drop out of the sample from one year to the next.

6. The decline in segregation may be a function of the districts sampled and the measure of segregation. Gary Orfield and Franklin Monfort provide information that 1984 segregation levels for Hispanics exceeded those for blacks. Their data also show that Hispanic segregation increased from 1968 to 1984 (1988, p. 327).

7. Having segregation scores up to 1976 only is not as serious a problem as it seems. Very little desegregation occurred in the United States after 1976. A recent article (Berlowitz and Sapp 1987) is highly critical of the Taeuber index as a measure of segregation. Essentially, their criticisms contend that the Taeuber index only measures formal desegregation, not the amount of interaction between minority and Anglo students. We share this concern, but for the purposes of estimating Anglo enrollment decline, the Taeuber index is adequate.

8. This measure contains both Catholic school and other private schools. In assessing white enrollment declines in regard to black desegregation, this is not a major problems since few blacks are Catholic. With Hispanics, this is not the case. Anglo students are unlikely to avoid Hispanic students by transferring to Catholic schools, given the high percentage of Hispanics who are Catholic.

Chapter 7

Hispanics and
Equal Access to Education

Although Hispanic education has not been examined with the same scrutiny as black education, substantial information is known about the status of Hispanic education in the United States. The historical patterns of exclusion from education that greatly handicapped blacks also applied to Hispanics, even though the precise methods of exclusion differed. Hispanics were trapped in a legal limbo, at times being considered "white" and at other times being considered "non-white." Regardless of how Hispanics were considered, however, the designation was used to limit Hispanic access to educational opportunities.

Because the courts were slow to consider Hispanics as a separate minority group for civil rights purposes, the Hispanic legal struggle for equal education did not develop as quickly as the black struggle. Hispanics frequently sought access to Anglo institutions of education, but even when victorious in court were often denied access through administrative action. When Hispanics finally received legal recognition from the courts, the great wave of school desegregation action had ended. Sweeping remedies for unequal education were no longer possible.

This chapter recapitulates our research findings. The empirical results are probed for their relevance to equal access to education. The second portion of the chapter is more normative. It seeks solutions to the policy problems revealed by this research. Policy changes that address the access of Hispanics to equal education are presented and evaluated.

The Status of Equal Education

Hispanic students in the major urban educational systems of the United States are not receiving educational opportunities equal to those received by their Anglo classmates. School districts remain segregated. Gary Orfield and Franklin Monfort found that 70.6

percent of Hispanic students in 1984 attended schools where more than one-half the students were minorities. In the northeast, the figure was 77.5 percent (1988, p. 327).

Given the political realities in the United States and the amount of school desegregation that has occurred in the last decade, few desegregation gains are likely. Yet current segregation measures only sense the tip of the segregation iceberg; they measure the racial mixture at the school level but do not tap racial distributions in classrooms, in social activities, and in other school functions. This book addressed some of the secondary aspects of school segregation that limit the interracial contact among students.

A school system can restrict the interaction between Hispanic and Anglo students, even if the system is totally desegregated, by a variety of common educational practices, most specifically the use of academic grouping. Academic grouping is the process of grouping students into homogeneous groups for instructional purposes. Special education is a grouping practice that separates students who can benefit from the regular school curriculum from those who cannot. Special education students are further grouped according to specific problems or severity of problems. Bilingual education is used to group students by English-language skills, separating out those targeted for bilingual instruction. Within the regular curriculum, ability grouping is common. Students are grouped by academic potential and taught in homogeneous groups. At the junior and senior high levels, curriculum tracking is frequently used; curriculum tracking separates students according to educational and career aspirations with curricula designed specifically for each track.

Grouping, regardless of its form, creates several problems. First, it separates students from those who are different from themselves and has them interact only with students similar to themselves. Second, even though efforts may be made to avoid such distinctions, the groups are of different status in the education system and, therefore, in the eyes of the students. Some students are ranked above other students. Both actions are contrary to the notion of integration—the mixing of students in an equal status environment.

The first two problems are exacerbated by the third. Grouping appears to benefit students only in infrequent situations, and then only for higher-status groups. Individuals grouped into special education, lower-level ability groups, or vocational or basic tracks perform less well than similar students who are not grouped (see chapter 1). The reasons why are fairly obvious. Students in higher-status groups normally receive greater attention, more resources, and better quality instruction from teachers with higher expectations (see Oakes 1988). In short, grouping creates inequalities in access to education among students.

The fourth problem is that Hispanic students are not equitably distributed among the various academic groups. Data are not collected on all forms of academic grouping; in fact, available data only provide a small glimpse of the overall grouping pattern. An Hispanic student is approximately 50 percent more likely to be assigned to a class for the educable mentally retarded than is an Anglo student. Compared to Anglo students, Hispanic students are overrepresented by 15 to 25 percent in classes for the trainable mentally retarded, and 3,000 percent overrepresented in bilingual education classes. For high-status classes, the pattern is the opposite. An Anglo student is three to four times more likely to be placed in a gifted class than is an Hispanic student.

The patterns noted above are visible only because a federal agency requires school districts to submit data on these classes. For other forms of grouping, which in combination dwarf the impact of these forms, no comparable data exist. Evidence from cases studies or single-school statistical analyses, however, suggests that similar patterns occur in other forms of grouping. Hispanics and other minorities are routinely placed at the bottom levels of the academic-grouping pyramid.

Academic-grouping patterns are reinforced by disparities in disciplinary actions. By the selective use of discipline, schools can discourage individual students. A minority student may be punished for offenses that are permitted other students or may be punished simply for being different (e.g., speaking Spanish). Although the differences were not great, Hispanic students were more likely to receive corporal punishment than were Anglo students in the same schools. They were also more likely to be suspended from school and two-to-three times more likely to be expelled from school.

An Hispanic student seeking an education faces a difficult challenge. Through grouping into lower-level academic groups, that child receives a less stimulating education than his or her Anglo schoolmates. In addition, with disparities in discipline, Hispanic students are encouraged to leave school. Those who remain in school, while better off than their cohorts who drop out, will graduate with an education that has been less valuable to them than the education received by Anglo students (see chapter 6). Numerous studies have documented the high dropout rate for Hispanic students. Our study reveals that Hispanic high school graduation rates trail those of Anglos by as much as 50 percent.

Patterns of Education

If ethnic disparities in the areas examined were isolated cases, then we would have cause for concern but not alarm. Ethnic disparities in grouping, discipline, and educational attainment followed a reasonably consistent pattern. First, in all cases where the situation investigated had negative connotations, Hispanics were overrepresented compared to Anglos. In all cases where the situation had positive connotations, Hispanic students were underrepresented.

Second, ethnic disparities in one area were related to ethnic disparities in other areas. Using both correlation patterns and factor analysis, the disparities in grouping, discipline, and educational attainment clustered into two groups. One group consisted of the Hispanic policy ratios for EMR classes, TMR classes, corporal punishment, suspensions, expulsions, and dropouts. Disproportionate special education placements and disproportionate discipline were common in the same school districts. The linkage between discipline and special education was also found in the historical literature. Together they suggest that special education assignments for Hispanics are used in the same manner as punishment of Hispanic students, for the purpose of removing them from classes.

The second dimension encompassed the Hispanic policy ratios for bilingual education classes, gifted classes, and high school graduation rates. Schools with little Hispanic-Anglo contact in bilingual classes had fewer Hispanics in gifted classes and fewer Hispanic students graduating from high school. This pattern appears to be the rewards side of education (just as the prior dimension was the punishment side). Gifted classes are conceded to be the best education offered by a school system. High school graduation rates indicate the success of a school system at retaining its students until the completion of their education.

Bilingual classes and their linkage requires some discussion. For students with limited English proficiency, bilingual instruction or instruction to provide a transition from Spanish to English is a

necessity. What evidence exists on the content of bilingual programs suggests that few true bilingual-bicultural programs exist.
True bilingual-bicultural education requires that Anglo students
share the same educational experiences as Hispanic students. The
data show that extremely few Anglo students are in bilingual education classes.

Instead, bilingual classes for Hispanic students are composed
almost exclusively of Hispanic students. These programs are generally transitional rather than bilingual. A larger bilingual class
ratio means that a school district either puts more Hispanic students into bilingual classes or keeps those placed there longer.
Regardless of how much Hispanic students are helped by these
transitional bilingual classes, they are hurt greatly by the separation from Anglo students. When they rejoin their Anglo classmates, they are less likely to gain access to the best educational
opportunities within the school district (e.g., gifted classes) and
less likely to graduate.[1]

One exception to the bilingual pattern exists. In districts with a
preponderance of Cuban Americans, bilingual programs have positive rather than negative impacts. The reasons why are obvious.
Cuban Americans are much more likely to be middle-class and
much more likely to live in cities (primarily Miami) where Spanish
is a coequal if not dominant language. In such cities, bilingualism
is a definite economic advantage.

The overall pattern of racial disparities has been termed "second-generation education discrimination." While this designation
has been used primarily for blacks, the pattern discovered here is
consistent with the notion of second-generation discrimination,
albeit a different form than that affecting black students. For
blacks, the policy ratios form a single dimension. For Hispanics,
two dimensions exist, one with special education and punishment,
the other for bilingual education, gifted classes, and graduation
from high school.

Institutional Versus Intentional

Discrimination is often considered to have two parts—a detrimental impact and also some intention to discriminate. This
research has revealed the detrimental impact. Nothing has
addressed the question of intent. In fact, "intent" in the common
meaning of the term may well be absent. Instead, a form of discrimination called institutional discrimination may account for

the patterns of ethnic disparity (Feagin and Feagin 1986).

Institutional discrimination occurs when the rules or procedures of an organization are such that the neutral application of these rules and procedures results in a disproportionate impact on minorities. That the patterns presented here result from rules and procedures is unquestioned. The use of grouping techniques is one of the most widely accepted educational norms in the United States. "Good educational practices" encourage teachers to group students in homogeneous groups so that each student can receive instruction tailored for his or her specific needs. Scientific techniques have been developed to facilitate grouping and give it an aura of rationalism. Counseling and guidance professionals are employed to assist in this process. Acceptance of grouping and the role of testing to create groups is virtually universal in American school districts.

Discipline is also part of the institutional procedures of all school districts. Students cannot learn if order is not maintained. Rules are issued to students, and punishment is dispensed for rule violations. Procedures are established for the use of more serious punishments, with some of checks against abuse.

Both grouping and discipline form part of the educational process that leads to students either completing or not completing school. Students unwilling or unable to learn drop out and may be better for it. Students who remain must perform up to certain standards to receive a diploma.

Institutional discrimination implies that discrimination is inherent in the rules and procedures of the institution. The normal application of discriminatory rules and procedures will have discriminatory effects, even if the person applying the rules does not intend to discriminate. The person who makes decisions on grouping or discipline, therefore, might well be part of a pattern of discrimination without even being cognizant of any discrimination.

Distinguishing between institutional discrimination and intentional discrimination is difficult and, with the data available to us, impossible. Simply put, we cannot empirically determine if the discrimination against Hispanic students results solely from institutional sources or if it comes from individual designs. On the one hand, this question can be deemed irrelevant since Hispanic students are negatively affected by such decisions, whether or not the intent was to discriminate. On the other hand, it does matter since it influences how such policies can be changed.

Policy Interrelationships

Without resolving the intentional versus institutional debate, chapter 6 addressed a series of questions that peripherally bear on the issue—policy interrelationships, linkage to desegregation, linkage to Anglo enrollment declines, and the relationship to educational performance. Except for our previous work on blacks (see Meier, Stewart, and England 1989), the linkages between the various indicators of second-generation discrimination has been almost totally ignored (two exceptions are Finn 1982 and Velez 1989). Because the clustering of measures differs for Hispanics, compared to blacks, and because bilingual classes affect Hispanics but generally not blacks, the policy interrelationships merited study. By examining the correlations between the various indicators of second-generation discrimination, stable relationships were identified.

Perhaps one of the most interesting trends in academic grouping is the gradual reduction in size of classes for the educable mentally retarded and the decoupling of the linkage between EMR classes and classes for the trainable mentally retarded. Our study found that a one percent increase in the Hispanic EMR disproportion ratio was associated with a .21 percent increase in disproportionate TMR assignments. The linkage between the two forms of classes, however, declined greatly since 1976 and actually disappeared briefly in 1984.

Even though gifted classes loaded on a different dimension of second-generation discrimination from EMR classes, a linkage still remained. A one percent increase in the Hispanic EMR ratio resulted in a .12 percent decline in the Hispanic gifted class ratio. Similarly, a one percent increase in the Hispanic bilingual class ratio was associated with a .21 percent decline in Hispanic gifted class assignments. The relationship between bilingual class assignments and lack of access to gifted classes increased in strength over the ten years studied.

Corporal punishment ratios for Hispanics were linked strongly to EMR ratios and weakly to bilingual class ratios. A one percent increase in the Hispanic EMR ratio covaried with a .35 percent increase in the Hispanic corporal punishment ratio. A one percent increase in Hispanic bilingual class ratios generated a .04 percent increase in Hispanic corporal punishment ratios.

Hispanic suspension ratios in turn were predicted by EMR

ratios and corporal punishment ratios. A one percent increase in Hispanic EMR ratios was associated with a .31 percent increase in the Hispanic suspension ratio. A one percent increase in corporal punishment ratios was related to a .17 percent increase in Hispanic suspensions. A one percent increase in the Hispanic suspension ratio, then, resulted in a .74 percent increase in the Hispanic expulsion ratio.

Perhaps the most surprising linkage was for educational attainment, given the generally indirect linkage between educational policies and high school graduation rates. A one percent increase in Hispanic gifted class ratios was associated with a .1 percent increase in Hispanic graduation rates. A one percent increase in Hispanic bilingual class assignments was similarly associated with a .14 percent decline in high school graduation rates, and a one percent increase in corporal punishment produced a .17 percent decline in Hispanic high school graduation rates.

The specification of the precise linkages of the various elements of second-generation discrimination to each other underscores the commonality possessed by the various actions. While the results clearly demonstrate that not every instance of grouping and discipline is a case of discrimination (if it were, the relationships would be much stronger), the results illustrate that each action is not a discrete event. Academic grouping actions are related to disciplinary actions, and both are related to educational attainment. Such a pattern is consistent with either institutional discrimination or intentional discrimination.

The relationship between the various academic grouping and discipline measures and Anglo enrollments also suggests discrimination. Hispanic disproportions in discipline and lower-level academic grouping were associated with increases in Anglo enrollment, while Hispanic assignments to gifted classes were associated with decreases in Anglo enrollment. If the ratios indicate greater contact between Anglo and Hispanic school children, then greater contact increases the likelihood that Anglo students will leave the school system. An hypothesis of intentional discrimination would suggest that school administrators perceive the importance of retaining Anglo enrollments and make an effort to keep these enrollments by limiting Hispanic-Anglo contact. Alternatively, the institutional discrimination hypothesis would treat Anglo student enrollments as a response by Anglo students to institutional actions of the school system rather than the school system's response to Anglo enrollment declines.

Distinguishing between institutional discrimination and intentional discrimination with aggregate data is simply impossible. We are skeptical, in fact, that any form of data, barring the ability to read the minds of teachers, counselors, and administrators, can resolve this debate. While the resolution of this debate is important in academic terms, in practical terms the debate need not be resolved. The concern is with limitations on the access of Hispanic students to equal education. Limitations imposed by institutional discrimination need to be addressed, just as limitations based on individual discrimination must be addressed.

The Politics of Second-Generation Discrimination

Throughout this research project, we viewed education as a political process. Accordingly, chapter 1 presented a political theory to explain Hispanic disproportions in academic grouping, discipline, and educational attainment. School district size, group competition, Hispanic political resources, and Hispanic representation were the four forces hypothesized to affect Hispanic student access to equal educational opportunities.

The power thesis of group relations holds that groups compete for scarce resources and that intergroup hostility is a function of differences between groups. The power thesis suggests that Hispanic students will fare better in an educational system when the system contains a larger number of lower-class Anglos and a larger number of blacks. While the number of lower-class Anglos had a significant impact in only two areas (bilingual education and graduation rates), the proportion of black students significantly affected seven of the nine policies (all except bilingual education and Hispanic graduation rates; see chapter 5). As black students increased proportionately, lower-level academic grouping and discipline affected more black students. Hispanic students, in turn, were affected less. The relationships suggest that a substitution exists; when there are large black enrollments, second-generation discrimination will be directed at blacks. When the number of blacks is small, second-generation discrimination will be focused on Hispanics.

School district size had a significant impact on two policies (suspensions and graduation rates). As predicted, larger school districts were less likely to have disproportionate Hispanic ratios in these areas. This finding was linked to the greater levels of professionalism in larger school districts and the visibility of these districts to both courts and the federal government.

Unlike the situation for blacks (see Meier, Stewart, and England 1989), political resources for Hispanics had only modest impact on the levels of second-generation discrimination. Income was associated with lower EMR ratios and higher gifted ratios; education is associated with more Hispanic graduates. One possible reason might be the relatively low level of political resources possessed by Hispanics compared to levels possessed by blacks.

Political resources, the size of the school district, and the proportion of blacks in the school district are forces over which the Hispanic community has little, if any, control. Hispanic representation, on the other hand, is a variable that the Hispanic community can potentially affect. School districts with greater Hispanic representation on the school board and among teachers placed fewer Hispanic students in EMR, TMR, and bilingual classes, placed more Hispanic students in gifted classes, and eventually had more Hispanic students graduate from high school. School districts with more Hispanic representation also had lower corporal punishment, suspension, expulsion, and dropout ratios.

The crucial nature of Hispanic representation in educational policy positions is both a pessimistic and an optimistic finding. It is pessimistic because Hispanic representation levels are extremely low (see chapter 4). Hispanics have only one-third the number of teachers that blacks do nationwide, and representation on the school board also lags greatly. On the optimistic side, these are variables that can be changed with concerted political efforts and appropriate policy decisions. Since 1972, Hispanic teacher representation has doubled.

The essential role of representation in affecting public policy makes the study of Hispanic representation extremely important. Chapter 4 revealed that the prime determinant of the proportion of Hispanic teachers was the proportion of Hispanic administrators. The proportion of Hispanic administrators, in turn, was affected by the number of Hispanics in the school district and the proportion of Hispanics serving on the school board. The three forms of representation are inexorably linked.

Hispanic representation on the school board was affected by four forces. First, Hispanic political resources (numbers and education) increased the level of Hispanic representation. Second, group competition had an impact; in districts with more lower-class Anglos and more blacks, Hispanics achieved greater representation. Third, electoral structure was important; at-large election systems reduced the level of Hispanic representation, especially in those school districts where Hispanics were a voting minority. Fourth, the recency of immigration had a detrimental impact on school board representation.

Differences Within the Hispanic Communities

This study also explored Hispanic access to educational opportunities for subsets of school districts that were predominantly Mexican-American, Cuban-American, or Puerto Rican. While each group of Hispanics did reasonably well in attaining school board seats, there were some slight differences. Controlling for available resources, electoral structure, and other forces, Mexican Americans achieved the greatest electoral success, with Puerto Ricans following closely behind, and Cuban Americans right behind Puerto Ricans.

Access to other policy-making positions, however, is where the subgroups of Hispanics differ the most. Mexican Americans do poorly in attaining administrative representation (with controls for political resources and other representation), yet do significantly better than both Cuban Americans and Puerto Ricans. Cuban Americans do about half as well as Mexican Americans in administrative settings; Puerto Ricans, however, do so poorly that their relative level of administrative representation is almost nonexistent.

Since teacher representation is greatly influenced by administrative representation, the extremely low levels of representation for all three groups should come as no surprise. While Cuban Americans and Puerto Ricans do relatively better than Mexican Americans, this results from their poor representation among administrators rather than from success in gaining access to teaching positions.

The great variation in representation levels for Mexican Americans, Cuban Americans, and Puerto Ricans cannot but affect the patterns of access to equal education. Mexican Americans, because they are the largest group, have a pattern that is most similar to Hispanics in general. Mexican-American students are most overrepresented in EMR and TMR classes, highly underrepresented in gifted classes, and among the three groups of Hispanics the least likely to be segregated via bilingual classes. Overall, Mexican Americans suffer the greatest disproportionate discipline. The combination of these factors results in a low high school graduation rate.

Puerto Ricans follow a completely different pattern. Puerto Rican students are not subject to large disparities in EMR or TMR assignments. Bilingual classes are large, with little Anglo contact. They have the greatest access to gifted classes of the three groups but are still significantly underrepresented. Corporal punishment and suspensions do not disproportionately affect Puerto Ricans. Despite the low level of suspensions and corporal punishment, Puerto Rican students are expelled in large numbers. Despite this more moderate collection of indicators, the Puerto Rican high school graduation rate is extremely low, the lowest for any of the three groups. How equal education policies affect Puerto Ricans remains somewhat of a mystery. Indicators that should result in higher levels of educational attainment do not do so. Clearly more subtle influences are discouraging Puerto Ricans from staying in school.

One possible influence is migration patterns. Unlike Mexican Americans and Cuban Americans, many Puerto Ricans desire to return to their homeland, and many do. Although education is a virtual necessity in American life, it is less valued in the depressed island economy. Puerto Rican students, therefore, might perceive less payoff to staying in school than do other Hispanics.

For Cuban Americans, a third pattern of access to equal educational opportunity results. Cuban Americans have the lowest level of EMR assignments, a ratio approaching that of Anglos. While their bilingual class ratios are the highest of any group, they are also declining rapidly and are the only set of bilingual classes to be positively related to high school graduation rates. Gifted class enrollments are low, but so are the disciplinary ratios. In fact, Cuban Americans are about as likely to be disciplined as are Anglos. The end result is a high school graduation rate that is slightly higher than that for their Anglo classmates.

Important in viewing the Cuban-American educational experiences are the differences between Cuban Americans and other Hispanic groups. Their origin as political refugees provided them with assistance in resettling in the United States. Miami has become a bilingual-bicultural city. The middle-class status of many Cuban Americans meant that they had greater economic and political resources that could be used to gain access to equal education. The policy ratios indicate that they have been successful in doing so. Except for their inability to gain access to gifted classes, they have avoided many of the second-generation problems that affect Mexican Americans and Puerto Ricans. Because the economic and political differences between Cuban Americans *and* Mexican Americans and Puerto Ricans are so great, Cuban-American experiences provide little policy guidance for either Mexican Americans or Puerto Ricans.

Policy Recommendations

Students of public policy are concerned both with examining how policies exist in the world and proposing changes in those policies (Simon 1969). Our interest in equal access to education is driven by both concerns. While our approach to this point has been empirical with emphasis on how politics affects public policy, much has been learned in the process about how policies might be changed to provide Hispanic students greater access to equal educational opportunities. Our policy recommendations concern federal agencies, local school policies of grouping, local school policies of discipline, procedures for increasing Hispanic representation, and political recommendations.

Federal Agencies

Absent from this analysis has been a discussion of the role of federal agencies in combating second-generation discrimination. This absence of discussion is easily explained by the absence of policy actions taken by federal agencies. The lead federal agency in educational discrimination is the Office for Civil Rights, located in the Department of Education. At one time OCR was an aggressive advocate of equal education (see Bullock 1980). OCR's aggressiveness during the early months of the Nixon administration resulted in OCR losing its power to cut off funds to discriminatory school districts. Later, federal courts stripped away OCR's ability to set priorities by forcing it to respond to all complaints (Bullock and Stewart 1978).

Over time, OCR has become an agency that collects data and, during periods with sympathetic presidents, an agency that encourages equality in education. As much as we would like to see an active OCR combating second-generation discrimination, we recognize that political realities at the national level prevent this. Even with a sympathetic president, the likelihood of an extensive new initiative in civil rights is unlikely. If a miracle should occur, however, legislation should provide OCR with the ability to set enforcement priorities and the power to restrict federal funds to discriminatory school districts. Reestablishment of the 20 percent guideline (20 percent overrepresentation in special education class would trigger a review) for various forms of second-generation discrimination would be a start.

Even if OCR remains a data-gathering organization, some improvements are possible. While we consistently found OCR personnel helpful in providing access to information, we were frequently dismayed at the format of the data. OCR data sets are extremely inefficient and difficult to use; colleagues of ours who teach at universities without IBM mainframes often find the data impossible to read. We suspect that the reason why little quantitative work has been done on second-generation discrimination is that data problems overwhelm potential analysts. Accessible, machine-readable data is a necessity both for research purposes and enforcement purposes.

The type of data gathered is also problematic. OCR has changed the data gathered several times, and at times even redefined terms. Especially of concern are the data that are never gathered. No data on curriculum tracking relative to race or ethnicity are gathered. Even if currently gathered data on industrial arts classes were gathered with breakdowns by race rather than just by sex, some curriculum tracking analysis could be done. Perhaps the best solution to the problem is for a small number of school districts (say 25-50) be surveyed in more detail. These districts might be required to report racial distributions for curriculum tracks, ability groups, other forms of discipline, and classroom composition. While such information gathering would be a formidable task, a pilot project with a few schools would provide extremely valuable data for research purposes.

OCR might also rethink the sample of districts that it uses. Every two years, some three thousand school districts are sampled in the Elementary and Secondary Education Survey. Nothing is more frustrating than to examine a single school district over time and find that the school district was not included in one or more of the samples. Despite sampling techniques to over-sample larger school districts, literally hundreds of extremely small school districts are included. The value of information on school districts with less than ten students (there are numerous such districts in every sample) is questionable. Rather than using scarce resources and taking up data space with such districts, a greater weight on large school districts would be beneficial. In an ideal world, every school district would be sampled every year. When tradeoffs are made, however, greater weight should be given to continuous inclusion of larger school districts.

The Equal Employment Opportunity Commission (EEOC) is the agency charged with gathering data on the racial composition of teachers and administrators in school districts. EEOC data on these distributions are not released by school district, ostensibly to avoid identifying individual employees. While we admire EEOC's concern for privacy, we fail to see how individuals could be identified from statistics aggregated at the school district level. Research on the racial composition of the teaching corps has been so scarce undoubtably because the best source of data, EEOC, does not allow access. This policy needs to be changed so that policy-makers and scholars have access to aggregate district level data on teachers, administrators, and other school district employees.

The final federal policy recommendation concerns Congress. School districts can rightly point to federal laws that require students to be grouped in homogeneous units to provide some form of mandated instruction. Federal funding requirements not only provide incentives to group students, but they also provide incentives to group as many students as possible. The ballooning size of special education can be attributed to the stimulus of federal funds (Magnetti 1982). Too many local pressures encourage school districts to use methods that can be discriminatory; additional federal incentives to take such actions are extremely harmful.

A variety of ways exist to provide federal money and eliminate the incentives for separatism. Block grants are one possibility; funding tied to program successes (e.g., number of special education students returned to regular classes or proportion of minority high school graduates) is another; vigorous enforcement of civil rights regulations is a third. Similarly, federal monies should be used to encourage innovation in these areas. The literature is filled with literally hundreds of proposed methods of educating children. Even within the smaller area of bilingual education, scores of different methods of instruction appear to exist. Federal funds should encourage this innovation and provide technical assistance so that innovations can be effectively evaluated.

Political Recommendations

This study joins numerous others that demonstrate the detrimental impact of at-large elections on minority representation. This impact is especially severe when the minority under consideration is a voting minority in the school district. Not only do ward elections increase the probability of minority representation, but they also increase the probability of representatives who are likely to be strong advocates of minority interests. Work by Polinard and Wrinkle (1988) finds that movement to ward elections increases the likelihood that minority candidates will reside in minority neighborhoods. Their research suggests that Hispanics are better represented in ward systems, which permit Hispanics to select their own representatives, than in at-large systems where non-Hispanics play a major role in selecting any Hispanic representatives.

Because representation plays such a vital role in the policy process, the inescapable conclusion is that at-large elections should be eliminated. We are under no illusion that such a policy will be implemented quickly or easily. We expect that this will be done on a district-by-district basis as a result of lawsuits filed by Hispanic voters. In the long run, we expect that all school districts will move to ward elections, but the long run is extremely long. The United States Justice Department could greatly aid this effort if they examined all the evidence on at-large elections and then filed amicus curiae briefs opposing the continued use of at-large elections. The U.S. Congress could provide even greater assistance by banning at-large elections in districts covered by the Voting Rights Act. Neither shortcut is likely to come to fruition.

The evidence regarding Hispanic-black coalitions suggests that electoral strategies need to be adjusted to potential Anglo actions. Anglo politicians are unlikely to passively let a rainbow coalition develop that will oust it from power. More likely, Anglo politicians will seek coalitions with Hispanics to avoid black electoral victories. Hispanic candidates should recognize that Anglo politicians in many school districts have no choice but to form a coalition with Hispanics. In exchange for coalition support, Hispanic leaders need to insist on selecting their own representatives and insist on policy changes that increase Hispanic students' access to educational opportunities. Coalition participation should only proceed if the coalition partners are equal participants.

Teachers

Attracting more minority teachers is an effective way to improve the educational experiences of minority students. A strong relationship was found for black students (see Meier, Stewart, and England 1989) and a similar, though not quite as strong a relationship, was found for Hispanics. While increasing the number of Hispanic teachers and administrators is feasible, it is not something that can be done easily. The major constraint is that the number of minority teachers is limited and minority enrollments in schools of education are declining. In fact, between 1975 and 1980 the proportion of Hispanic high school graduates entering college dropped from 35.4 percent to 29.9 percent (Valverde 1987, 320).

The strongest influence on the number of Hispanic teachers is the number of Hispanic administrators. Hispanic administrators in all likelihood make the school environment more attractive to Hispanic teachers. Increasing the number of Hispanic administrators is significantly easier than increasing the number of Hispanic teachers. Administrative skills are taught in a variety of settings. School districts could look to the private sector, other government agencies, and the military for trained Hispanic administrators. Aggressive affirmative action efforts are likely to pay dividends by increasing the total number of Hispanic school administrators.

Recruiting teachers is more difficult. The first effort should be focused at increasing the enrollments of Hispanic students in schools of education. This might be done with scholarship and loan programs with loan forgiveness provisions to students who teach for a given period of time. A local school district might undertake its own program by raising private-sector money for such aid, identifying promising students among those in the district, and establishing a program for their return after graduation. The Los Angeles school system's magnet school for future teachers is another innovative idea that might merit copying.

Several states have experimented with alternative teacher certification programs to attract individuals who want to teach but do not have a degree in education. New Jersey's program is highly successful; its provisional teachers not only are more likely to remain as teachers, but they also score higher on the New Jersey subject evaluation tests. Licensing programs in general should be reexamined to determine if they are valid determinants to teacher competence. Where relationships between licensing requirements and future performance cannot be demonstrated, perhaps licensing should be eliminated and school districts allowed to evaluate potential teachers using their own criteria.

A related phenomenon is the recent increase in teacher competency testing. Numerous states have implemented programs to test teachers without serious efforts to validate such tests. Dometrius and Sigelman (1988) have found that the implementation of competency testing has a negative impact on black teachers. Although little information exists, we suspect that such tests might have a similar impact on Hispanic teachers. Given the crucial nature of Hispanic teachers in attaining equal educational opportunities and the lack of demonstrated validity for teaching competency tests, a reasonable policy would be to not implement such testing until a full evaluation of its validity is conducted.

Grouping Recommendations

The disadvantages of academic grouping in all of its forms clearly exceed the benefits of such practices. Despite the overwhelming evidence, grouping practices are flourishing. Our initial preference is to ban all academic grouping. Effective teaching techniques for teaching students of differing abilities are widely available (see a review by Eyler, Cook and Ward 1983, 152-56). Cooperative learning, where students form teams to assist each other, is one approach that has received a great deal of attention (Slavin 1982). Wang and Birch's (1984) Adaptive Learning Environments Model with individually structured education plans within mainstreamed classrooms is another. The decision concerning which method of nongrouped teaching is most effective should be left to the experts, the local teachers. Sufficient options exist.

Since we hardly expect school district to recognize the ill effects of all grouping, given the resilience of academic grouping in American schools, we also support some more limited policy reforms. Special education classes, particularly those for the mildly retarded, need to be reduced in size as much as possible, given the correlation between program size and minority disparities in placement (see Finn 1982). The national trend in reduced EMR classes is encouraging (Reschly and Gresham 1988, 264). Unlike others, we did not find racial and ethnic disparities in specific learning disability classes; still, careful monitoring of such classes is necessary as long as discrimination remains a possibility.

Our view of special education is that it should be thought of as compensatory. Placement of a student in special education should not be permitted until a school district can demonstrate that the student has been exposed to effective instruction and was not able to learn (Heller, Holtzman, and Messick 1982, 68). The use of IQ tests for placement purposes should be prohibited. More appropriate are tests of adaptive behavior (see Mercer 1972; Mercer and Richardson 1985; Heller, Holtzman, and Messick 1982, 62). Since students progress at widely varying rates, special education students need to be reevaluated at least twice a year to determine if their current placement is appropriate. Placement of a student in special education should be accompanied by specific goals for the student and a timetable for when that student is likely to rejoin regular classes. Programs should be evaluated on how successful they are in providing students assistance and giving them the tools to take advantage of regular class instruction.

While special education is probably a necessary evil, ability grouping and curriculum tracking are not. Quite clearly a demand exists for high-quality education, and parental support plays a major role in the retention of gifted programs and college prep tracks. What is unclear is who is demanding the lower-quality education provided by lower-ability groups and vocational curriculum tracks? The labor market demand for blue collar workers is clearly declining. A basic education track for lower-level service workers is not the function of a school district; a proposed magnet school in Milwaukee for food service workers shows just how far such grouping might progress.

Education received in a basic or vocational track no longer prepares an individual for a lifetime of employment. Most high school graduates of today in thirty years will be working at jobs that do not exist at the present time. While some firms can temporarily avoid problems by "dumbing down" their jobs, such techniques are useful only to the extent that jobs are simple and repetitive. The labor market is far better served, as are the students, by as high a quality education as possible. Students will need to retrain several times in their careers, and the support of a good secondary education will assist that retraining. Our position is that the quality education offered to the "best" students in the district should be offered to all. Pressure to upgrade the quality of instruction for one group of students needs to be translated into support for upgrading the instruction for all groups of students. Only when education is not a ethnic zero-sum game (i.e., when Anglos do not benefit at the expense of Hispanics) can educational opportunities be equalized.

Bilingual Education

No recommendations are more difficult to make than those for bilingual education. Our research and reading of the literature convinces us that effective bilingual education is an educational necessity. An effective bilingual education program would have a variety of characteristics. First, it would be integrated (see Fernández and Guskin 1981, 133). Separating Hispanic students from

Anglos begins the process of separation that eventually produces inequalities in education. The benefits of bilingual instruction for Anglo students should be obvious. Anglo students will learn to function in the bilingual communities that exist in many cities. In addition, they should gain an appreciation of the multicultural nature of American society. Those who are studying a foreign language are afforded an enhanced opportunity to learn that language in a meaningful context. Given current birth rates, Anglos will eventually become a minority of the population. Now is an appropriate time to adjust.

Second, education needs to be multicultural, whether in bilingual education or—preferably—in the regular classroom. Much of the support for bilingual education among Hispanics is in fact a demand for cultural respect, something lacking in many urban districts. Integration of schools is not possible if some cultures are valued more than others. Biculturalism virtually requires integrated classes since cultural exchange is impossible without the interaction of students from both cultures (Orfield 1978, 229).

Third, no matter how bilingual education is structured, it must not be allowed to become an Hispanic track. If integrated bilingual classes are not permitted, then the amount of separate instruction should be limited. Programs should permit early exit to regular classrooms as soon as students can make the transition.

Our support for effective bilingual education rests on our research that shows the harmful impacts of many bilingual programs as they are currently operated. The Mexican-American Legal Defense Fund characterized bilingual programs in the southwest as the functional equivalent of the old Mexican Rooms in Texas schools (see Orfield 1978, 212). The reader should not confuse our criticism of current bilingual programs with support for the elimination of bilingual education or support for the bizarre proposals to make English the official language. The economic system in the United States already provides severe economic penalties for not knowing English. These alone create an incentive for Hispanics to learn English, just as they have for other immigrants, both previous and current. Additional government policies that punish Spanish-speaking citizens are simply irrational.

Discipline

School districts need to consider racial disparities in discipline as serious problems. In one area, corporal punishment, the solution is simple. Our review of the literature and our research on black students (Meier, Stewart, and England 1989) could find no evidence that corporal punishment is more effective than other forms of punishment. Corporal punishment is a primitive response to behavioral problems. We recommend that states that have not done so ban the use of corporal punishment in schools.

Suspensions, as currently administered, are an irrational punishment. A student is told that unacceptable behavior in school will result in the student being prevented from attending school. Such a punishment makes sense if the student values school attendance. A student who is not particularly interested in attending school might well perceive a suspension as a reward. In addition, suspensions provide students with greater opportunities for contacts with other role models who are not in school. Unless suspensions are vigorously reinforced by parents, they do not appear to be an appropriate punishment.

Radin (1988) provides an extensive review of alternatives to suspensions. In-school suspensions are a particularly promising alternative. Disciplined students are sent to a specified classroom within the school where the student serves his/her suspension time under teacher supervision. Class assignments are given to the student, and in some cases additional work is also assigned. An alternative form of in-school suspension is the use of the Saturday school option where Saturday classes are required as a student punishment. Radin reports that one Saturday school program reduced repeated suspensions by 25 percent (1988, p. 480).

A more elaborate version of an in-school suspensions system is the alternative school model. Students with disciplinary problems are assigned to a special school with low student-teacher ratios and individualized instruction. Despite the potential for segregation if not properly monitored, Radin reports that alternative schools have resulted in improved student grades and behavior (p. 482).

A third alternative to suspension is behavior contracting. In this situation, a written contract is drawn between the student and the school. Violations of the contract can be enforced by both parties. Radin reports that behavioral contracts have been used to reduce greatly the number of suspensions (p. 483).

The type of transgression that produces discipline, particularly suspensions, needs to be reevaluated. Many students are suspended for not attending classes. How a school system perceives that a suspension will be considered a penalty by a student who has failed to attend class is beyond logic. Attendance violations should not be a reason for suspending a student unless the school adopts one of the alternative forms of discipline described above. Without such changes, suspensions for skipping class merely reward a student for not attending school.

Expulsions are an admission by the school system that it has failed to educate a child. Schools should frequently evaluate their expulsions to determine what offenses result in expulsions and if racial or ethnic disparities are apparent. If such disparities exist, aggressive action needs to be taken to eliminate any discrimination in the administration of discipline.

Conclusion

The policy changes recommended here will not be implemented quickly or easily. School systems are bureaucratic organizations, and bureaucratic organizations are slow to change. Relying on such organizations to reform themselves is not a promising alternative. Outside pressure will be needed to encourage school systems to provide equal educational opportunities for all students.

Although the federal government was the source of much outside pressure in desegregating schools, the current political climate makes federal intervention unlikely. The source of change will of necessity need to be local. The most promising local source is the political system. This study demonstrated that the election of school board members had a critical impact on the educational opportunities afforded to Hispanic students. While we may well be guilty of advocating the politicization of school systems, we think school systems have always been political. We are merely advocating that the range of political pressures that school systems respond to must be increased. The result could be the fundamental restructuring of schools as we know them; greater political responsiveness is a small price to pay to provide equal educational opportunities for all Americans.

Notes

1. This is not a function of the size of the Hispanic community. Controls for that variable and for the percentage of Hispanic students designated as limited English-proficient did not affect these relationships.

Appendix A

Table A–1   **Policy Intercorrelations: 1973**

	Suspensions	EMR Classes	Expulsions
EMR Classes	.26*	—	—
Expulsions	.54*	.22	—
TMR Classes	.01	-.03	—

*p <.05

Table A–2   **Policy Intercorrelations: 1974**

	Suspensions	EMR Classes	Expulsions
EMR Classes	.21*	—	—
Expulsions	.31#	-.06	—
TMR Classes	.01	.07	-.02

*p <.05
#p <.1

Table A–3   **Policy Intercorrelations: 1976**

	Suspend	EMR	Punish	Expel	TMR	Grads	Gifted
EMR	.46*	—	—	—	—	—	—
Punish	.41*	.33*	—	—	—	—	—
Expel	.33*	.25*	.20	—	—	—	—
TMR	.22*	.37*	.06	.37*	—	—	—
Graduates	.18*	.03	-.18	.04	.23*	—	—
Gifted	-.08	.07	-.01	.02	.07	-.06	—

*p <.05
#p <.1

Table A–4 **Policy Intercorrelations: 1978**

	Suspend	EMR	Punish	Expel	TMR	Grads
EMR	.51*	—	—	—	—	—
Punishment	.25*	.43*	—	—	—	—
Expel	.31*	.34*	.31#	—	—	—
TMR	.38*	.29*	.09	.04	—	—
Graduates	.02	-.14	-.27*	.04	-.06	—
Gifted	.09	-.07	-.22#	-.14	.16	.16

*p <.05
#p <.1

Table A–5 **Policy Intercorrelations: 1980**

	Suspend	EMR	Punish	Expel	TMR	Grads
EMR	.37*	—	—	—	—	—
Punishment	.41*	.41*	—	—	—	—
Expel	.48*	.42*	.29#	—	—	—
TMR	.21#	.29*	.14	-.16	—	—
Graduates	.17#	.03	-.10	.10	.02	—
Gifted	-.20*	-.31*	-.15	-.21	.09	.21*

*p <.05
#p <.1

Table A–6 **Policy Intercorrelations: 1982**

	Suspend	EMR	Punish	TMR	Grads
EMR	.47*	—	—	—	—
Punishment	.48*	.37*	—	—	—
TMR	.12	.24#	.04	—	—
Graduates	.07	-.22#	-.10	.05	—
Gifted	-.16	-.14	-.16	-.02	.44

*p <.05
#p <.1

Appendix B

List of Districts Included in the Survey

Arizona: Alhambra 068; Chandler Unified; Flagstaff Unified; Glendale; Phoenix Union; Roosevelt; Sunnyside Unified; Tempe Union; Washington; Yuma.

California: ABC Unified; Alhambra City; Alum Rock Union; Anaheim Union; Anaheim Elementary; Baldwin Park Unified; Bassett Unified; Berryessa Union; Campbell Union; Centinela; Chaffey Union; Coachella Valley; El Monte; El Rancho Unified; Fairfield-Suisun; Franklin-McKinley; Fresno City; Grant Joint Unified; Hacienda-La Puente Unified; Hayward Unified; Huntington Beach Union; La Habra City; Los Angeles Unified; Manteca; Merced Union; Montebello; Monterey Peninsula; Napa Valley Unified; Orange Unified; Oxnard Union; Pasadena Unified; Pittsburg Unified; Pleasant Valley; Pomona Unified; Richmond Unified; Sacramento City; San Bernardino City; San Diego City; San Mateo Union; Stockton City; Sanger Unified; Santa Monica; Sequoia; Union; Sunnyvale; Vallejo City.

Colorado: Adams-Arapahoe; Colorado Springs; Denver; Harrison; Pueblo; Mesa Valley; Thompson; Westminster; Widefield.

Connecticut: Bridgeport.

Florida: Dade County; Hillsborough County; Orange County.

Idaho: Nampa 131.

Illinois: Chicago; Bloom Township High; Joliet Township High.

Kansas: Kansas City; Topeka; Wichita 259.

Maryland: Montgomery County.

Massachusetts: Holyoke.

Michigan: Lansing; Adrian.

Minnesota: St. Paul.

Nevada: Clark County; Washoe County.

New Jersey: Camden; Hoboken; Jersey City; New Brunswick; Newark; Passaic; Patterson; Pemberton Borough; Plainfield.

New Mexico: Alamogordo; Carlsbad; Farmington; Gadsden; Gallup; Grants Ciboloa; Las Cruces; Roswell; Santa Fe.

New York: Buffalo; Middletown; New York City; Rochester.

Oklahoma: Lawton.

Pennsylvania: Allentown; Philadelphia.

Texas: Abilene ISD; Austin ISD; Brownsville ISD; Carrollton Farmers; Dallas ISD; Deer Park ISD; Denton; Ector County ISD; Edgewood ISD; El Paso ISD; Fort Worth; Galena Park ISD; Galveston ISD; Grand Prairie ISD; Houston ISD; Kingsville ISD; La Porte; Lamar Consolidated; Lubbock ISD; Midland ISD; Misson ISD; North East ISD; Northside ISD; Pharr-San Juan-Alamo ISD; San Antonio ISD; Seguin ISD; South San Antonio ISD; Temple ISD; Tyler ISD; Waco ISD; Weslaco ISD; Wichita Falls ISD.

Utah: Salt Lake City; Odgen City.

Virginia: Arlington County.

Wisconsin: Kenosha; Milwaukee.

Wyoming: Laramie County.

References

Acuña, Rudolfo. 1972. *Occupied America: The Chicano's Struggle Toward Liberation*. San Francisco: Canfield Press.

Adair, Alvis V. 1984. *Desegregation: The Illusion of Black Progress*. New York: University Press of America.

Alexander, Karl L. and Bruce K. Eckland. 1975. "Contextual Effects in the High School Attainment Process," *American Sociological Review* 40 (June), 402–16.

Alexander, Karl L. and Edward L. McDill. 1976. "Selection and Allocation Within Schools," *American Sociological Review* 41 (December), 969–80.

Allport, Gordon W. 1954. *The Nature of Prejudice*. Reading, MA: Addison-Wesley.

Allsup, Carl. 1977. "Education Is Our Freedom: The American G.I. Forum and the Mexican American School Segregation in Texas, 1948–1957," *Aztlan* 8 (Spring), 27–49.

Ambert, Alba N. and Sarah E. Melendez. 1985. *Bilingual Education: A Source Book*. New York: Teachers College Press.

American Institutes of Research. 1977. *Evaluation of the Impact of ESEA Title VII Spanish/English Bilingual Education Program, Vol 1: Study Design and Interim Findings*. Palo Alto, CA.

Anastasi, Anne, and Fernando A. Cordova. 1972. "Some Effects of Bilingualism Upon the Intelligence Test Performance of Puerto Rican Children in New York City." In Francesco Cordasco and Eugene Bucchiono, eds., *The Puerto Rican Community and Its Children on the Mainland*. Metuchen, NJ: Scarecrow Press, 318–32.

Anderson, James E., David W. Brady, Charles Bullock, and Joseph Stewart, Jr. 1984. *Public Policy and Politics in America*. Monterey, CA: Brooks/Cole.

Andersson, Theodore and Mildred Boyer. 1970a. *Bilingual Schooling in*

the United States: History, Rationale, Implications, and Planning,
Volume I. Austin, TX: Southwest Educational Development Library.

Andersson, Theodore and Mildred Boyer. 1970b. *Bilingual Schooling in the United States: History, Rationale, Implications, and Planning,* Volume II. Austin, TX: Southwest Educational Development Library.

Andrews, David F. 1974. "A Robust Method for Multiple Linear Regression," *Technometrics* 16 (November), 523–31.

Arias, M. Beatriz. 1985. "Hispanics, School Desegregation and Educational Opportunity." In Marguerite Ross Barnett and Charles C. Harrington, eds., *Readings in Equal Education,* Volume 8. New York: AMS Press, 207–18.

Arias, M. Beatriz. 1986. "The Context of Education for Hispanic Students: An Overview," *American Journal of Education* (November), 26–57.

Armor, David J. 1978. *White Flight, Demographic Transition, and the Future of School Desegregation.* Santa Monica, CA: Rand Corporation (R–5931).

Armor, David J. 1980. "White Flight and the Future of School Desegregation." In Walter G. Stephan and Joe R. Feagin, eds. *School Desegregation: Past, Present, and Future.* New York: Plenum Press, 187–226.

Arnez, Nancy L. 1978. "Implementation of Desegregation as a Discriminatory Process," *Journal of Negro Education* 47 (Winter), 28–45.

Austin, Mary C. and Coleman Morrison. 1963. *The First R: The Harvard Report on Reading in Elementary School.* New York: MacMillian.

Bach, Robert L. 1980. "The New Cuban Immigrants: Their Background and Prospects," *Monthly Labor Review* 103 (October), 30–46.

Baker, James N. with Daniel Shapiro, Pat Wingert, and Nadine Joseph. 1987. "Paddling: Still a Sore Point," *Newsweek* (June 22), 61.

Baker, Keith and Adriana de Kanter. 1983. *Bilingual Education: A Reappraisal of Federal Policy.* Lexington, MA: Lexington Books.

Bancroft, Hubert Howe. 1962. *History of Arizona and New Mexico.* Albuquerque: Horn and Wallace.

Banfield, Edward C. and James Q. Wilson. 1963. *City Politics.* New York: Vintage.

Banks, James A. 1982. "Educating Minority Youths: An Inventory of Current Theory," *Education and Urban Society* 15 (November), 88–103.

Barbagli, Marzio and Marcello Dei. 1977. "Socialization into Apathy and Public Subordination." In Jerome Karabel and A. H. Halsey, eds., *Power and Ideology in Education.* New York: Oxford University Press, 423–31.

Barr, Rebecca and Robert Dreeben. 1977. "Instruction in Classrooms." In L. S. Schulman, ed., *Review of Research in Education,* Volume 5. Itasca, IL: Peacock, 89–162.

Barrera, Mario. 1979. *Race and Class in the Southwest.* Notre Dame, IN: University of Notre Dame Press.

Bauer, Fran. 1989. "Minorities Rank Joblessness as Chief Problem, Survey Says," *The Milwaukee Journal* (January 27), 4B.

Baver, Sherrie. 1984. "Puerto Rican Politics in New York City: The Post–World War II Period." In James Jennings and Monte Rivera, eds., *Puerto Rican Politics in Urban America.* Westport, CT: Greenwood Press, 43–60.

Bean, Frank D. and Marta Tienda. 1987. *The Hispanic Population of the United States.* New York: Russell Sage Foundation.

Becker, Gary S. 1975. *Human Capital.* 2nd ed. New York: Columbia University Press.

Bell, Charles G. and Charles M. Price. 1984. *California Government Today.* 2nd ed. Homewood, IL: Dorsey Press.

Berlowitz, Marvin J. and Martin L. Sapp. 1987. "A Critique of the Taeuber Index as a Measure of School Desegregation," *Journal of Negro Education* 56 (Fall), 475–84.

Bernal, Joe. 1971. "Bilingual Education for La Raza." In Wayne Moquin with Charles Van Doren, ed., *A Documentary History of the Mexican Americans.* New York: Praeger, 366–70.

Berry, William D. and Stanley Feldman. 1985. *Multiple Regression in Practice.* Beverly Hills, CA: Sage Publications.

Bickel, William E. 1982. "Classifying Mentally Retarded Students: A Review of Placement Practices in Special Education." In Kirby A. Heller, Wayne H. Holtzman, and Samuel Messick, eds., *Placing Children in Special Education.* Washington, DC: National Academy Press, 182–229.

Blutstein, Howard K., et al. 1971. *Area Handbook for Cuba.* Washington, DC: Government Printing Office.

Boss, Michael O. and Harmon Zeigler. 1977. "Experts and Representatives: Comparative Basis of Influence in Educational Policy-Making," *Western Political Quarterly* 30 (June), 255–63.

Boswell, Thomas D. and James R. Curtis. 1983. *The Cuban-American Experience.* Totowa, NJ: Rowman and Allanheld.

Bou, Ismael Rodriquez. 1966. "Significant Factors in the Development of Education in Puerto Rico." In *Status of Puerto Rico: Selected Background Studies.* Washington, DC: United States-Puerto Rican Commission on the Status of Puerto Rico, 147–314.

Brierly, Allen Bronson and David Moon. 1988a. "Hispanic Attitudes Toward Metropolitan Reform in Greater Miami." Working paper Number 88–7, University of Miami, School of Business.

Brierly, Allen Bronson and David Moon. 1988b. "The Effect of Ethnic Cleavages on Metropolitan Reform in Greater Miami." Working Paper Number 88–5, University of Miami, School of Business.

Brim, Orville G. and Stanton Wheeler. 1966. *Socialization After Childhood.* New York: John Wiley & Sons.

Brookover, Wilbur B. and Edsel L. Erickson. 1975. *The Sociology of Education.* Homewood, IL: Dorsey Press.

Brophy, Jere E. 1983a. "Research on the Self-Fulfilling Prophecy and Teacher Expectations," *Journal of Educational Psychology* 75 (October), 631–61.

Brophy, Jere E. 1983b. "Classroom Organization and Management," *Elementary School Journal* 83 (March), 265–85.

Brophy, Jere E. and Thomas L. Good. 1970. "Teachers' Communication of Differential Expectations for Children's Classroom Performance." *Journal of Educational Psychology* 61 (October), 365–74.

Brophy, Jere E. and Thomas L. Good. 1974. *Teacher Student Relationships: Causes and Consequences.* New York: Holt, Reinhart, and Winston.

Brouthers, Lance Eliot and David Lawson McClure. 1984. "The Effect of Council Size and District Elections on City Council Representation," *Aztlan* 15 (Fall), 263–76.

Brown, George H., Nan L. Rosen, Susan T. Hill, and Michael A. Olivas. 1980. *The Condition of Education for Hispanic Americans.* Washington, DC: National Institute of Education.

Browning, Rufus P., Dale Rogers Marshall, and David H. Tabb. 1984. *Protest Is Not Enough.* Berkeley, CA: University of California Press.

Bullock, Charles S., III. 1976. "Compliance with School Desegregation Laws: Financial Inducements and Policy Performance." Paper presented at the annual meeting of the American Political Science Association, Chicago, September, 2–5.

Bullock, Charles S., III. 1980. "The Office of Civil Rights and Implementation of Desegregation Programs in the Public Schools," *Policy Studies Journal* 8 (Special Issue # 2), 597–615.

Bullock, Charles S., III and Charles M. Lamb, eds. 1984. *Implementation of Civil Rights Policy.* Monterey, CA: Brooks/Cole.

Bullock, Charles S., III and Joseph Stewart, Jr. 1978. "Complaint Processing as a Strategy for Combating Second Generation Discrimination." Paper presented at the annual meeting of the Southern Political Science Association, Atlanta.

Bullock, Charles S., III and Joseph Stewart, Jr. 1979. "Incidence and Correlates of Second-Generation Discrimination." In Marian L. Palley and Michael B. Preston, eds., *Race, Sex, and Policy Problems.* Lexington, MA: Lexington Books, 115–29.

Bullock, Charles S., III and Joseph Stewart, Jr. 1984. "New Programs in 'Old' Agencies: Lessons in Organizational Change from the Office for Civil Rights," *Administration and Society* 15 (February), 387–412.

Buriel, Raymond. 1983. "Teacher-Student Interactions and Their Relationship to Student Achievement: A Comparison of Mexican-American and Anglo-American Children," *Journal of Educational Psychology* 75 (December), 889–97.

Cabinet Committee on Opportunities for Spanish Speaking People. 1971. *Annual Report.* Washington, DC: Government Printing Office.

Cafferty, Pastora San Juan and Carmen Rivera-Martínez. 1981. *The Politics of Language: The Dilemma of Bilingual Education for Puerto Ricans.* Boulder, CO: Westview Press.

Camarillo, Albert. 1979. *Chicanos in a Changing Society.* Cambridge, MA: Harvard University Press.

Campbell, David and Joe Feagin. 1975. "Black Politics in the South: A Descriptive Analysis," *Journal of Politics* 37 (February), 129–59.

Cardenas, Jose A. 1975. "Bilingual Education, Segregation, and a Third Alternative," *Inequality in Education* 19 (February), 19–22.

Carlberg, Conrad and Kenneth Kavale. 1980. "The Efficacy of Special Versus Regular Class Placement for Exceptional Children: A Meta-Analysis," *Journal of Special Education* 14 (Fall), 295–309.

Carrión, Arturo Morales. 1983. *Puerto Rico: A Political and Cultural History.* New York: W. W. Norton and Company.

Carter, Thomas P. 1970. *Mexican Americans in School: A History of Educational Neglect.* New York: College Entrance Examination Board.

Carter, Thomas P. and Roberto D. Segura. 1979. *Mexican Americans in School: A Decade of Change.* New York: College Entrance Examination Board.

Cataldo, Everett F. and John D. Holm. 1983. "Voting on School Finance: A Test of Competing Theories," *Western Political Quarterly* 36 (December), 619–32.

Cayer, N. Joseph and Lee Sigelman. 1980. "Minorities and Women in State and Local Government: 1973–1975," *Public Administration Review* 40 (September/October), 443–50.

Center for Education Statistics. 1987. *The Condition of Education: A Statistical Report.* Washington, DC: U.S. Department of Education.

Cervantes, Robert A. 1984. "Ethnocentric Pedagogy and Minority Student Growth," *Education and Urban Society* 16 (May), 274–93.

Chandler, John T. and John Plakos. 1969. "Spanish-Speaking Pupils Classified as Educable Mentally Retarded," *Integrated Education* 7 (November/December), 28–32.

Chesler, Mark A. and William M. Cave. 1981. *Sociology of Education.* New York: MacMillian.

Children's Defense Fund. 1974. *Children Out of School in America.* Washington, DC: Children's Defense Fund of the Washington Research Project, Inc.

Children's Defense Fund. 1975. *School Suspensions: Are They Helping Children?* Washington, DC: Children's Defense Fund of the Washington Research Project, Inc.

Children's Defense Fund. 1977. *The Elementary and Secondary School Civil Rights Survey: 'Bureaucratic Balderdash' or the Cornerstone of Civil Rights Compliance in Public Schools?* Washington, D.C.: The Children's Defense Fund of the Washington Research Project, Inc.

Chinn, Philip C. and Selma Hughes. 1987. "Representation of Minority Students in Special Education Classes," *Remedial and Special Education* 8 (July/August), 41–46.

Cicourel, Aaron V. and John I. Kitsuse. 1963. *The Educational Decision-Makers.* Indianapolis, IN: Bobbs-Merrill.

Cistone, Peter J. 1975. "The Recruitment and Socialization of School

Board Members." In Peter J. Cistone, ed., *Understanding School Boards*. Lexington, MA: D.C. Heath, 47–62.

Claridge, Roy M. 1972. "Education." In Members of the Faculty of the University of Arizona, *Arizona: Its People and Resources* rev., 2nd ed. Tucson: University of Arizona Press, 329–41.

Cohen, Yinon and Andrea Tyree. 1986. "Escape From Poverty: Determinants of Intergenerational Mobility of Sons and Daughters of the Poor," *Social Science Quarterly* 67 (December), 803–13.

Cole, Leonard A. 1974. "Electing Blacks to Municipal Office," *Urban Affairs Quarterly* 10 (September), 17–39.

Cole, Leonard A. 1976. *Blacks in Power.* Princeton: Princeton University Press.

Coleman, James S. 1976. "Liberty and Equality in School Desegregation," *Social Policy* 6 (January/February), 9–13.

Coleman, James S. 1981. "The Role of Incentives in School Desegregation." In Adam Yarmolinsky, Lance Liebman, and Corinne S. Schelling, eds., *Race and Schooling in the City.* Cambridge, MA: Harvard University Press, 182–93.

Coleman, James S., Ernest Q. Campbell, Carol J. Hobson, James McPartland, Alexander B. Mood, Frederic D. Weinfeld, and Robert L. York. 1966. *Equality of Educational Opportunity.* Washington, DC: Government Printing Office.

Coleman, James S., Sara D. Kelly, and John A. Moore. 1975. *Trends in School Segregation, 1968–73.* Working Paper 722–03–01. Washington, DC: Urban Institute.

Connecticut Advisory Committee to the U.S. Commission on Civil Rights. 1973. *El Boricua: The Puerto Rican Community in Bridgeport and New Haven.* Washington, DC: Government Printing Office.

Cooke, W. Henry. 1971. "Segregation of Mexican-American School Children." In Wayne Moquin with Charles Van Doren, ed., *A Documentary History of Mexican Americans.* New York: Praeger, 325–28.

Cordasco, Francesco. 1972. "The Puerto Rican Child in the American School." In Francesco Cordasco and Eugene Bucchiono, eds., *The Puerto Rican Community and Its Children on the Mainland.* Metuchen, NJ: Scarecrow Press, 341–48.

Cordasco, Francesco, ed. 1978. *Bilingual Education in New York City.* New York: Arno Press.

Cordasco, Francesco and Eugene Bucchioni. eds. 1968. *Puerto Rican Children in Mainland Schools.* Metuchen, NJ: Scarecrow Press.

Corman, Louise and Jay Gottlieb. 1978. "Mainstreaming Mentally Retarded Children: A Review of Research." In Norman R. Ellis, ed., *International Review of Research in Mental Retardation.* New York: Academic Press, 251–76.

Coser, Lewis A. 1956. *The Functions of Social Conflict.* New York: The Free Press.

Cotton, Jeremiah. 1985. "More on the 'Cost' of Being a Black or Mexican American Male Worker," *Social Science Quarterly* 66 (December), 867–85.

Council of Great City Schools. 1986. *Special Education: Views from America's Cities.* Washington, DC: Council of Great City Schools.

Crow, John E. 1971. "City Politics in Arizona." In Robert D. Wrinkle, ed., *Politics in the Urban Southwest.* Albuquerque, NM: University of New Mexico, Division of Government Research, 22–34.

Culver, John H. and John C. Syer. 1984. *Power and Politics in California.* New York: John Wiley and Sons.

Dahl, Robert A. 1961. *Who Governs?* New Haven, CT: Yale University Press.

Damico, Sandra Bowman and Christopher Sparks. 1986. "Cross-Group Contact Opportunities: Impact on Interpersonal Relationships in Desegregated Middle Schools," *Sociology of Education* 59 (April), 113–23.

Davidson, Chandler and George Korbel. 1981. "At-Large Elections and Minority Group Representation," *Journal of Politics* 43 (November), 982–1005.

Davis, O.L., Jr., and Carl R. Personke, Jr. 1968. "Effects of Administering the Metropolitan Readiness Test in English and Spanish to Spanish-Speaking School Entrants," *Journal of Educational Measurement* 5 (Fall), 231–34.

De Avila, Edward A., and Barbara E. Havassy. 1975. "Piagetian Alternative to IQ: Mexican-American Study." In Nicholas Hobbs, ed., *Issues in the Classification of Children,* Vol. 2. San Francisco: Josey-Bass, 246–65.

de la Garza, Rudolph O. 1974. "Voting Patterns in 'Bi-Cultural El Paso'." In F. Chris Garcia, ed., *La Causa Politica.* Notre Dame, IN: University of Notre Dame Press, 250–65.

de la Garza, Rudolph O. 1979. "The Politics of Mexican Americans." In Arnulfo D. Trejo, ed., *The Chicanos: As We See Ourselves.* Tucson, AZ: University of Arizona Press, 101–20.

de la Garza, Rodolfo O. 1984. "'And then there were some . . .:' Chicanos as National Political Actors, 1967–1980," *Aztlan* 15 (Spring), 1–24.

de la Garza, Rudolfo O. and Janet Weaver. 1985. "Chicano and Anglo Public Policy Perspectives in San Antonio: Does Ethnicity Make a Difference?" *Social Science Quarterly* 66 (September), 576–86.

de los Angeles Torres, Maria. 1988. "From Exiles to Minorities: The Politics of Cuban Americans." In F. Chris Garcia, ed., *Latinos and the Political System.* Notre Dame, IN: University of Notre Dame Press, 81–98.

DeMeis, Debra K. and Ralph R. Turner. 1978. "Effects of Students' Race, Physical Attractiveness and Dialect on Teachers' Evaluations," *Contemporary Educational Psychology* 3 (January), 77–86.

Dennis, Jack. 1968. "Major Problems in Political Socialization," *Midwest Political Science Review* 12 (February), 85–114.

Denton, Nancy A. and Douglas S. Massey. 1988. "Residential Segregation of Blacks, Hispanics, and Asians by Socioeconomic Status and Generation," *Social Science Quarterly* 69 (December), 797–817.

Dometrius, Nelson C. 1984. "Minorities and Women Among State Agency Leaders," *Social Science Quarterly* 37 (March), 127–37.

Dometrius, Nelson C. and Lee Sigelman. 1984. "Assessing Progress Toward Affirmative Action Goals in State and Local Government," *Public Administration Review* 44 (May/June), 241–46.

Dometrius, Nelson C. and Lee Sigelman. 1988. "Teacher Testing and Racial-Ethnic Representativeness in Public Education," *Social Science Quarterly* 69 (March), 70–82.

Dominguez, John R. 1977. "School Finance: The Issues of Equity and Efficiency," *Aztlan* 8 (Spring), 175–99.

Downs, Anthony. 1967. *Inside Bureaucracy.* Boston: Little, Brown.

Downs, Anthony. 1970. *Racism in America and How to Combat It.* Washington, D.C.: U.S. Commission on Civil Rights.

Duncan, Greg J. 1984. *Years of Poverty, Years of Plenty.* Ann Arbor, MI: Institute for Social Research, University of Michigan.

Dunn, Lloyd M. 1968. "Special Education for the Mildly Retarded—Is Much of It Justifiable?" *Exceptional Children* 35 (September), 5–22.

Durán, Richard P. 1983. *Hispanics Education and Background.* New York: College Entrance Examination Board.

Dusek, Jerome B. and Gail Joseph. 1983. "The Bases of Teacher

Expectancies: A Meta-Analysis," *Journal of Educational Psychology* 75 (June), 327–46.

Dutcher, Nadine. 1982. *The Use of First and Second Languages in Primary Education*. Washington, DC: The World Bank.

Dye, Thomas R. and James Renick. 1981. "Political Power and City Jobs: Determinants of Minority Employment," *Social Science Quarterly* 62 (September), 475–86.

Eder, Donna. 1981. "Ability Grouping as a Self-Fulfilling Prophecy," *Sociology of Education* 54 (July), 151–62.

Edgar, Eugene and Alice H. Hayden. 1984–85. "Who Are the Children Special Education Should Serve and How Many Children Are There?" *The Journal of Special Education* 18 (Winter), 521–39.

Edgar, Eugene and M. Maddox. 1984. "What Happens to Students Placed in Special Education?" University of Washington: mimeo.

Edwards, John. 1980. "Critics and Criticisms of Bilingual Education," *Modern Language Journal* 64 (Winter), 409–15.

Eisinger, Peter K. 1982a. "Black Employment in Municipal Jobs: The Impact of Black Political Power," *American Political Science Review* 76 (June), 330–92.

Eisinger, Peter K. 1982b. "The Economic Conditions of Black Employment in Municipal Bureaucracies," *American Journal of Political Science* 26 (November), 754–71.

Elliot, Rogers. 1987. *Litigating Intelligence*. Dover, MA: Auburn House.

England, Robert E. and Kenneth J. Meier. 1985. "From Desegregation to Integration: Second Generation Discrimination as an Institutional Impediment," *American Politics Quarterly* 13 (April), 227–47.

England, Robert E. and David R. Morgan. 1986. *Desegregating Big City Schools: Strategies, Outcomes, and Impacts*. New York: Associated Faculty Press.

Engstrom, Richard L. and Michael D. McDonald. 1981. "The Election of Blacks to City Councils," *American Political Science Review* 75 (June), 344–54.

Engstrom, Richard L. and Michael D. McDonald. 1982. "The Underrepresentation of Blacks on City Councils," *Journal of Politics* 44 (November), 1088–1105.

Epstein, Joyce L. 1985. "After the Bus Arrives: Resegregation in Desegregated Schools," *Journal of Social Issues* 41 (Number 3), 23–43.

Estrada, Leobardo F., F. Chris Garcia, Reynaldo Flores Macias, and Lionel Maldonado. 1988. "Chicanos in the United States: A History of Exploitation and Resistance." In F. Chris Garcia, ed., *Latinos and the Political System*. Notre Dame, IN: University of Notre Dame Press, 28–64.

Eulau, Heinz and Paul D. Karps. 1977. "The Puzzle of Representation: Specifying Components of Responsiveness," *Legislative Studies Quarterly* 2 (August), 233–54.

Eulau, Heinz, John C. Wahlke, William Buchanan, and Leroy C. Ferguson. 1959. "The Role of the Representative: Some Empirical Observations on the Theory of Edmund Burke," *American Political Science Review* 53 (September), 742–56.

Everhart, Robert B. 1983. *Reading, Writing, and Resistance*. London: Routledge and Kegan Paul.

Evertson, Carolyn M. 1986. "Do Teachers Make a Difference? Issues for the Eighties," *Education and Urban Society* 18 (February), 195–210.

Eyler, Janet, Valerie J. Cook, Rachel Thompkins, William Trent, and Leslie E. Ward. 1981. "Resegregation: Segregation Within Desegregated Schools." In Christine H. Rossell, et al., eds., *Assessment of Current Knowledge About the Effectiveness of School Desegregation Strategies*. Nashville, TN: Institute of Public Policy Studies, Vanderbilt University, 210–329.

Eyler, Janet, Valerie J. Cook, and Leslie E. Ward. 1983. "Resegregation: Segregation Within Desegregated Schools." In Christine H. Rossell and Willis D. Hawley, eds., *The Consequences of School Desegregation*. Philadelphia: Temple University Press, 126–62.

Faculty of the University of Arizona. 1972. *Arizona: Its People and Resources*. Tucson, AZ: University of Arizona Press.

Fagen, Richard R., Richard A. Brody, and Thomas J. O'Leary. 1968. *Cubans in Exile: Disaffection and the Revolution*. Stanford, CA: Stanford University Press.

Falcón, Angelo. 1984. "A History of Puerto Rican Politics in New York City: 1860s to 1945." In James Jennings and Monte Rivera, eds., *Puerto Rican Politics in Urban America*. Westport, CT: Greenwood Press, 15–42.

Falcón, Angelo. 1988. "Black and Latino Politics in New York City: Race and Ethnicity in a Changing Urban Context." In F. Chris Garcia, ed., *Latinos and the Political System*. Notre Dame, IN: University of Notre Dame Press, 171–94.

Farley, Reynolds. 1975. "Racial Integration in the Public Schools, 1967 to 1972: Assessing the Effects of Governmental Politics," *Sociological Forces* 8 (January), 3–26.

Farley, Reynolds, Toni Richards, and Clarence Wurdock. 1980. "School Desegregation and White Flight: An Investigation of Competing Models and their Discrepant Findings," *Sociology of Education* 53 (July), 123–39.

Feagin, Joe R. 1980. "School Desegregation: A Political-Economic Perspective." In Walter G. Stephan and Joe R. Feagin, eds., *School Desegregation: Past, Present, and Future.* New York: Plenum Press, 25–50.

Feagin, Joe R. and Clairece Booher Feagin. 1986. *Discrimination American Style,* 2nd ed. Malabar, FL: Robert E. Krieger.

Felmlee, Diane and Donna Eder. 1983. "Contextual Effects in the Classroom: The Impact of Ability Groups on Student Attention," *Sociology of Education* 56 (April), 77–87.

Fernández, Ricardo R. and Judith T. Guskin. 1981. "Hispanic Students and School Desegregation." In Willis D. Hawley, ed., *Effective School Desegregation.* Beverly Hills, CA: Sage, 107–40.

Fernández, Ricardo R. and William Velez. 1985. "Race, Color, and Language in the Changing Public Schools." In Lionel Maldonado and Joan Moore, eds. *Urban Ethnicity in the United States.* Beverly Hills, CA: Sage, 123–44.

Findley, Warren and Miriam Bryan. 1975. *The Pros and Cons of Ability Grouping.* Bloomington, IN: Phi Delta Kappa Educational Foundation.

Finn, Jeremy D. 1982. "Patterns in Special Education Placement as Revealed by the OCR Surveys." In Kirby A. Heller, Wayne H. Holtzman, and Samuel Messick, eds., *Placing Children in Special Education.* Washington, DC: National Academy Press, 322–81.

Fitzpatrick, Joseph P. 1971. *Puerto Rican Americans: The Meaning of Migration to the Mainland.* Engelwood Cliffs, NJ: Prentice-Hall.

Flaxman, Erwin, ed. 1976. *Educating the Disadvantaged.* New York: AMS Press.

Fraga, Luis R., Kenneth J. Meier, and Robert E. England. 1986. "Hispanic Americans and Educational Policy: Limits to Equal Access," *Journal of Politics* 48 (November), 850–76.

Franseth, Jane. 1966. "Does Grouping Make a Difference in Pupil Learning?" In Anne Morgenstern, ed., *Grouping in Elementary School.* New York: Pitman, 14–21.

Free, Lloyd A. and Hadley Cantril. 1968. *The Political Beliefs of Americans*. New York: Simon and Schuster.

Freeman, Donald M. 1974. "Party, Vote and the Mexican American in South Tucson." In F. Chris Garcia, ed., *La Causa Politica*. Notre Dame, IN: University of Notre Dame Press, 55–66.

Friere, Paulo. 1970. *Pedagogy of the Oppressed*. New York: Herder and Herder.

Friesema, H. Paul and Ronald D. Hedlund. 1974. "The Reality of Representational Roles." In Norman R. Luttbeg, ed., *Public Opinion and Public Policy*. Homewood, IL: Dorsey Press, 413–17.

Fuentes, Luis. 1984. "Puerto Ricans and New York City School Board Elections: Apathy or Obstructionism?" In James Jennings and Monte Rivera, eds., *Puerto Rican Politics in Urban America*. Westport, CT: Greenwood Press, 127–38.

Gallagher, James J. 1972. "The Special Education Contract for Mildly Handicapped Children," *Exceptional Children* 38 (March), 527–35.

García, Eugene E. 1986. "Bilingual Development and the Education of Bilingual Children During Early Childhood," *American Journal of Education* 95 (November), 96–121.

Garcia, F. Chris. 1974a. "Mexican Americans and Modes of Political Participation." In F. Chris Garcia, ed., *La Causa Politica*. Notre Dame, IN: University of Notre Dame Press, 67–85.

Garcia, F. Chris. 1974b. "Manitos and Chicanos in New Mexico Politics." In F. Chris Garcia, ed., *La Causa Politica*. Notre Dame, IN: University of Notre Dame Press, 271–80.

Garcia, F. Chris, ed. 1974c. *La Causa Politica*. Notre Dame, IN: University of Notre Dame Press.

Garcia, F. Chris and Rudolph O. de la Garza. 1977. *The Chicano Political Experience*. North Scituate, MA: Duxbury Press.

Garcia, F. Chris and Robert D. Wrinkle. 1971. "New Mexico: Urban Politics in a State of Varied Political Cultures." In Robert D. Wrinkle, ed., *Politics in the Urban Southwest*. Albuquerque, NM: University of New Mexico, Division of Government Research, 35–49.

Garcia, John A. 1979. "An Analysis of Chicano and Anglo Electoral Patterns in School Board Elections," *Ethnicity* 6 (June), 168–83.

Garcia, John A. and Carlos H. Arce. 1988. "Political Orientations and Behaviors of Chicanos: Trying to Make Sense Out of Attitudes and

Participation." In F. Chris Garcia, ed., *Latinos and the Political System*. Notre Dame, IN: University of Notre Dame Press, 125–51.

Garcia, Joseph O. and Rubén W. Espinosa. 1977. "A Study of Credentialed Staff-Pupil Ratios by Ethnicity in the California Public Schools," *Aztlan* 8 (Spring), 217–36.

García, Juan Ramon. 1980. *Operation Wetback: The Mass Deportation of Mexican Undocumented Workers in 1954*. Westport, CT: Greenwood Press.

García, Maria C. 1982. "Quest for the Best: The Private School Explosion," *Miami Herald,* April 18, 1G.

Garrison, Mortimer and Donald D. Hammill. 1971. "Who Are the Retarded?" *Exceptional Children* 38 (September), 13–20.

Gartner, Alan and Dorothy Kerzner Lipsky. 1987. "Beyond Special Education: Toward a Quality System for All Students," *Harvard Educational Review* 57 (November), 367–95.

General Accounting Office. 1984. *Assessment of Audits of Bilingual Education Grants in Texas by U.S. Department of Education's Office of Inspector General*. Washington, DC.

General Accounting Office. 1987a. *Bilingual Education: Research and Evaluation Contracts*. Washington, DC.

General Accounting Office. 1987b. *Bilingual Education: A New Look at the Research Evidence*. Washington, DC.

Genevie, Louis and others. 1988. *The American Teacher 1988*. New York: Louis Harris and Associates.

Gersten, Russell and John Woodward. 1985. "A Case for Structured Immersion," *Educational Leader* 43 (September), 75–79.

Giles, Micheal W. 1975. "Black Concentration and School District Size as Predictors of School Segregation: The Impact of Federal Enforcement," *Sociology of Education* 48 (Fall), 11–19.

Giles, Micheal W. 1978. "White Enrollment Stability and School Desegregation: A Two-Level Analysis," *American Sociological Review* 43 (December), 848–64.

Giles, Micheal W. and Arthur S. Evans. 1985. "External Threat, Perceived Threat, and Group Identity," *Social Science Quarterly* 66 (March), 50–66.

Giles, Micheal W. and Arthur S. Evans. 1986. "The Power Approach to Intergroup Hostility," *Journal of Conflict Resolution* 30 (September), 469–86.

Giles, Micheal W. and Douglas S. Gatlin. 1980. "Mass Level Compliance with Public Policy: The Case of School Desegregation," *Journal of Politics* 37 (August), 722–46.

Gilliam, Franklin D., Jr. 1988. "The Politics of Cultural Diversity: Racial and Ethnic Mass Attitudes in California." Paper presented at the Conference on Comparative Ethnicity, June 1–4, Los Angeles.

Glazer, Nathan and Daniel P. Moynihan. 1963. *Beyond the Melting Pot.* Cambridge, MA: Harvard-MIT Press.

Goldberg, Miriam and A. Harry Passow. 1966. "The Effects of Ability Grouping." In Anne Morgenstern, ed., *Grouping in Elementary School.* New York: Pitman, 22–39.

Goldberg, Miriam L., A. Harry Passow, and Joseph Justman. 1966. *The Effects of Ability Grouping.* New York: Teachers College, Columbia University.

Good, Thomas L. 1970. "Which Pupils Do Teachers Call On?" *The Elementary School Journal* 70 (January), 190–98.

Good, Thomas L. and Harris M. Cooper. 1983. *Pygmalion Grows Up.* New York: Longman.

Grebler, Leo, Joan W. Moore, and Ralph C. Guzmán. 1970. *The Mexican American People.* New York: The Free Press.

Grebler, Leo, Joan Moore, and Ralph Guzmán. 1974. "Contact with Governmental Agencies." In F. Chris Garcia, ed., *La Causa Politica.* Notre Dame, IN: University of Notre Dame Press, 177–97.

Groff, Patrick J. 1962. "A Survey of Basic Reading Group Practices," *Reading Teacher* 15 (January), 232–35.

Guerra, Manuel H. 1979. "Bilingualism and Biculturalism: Assets for Chicanos." In Arnulfo D. Trejo, ed., *The Chicanos: As We See Ourselves.* Tucson, AZ: University of Arizona Press, 121–32.

Gutiérrez, Armando and Herbert Hirsch. 1974. "The Militant Challenge to the American Ethos: 'Chicanos' and 'Mexican Americans'." In F. Chris Garcia, ed., *La Causa Politica.* Notre Dame, IN: University of Notre Dame Press, 86–103.

Hakuta, Kenju and Laurie J. Gould. 1987. "Synthesis of Research on Bilingual Education," *Educational Leader* 44 (March), 38–45.

Hall, Grace and Alan Saltzstein. 1977. "Equal Employment Opportunity for Minorities in Municipal Government," *Social Science Quarterly* 57 (March), 864–72.

Harrington, Charles C. 1985. "Bilingual Education in the United States: A View from 1980." In Marguerite Ross Barnett and Charles C. Harrington, eds., *Readings in Equal Education,* Volume 8. New York: AMS Press, 185–205.

Hauser, Robert M., William H. Sewell, and Duane F. Alwin. 1976. "High School Effects on Achievement." In William H. Sewell, Robert M. Hauser, and David L. Featherman, eds., *Schooling and Achievement in American Society.* New York: Academic Press, 309–42.

Hawkins, Michael L. 1966. "Mobility of Students in Reading Groups," *Reading Teacher* 20 (November), 136–40.

Hawley, Willis and Susan Rosenholtz. 1984. "Good Schools: What Research Says About Improving Student Achievement," *Peabody Journal of Education* 61 (Summer), 1–178.

Hedlund, Ronald D. and H. Paul Friesema. 1972. "Representatives' Perceptions of Constituency Opinion," *Journal of Politics* 34 (August), 730–52.

Heilig, Peggy and Robert J. Mundt. 1984. *Your Voice at City Hall.* Albany, NY: SUNY Press.

Heller, Kirby A. 1982. "Effects of Special Education Placement on Mentally Retarded Children." In Kirby A. Heller, Wayne H. Holtzman, and Samuel Messick, eds., *Placing Children in Special Education.* Washington, DC: National Academy Press, 262–99.

Heller, Kirby A., Wayne H. Holtzman, and Samuel Messick, eds. 1982. *Placing Children in Special Education.* Washington, DC: National Academy Press.

Heohn, Arthur J. 1954. "A Study of Social Status Differentiation in the Classroom Behavior of Nineteen Third Grade Teachers," *Journal of Social Psychology* 39 (May), 269–92.

Hero, Rodney E. 1986. "Mexican Americans and Urban Politics: A Consideration of Governmental Structure and Policy," *Aztlan* 17 (Spring), 131–47.

Hero, Rodney. 1987. "The Election of Hispanics in City Government: An Examination of the Election of Federico Peña as Mayor of Denver," *Western Political Quarterly* 40 (March), 93–106.

Hero, Rodney and Kathleen M. Beatty. 1989. "The Election of Federico Peña as Mayor of Denver: Analysis and Implications," *Social Science Quarterly* 70 (June), 300–10.

Heyns, Barbara. 1974. "Social Selection and Stratification Within

Schools," *American Journal of Sociology* 79 (May), 1434–51.

Hobbs, Nicholas. 1975. *The Futures of Children: Categories, Labels, and Their Consequences.* San Francisco: Jossey-Bass.

Hochschild, Jennifer L. 1984. *The New American Dilemma: Liberal Democracy and School Desegregation.* New Haven, CT: Yale University Press.

Hoffman, Abraham. 1974. *Unwanted Mexican Americans in the Great Depression: Repatriation Pressures.* Tucson, AZ: University of Arizona Press.

Holland, Rick. 1986. "Bilingual Education: Recent Evaluations of Local School District Programs and Related Research on Second Language Learning." Washington, DC: Congressional Research Service.

Holliday, Bertha Garrett. 1985. "Differential Effects of Children's Self-Perceptions and Teachers' Perceptions on Black Children's Academic Achievement," *Journal of Negro Education* 54 (Winter), 71–81.

Holmes, Jack E. 1967. *Politics in New Mexico.* Albuquerque: University of New Mexico Press.

Hornberger, Nancy H. 1987. "Bilingual Education Success, But Policy Failure," *Language Society* 16: 205–26.

Hughes, Larry W., William M. Gordon, and Larry W. Hillman. 1980. *Desegregating America's Schools.* New York: Longman.

Hurtado, Aida and Patricia Gurin. 1987. "Ethnic Identity and Bilingualism Attitudes," *Hispanic Journal of Behavioral Sciences* 9 (March), 1–18.

Hyink, Bernard L., Seyom Brown, and Ernest W. Thacker. 1985. *Politics and Government in California.* New York: Harper and Row.

Illinois Advisory Committee to the U.S. Commission on Civil Rights. 1974. *Bilingual/Bicultural Education: A Privilege or a Right?* Washington, DC: U.S. Government Printing Office.

Jackman, Mary R. 1978. "General and Applied Tolerance," *American Journal of Political Science* 22 (May), 302–24.

Jackman, Mary R. 1981. "Education and Policy Commitment to Racial Integration," *American Journal of Political Science* 25 (May), 256–71.

Jackson, Gregg and Cecilia Cosca. 1974. "The Inequality of Educational Opportunity in the Southwest," *American Educational Research Journal* 11 (October), 3–23.

Jencks, Christopher, Marshall Smith, Henry Acland, Mary Jo Bane, David Cohen, Herbert Gintis, Barbara Heyns, and Stephan Michelson. 1972. *Inequality: A Reassessment of the Effect of Family and Schooling in America.* New York: Harper and Row.

Jennings, James. 1984a. "The Emergence of Puerto Rican Electoral Activism in Urban America." In James Jennings and Monte Rivera, eds., *Puerto Rican Politics in Urban America.* Westport, CT: Greenwood Press, 3–13.

Jennings, James. 1984b. "Puerto Rican Politics in Two Cities: New York and Boston." In James Jennings and Monte Rivera, eds., *Puerto Rican Politics in Urban America.* Westport, CT: Greenwood Press, 75–98.

Jennings, James and Monte Rivera, eds. 1984. *Puerto Rican Politics in Urban America.* Westport, CT: Greenwood Press.

Jones, Reginald L., ed., 1976. *Mainstreaming and the Minority Child.* Reston, VA: The Council for Exceptional Children.

Jones, Reginald L. and Frank Wilderson. 1976. "Mainstreaming and the Minority Child: An Overview of Issues and a Perspective." In Reginald L. Jones, ed., *Mainstreaming and the Minority Child.* Reston, VA: The Council for Exceptional Children, 1–14.

Juarez, Alberto. 1974. "The Emergence of El Partido De La Raza Unida." In F. Chris Garcia, ed., *La Causa Politica.* Notre Dame, IN: University of Notre Dame Press, 304–21.

Karnig, Albert K. 1976. "Black Representation on City Councils," *Urban Affairs Quarterly* 12 (December), 223–42.

Karnig, Albert K. 1979. "Black Resources and City Council Representation," *Journal of Politics* 41 (February), 134–49.

Karnig, Albert K. and Paula D. McClain. 1988. *Urban Minority Administrators: Politics, Policy and Style.* Westport, CT: Greenwood Press.

Karnig, Albert K. and Susan Welch. 1979. "Sex and Ethnic Differences in Municipal Representation," *Social Science Quarterly* 60 (December), 465–81.

Karnig, Albert K. and Susan Welch. 1980. *Black Representation and Urban Policy.* Chicago: University of Chicago Press.

Karnig, Albert K. and Susan Welch. 1982. "Electoral Structure and Black Representation on City Councils," *Social Science Quarterly* 63 (March), 99–114.

Keech, William. R. 1968. *The Impact of Negro Voting.* Chicago: Rand McNally.

Keller, Ernest. 1978. "The Impact of Black Mayors on Urban Policy," *The Annals* 439: 40–52.

Kingsley, J. Donald. 1944. *Representative Bureaucracy.* Yellow Springs, OH: Antioch Press.

Kirp, David L. 1973. "Schools as Sorters: The Constitutional and Policy Implications of Student Classification," *University of Pennsylvania Law Review* 121 (April), 705–97.

Kjolseth, Rolf. 1986. "Cultural Politics of Bilingualism," *Sociolinguistics Today* (May/June), 40–48.

Kloss, Heinz. 1977. *The American Bilingual Tradition.* Rowley, MA: Newbury House.

Knowlton, Clark. 1974. "Guerillas of Rio Arriba: The New Mexican Land Wars." In F. Chris Garcia, ed. *La Causa Politica.* Notre Dame, IN: University of Notre Dame Press, 331–40.

Krasker, William K. 1988. "Robust Regression." In Samuel Kotz and Norman L. Johnson, eds., *Encyclopedia of Statistical Sciences,* Vol. 8. New York: John Wiley and Sons, 166–69.

Kuklinski, James H. 1979. "Representative-Constituency Linkages: A Review Article," *Legislative Studies Quarterly* 4 (February), 121–40.

Kulik, Chen-Lin and James A. Kulik. 1982. "Effects of Ability Grouping on Secondary School Students," *American Educational Research Journal* 19 (Fall), 415–28.

Lanier, James and Wittmer, Joe 1977. "Teacher Prejudice in Referral of Students to EMR Programs," *The School Counselor* 24 (January), 165–70.

Laosa, Luis M. 1977a. "Multicultural Education: How Psychology Can Contribute," *Journal of Teacher Education* 28 (May/June), 26–30.

Laosa, Luis M. 1977b. "Inequality in the Classroom: Observational Research on Teacher-Student Interactions," *Aztlan* 8 (Spring), 51–67.

Lasswell, Harold D. 1936. *Politics: Who Gets What, When, How?* New York: McGraw-Hill.

Leacock, Eleanor B. 1969. *Teaching and Learning in City Schools.* New York: Basic Books.

Levine, Charles H. 1974. *Racial Conflict and the American Mayor.* Lexington, MA: Lexington Books.

Levitan, David M. 1946. "The Responsibility of Administrative Officials in a Democratic Society," *Political Science Quarterly* 61 (December), 562–98.

Levy, Mark R. and Michael S. Kramer. 1974. "Patterns of Chicano Voting Behavior." In F. Chris Garcia, ed., *La Causa Politica.* Notre Dame, IN: University of Notre Dame Press, 241–49.

Lineberry, Robert L. 1978. "Reform, Representation, and Policy," *Social Science Quarterly* 59 (June), 173–77.

Lineberry, Robert L. and Edmund P. Fowler. 1967. "Reformism and Public Policies in American Cities," *American Political Science Review* 61 (September), 701–16.

Lipsky, Michael. 1980. *Street Level Bureaucracy.* New York: Russell Sage Foundation.

Little, Wilson. 1944. *Spanish-Speaking Children in Texas.* Austin, TX: University of Texas Press.

Loehlin, John C., Garner Lindzey, and J.N. Spuhler. 1975. *Race Differences in Intelligence.* San Francisco: W.H. Freeman.

Lomotey, Kofi. 1987. "Black Principals for Black Students: Some Preliminary Observations," *Urban Education* 22 (July), 173–81.

Long, Norton E. 1952. "Bureaucracy and Constitutionalism," *American Political Science Review* 46 (September), 808–18.

Lopez, Manuel Mariano. 1981. "Patterns of Interethnic Residential Segregation in the Urban Southwest, 1960 and 1970," *Social Science Quarterly* 62 (March), 50–63.

Lucas, Isidro. 1984. "Puerto Rican Politics in Chicago." In James Jennings and Monte Rivera, eds., *Puerto Rican Politics in Urban America.* Westport, CT: Greenwood Press, 99–115.

Mackey, William Francis and Von Nieda Beebe. 1977. *Bilingual Schools for a Bicultural Community.* Rowley, MA: Newbury House.

Mackler, Bernard. 1969. "Grouping in the Ghetto," *Education and Urban Society* 2 (November), 80–96.

MacManus, Susan A. 1978. "City Council Election Procedures and Minority Representation: Are They Related?" *Social Science Quarterly* 59 (June), 153–61.

MacManus, Susan A., Charles S. Bullock, III, and Barbara P. Grothe. 1986. "A Longitudinal Examination of Political Participation Rates of Mexican American Females," *Social Science Quarterly* 67 (September), 604–12.

MacManus, Susan A. and Carol A. Cassell. 1988. "Mexican-Americans in City Politics: Participation, Representation, and Policy Preferences." In F. Chris Garcia, ed., *Latinos and the Political System.* Notre Dame, IN: University of Notre Dame Press, 201–12.

MacMilliam, Donald L., Irving G. Hendrick, and Alice V. Watkins. 1988. "Impact of *Diana, Larry P.,* and P.L. 94–142 on Minority Students," *Exceptional Children* 45 (February), 426–32.

Magnetti, Suzanne S. 1982. "Some Potential Incentives of Special Education Funding Practices." In Kirby A. Heller, Wayne H. Holtzman, and Samuel Messick, eds., *Placing Children in Special Education.* Washington, DC: National Academy Press, 300–21.

Maldonado, Lionel and Joan W. Moore, eds. 1985. *Urban Ethnicity in the United States.* Beverly Hills, CA: Sage Publications.

Maldonado-Denis, Manuel. 1972. *Puerto Rico: A Socio-Historical Interpretation.* New York: Random House.

Mann, Dale. 1974. "The Politics of Representation in Educational Administration," *Education in Urban Society* 6 (May), 297–317.

Manni, John L., David W. Winikur, and Maureen R. Keller. 1984. *Intelligence, Mental Retardation and the Culturally Different Child.* Springfield, IL: Charles C. Thomas.

Manuel, Herschel T. 1930. *The Education of Spanish-Speaking Children in Texas.* Austin, TX: University of Texas Press.

Manuel, Herschel T. 1965. *Spanish-Speaking Children of the Southwest.* Austin, TX: University of Texas Press.

Margolis, Richard J. 1968. *The Losers: A Report on the Puerto Ricans and the Public Schools.* New York: Aspira.

Marquez, Benjamin. 1987. "The Politics of Race and Class: The League of United Latin American Citizens in the Post–World War II Period," *Social Science Quarterly* 68 (March), 84–101.

Marquez, Benjamin. 1989. "The Politics of Race and Assimilation: The League of United Latin American Citizens, 1929–40," *Western Political Quarterly* 42 (June), 355–76.

Marshall, Harvey. 1979. "White Movement to the Suburbs: A Comparison of Explanations," *American Sociological Review* 44 (December), 975–94.

Marwit, Karen S., Samuel J. Marwit, and Elaine Walker. 1978. "Effects of Student Race and Physical Attractiveness on Teachers' Judgments of Transgressions," *Journal of Educational Psychology* 70 (December), 911–15.

Mazmanian, Daniel A. and Paul A. Sabatier. 1983. *Implementation and Public Policy.* Glenview, IL: Scott-Foresman.

McCleskey, Clifton and Bruce Merrill. 1974. "Mexican American Political Behavior in Texas." In F. Chris Garcia, ed. *La Causa Politica.* Notre Dame, IN: University of Notre Dame Press, 128–42.

McConahay, John B. 1981. "Reducing Racial Prejudice in Desegregated Schools." In Willis D. Hawley, ed., *Effective School Desegregation: Equity, Quality, and Feasibility.* Beverly Hills, CA: Sage, 35–53.

McLaughlin, Barry. 1985. *Second Language Acquisition in Childhood.* Hillsdale, NJ: Lawrence Erlbaum Associates.

McWilliams, Carey. 1968. *North From Mexico.* Westport, CT: Greenwood Press.

Meier, Kenneth J. 1984. "Teachers, Students and Discrimination: The Policy Impact of Black Representation," *Journal of Politics* 46 (February), 252–63.

Meier, Kenneth J. and Robert E. England. 1984. "Black Representation and Educational Policy: Are They Related?" *American Political Science Review* 78 (June), 392–403.

Meier, Kenneth J. and Lloyd G. Nigro. 1976. "Representative Bureaucracy and Policy Preferences," *Public Administration Review* 36 (July/August), 458–70.

Meier, Kenneth J., Joseph Stewart, Jr., and Robert E. England. 1989. *Race, Class and Education: The Politics of Second Generation Discrimination.* Madison, WI: University of Wisconsin Press.

Meier, Matt S. and Feliciano Rivera. 1972. *The Chicanos: A History of Mexican Americans.* New York: Hill and Wang.

Mercer, Jane R. 1972. "Discussion of Alternative Value Frames for Classification of Exceptional Children." Working paper prepared for the Project on Classification of Exceptional Children. Nashville, TN: Vanderbilt University.

Mercer, Jane R. 1973. *Labeling the Mentally Retarded: Clinical and Social System Perspectives on Mental Retardation.* Berkeley, CA: University of California Press.

Mercer, Jane R. and J. G. Richardson. 1975. "Mental Retardation." In Nicholas Hobbs, ed., *Issues in the Classification of Children*. San Francisco: Jossey-Bass, 463–96.

Metz, Mary Haywood. 1978. *Classrooms and Corridors: The Crisis of Authority in Desegregated Secondary Schools*. Berkeley: University of California Press.

Miles, Rufus E. 1978. "The Origin and Meaning of Miles' Law," *Public Administration Review* 38 (September/October), 399–403.

Miller, Warren E. and Donald E. Stokes. 1963. "Constituency Influence in Congress," *American Political Science Review* 57 (March), 45–56.

Milton, Sande. 1983. "Participation in Local School Board Elections," *Social Science Quarterly* 64 (September), 647–54.

Minar, David W. 1966. "The Community Basis of Conflict in School System Politics," *American Sociological Review* 31 (December), 822–35.

Minaya-Rowe, Liliana. 1986. "Sociocultural Comparison of Bilingual Education Policies and Programmes in Three Andean Countries and the United States," *Journal of Multicultural Development* 7 (December), 465–77.

Mindiola, Tatcho and Armando Gutierrez. 1988. "Chicanos and the Legislative Process: Reality and Illusion in the Politics of Change." In F. Chris Garcia, ed., *Latinos and the Political System*. Notre Dame, IN: University of Notre Dame Press, 349–62.

Mladenka, Kenneth R. 1989a. "Blacks and Hispanics in Urban Politics," *American Political Science Review* 83 (March), 165–92.

Mladenka, Kenneth R. 1989b. "Barriers to Hispanic Employment Success in 1,200 Cities," *Social Science Quarterly* 70 (June), 391–407.

Monroe, Alan D. 1975. *Public Opinion in America*. New York: Dodd, Mead.

Montejano, David. 1987. *Anglos and Mexicans in the Making of Texas, 1836–1986*. Austin, TX: University of Texas Press.

Moore, Helen A. and David R. Johnson. 1983. "A Reexamination of Elementary School Teachers Expectations: Evidence of Sex and Ethnic Segmentation," *Social Science Quarterly* 64 (September), 460–75.

Moore, Joan. 1989. "Is There a Hispanic Underclass?" *Social Science Quarterly* 70 (June), 265–84.

Moore, Joan W. and Harry Pachon. 1985. *Hispanics in the United States*. Engelwood Cliffs, NJ: Prentice-Hall.

Morgenstern, Anne. 1966. "Historical Survey of Grouping Practices in the Elementary School." In Anne Morgenstern, ed., *Grouping in the Elementary School*. New York: Pittman, 3–13.

Mosher, Frederick C. 1968. *Democracy and the Public Service*. New York: Oxford University Press.

Muñoz, Carlos, Jr. and Mario Barrera. 1988. "La Raza Unida Party and the Chicano Student Movement in California." In F. Chris Garcia, ed., *Latinos and the Political System*. Notre Dame, IN: University of Notre Dame Press, 213–35.

Muñoz, Carlos, Jr. and Charles Henry. 1986. "Rainbow Coalitions in Four Big Cities: San Antonio, Denver, Chicago, and Philadelphia," *PS* 19 (Summer), 598–609.

Muñoz-Hernández, Shirley and Isaura Santiago Santiago. 1985. "Toward a Qualitative Analysis of Teacher Disapproval Behavior." In Raymond V. Padilla, ed., *Theory, Technology and Public Policy on Bilingual Education*. Rosslyn, VA: National Clearing House for Bilingual Education, 99–112.

National Center for Education Statistics. 1975. *The Condition of Education*. Washington, DC: U.S. Government Printing Office.

National Center for Education Statistics. 1976. *Place of Birth and Language Characteristics of Persons of Hispanic Origin in the United States*. Washington, DC: U.S. Government Printing Office.

National Center for Education Statistics. 1978. *The Children's English and Services Study*. Washington, DC: U.S. Government Printing Office.

National Education Association. 1968. *Ability Grouping*. Washington, DC: National Education Association.

National Institute of Education. 1977a. *Conference Report: Desegregation and Education Concerns of the Hispanic Community*. Washington, DC: U.S. Government Printing Office.

National Institute of Education. 1977b. *Resegregation: A Second Generation School Desegregation Issue*. Washington, DC: U.S. Government Printing Office.

National Institute of Education. 1979. *In School Alternatives to Suspension*. Washington, DC: U.S. Government Printing Office.

National Journal. 1987. "A Lack of Political Power," January 24, 224.

Navarro, Armando. 1974. "The Evolution of Chicano Politics," *Aztlan* 5 (Spring), 57–84.

Nelson, William. 1972. *Black Politics in Gary.* Washington, DC: Joint Center for Political Studies.

Nelson, William and Phillip Meranto. 1976. *Electing Black Mayors.* Columbus, OH: Ohio State University Press.

Nordlinger, Eric A. 1981. *On the Autonomy of the Democratic State.* Cambridge, MA: Harvard University Press.

O'Connor, Karen and Lee Epstein. 1984. "A Legal Voice for the Chicano Community: The Activities of the Mexican American Legal Defense and Educational Fund, 1968–82," *Social Science Quarterly* 65 (June), 245–56.

Oakes, Jeannie. 1985. *Keeping Track: How Schools Structure Inequality.* New Haven, CT: Yale University Press.

Oakes, Jeannie. 1988. "Tracking: Can Schools Take a Different Route?" *National Education Association* (January), 41–47.

Office of Special Education, California State Department of Education. 1983. *A Status Report on Diana, et al., v. State Board of Education, et al.* Sacramento, CA: State of California.

Ogbu, John U. 1978. *Minority Education and Caste: The American System in Cross-Cultural Perspective.* New York: Academic Press.

Olivas, Michael A. 1983. "Research and Theory on Hispanic Education: Students, Finance, and Governance," *Aztlan* 14 (Spring), 111–46.

Orfield, Gary W. 1978. *Must We Bus?* Washington, DC: Brookings Institution.

Orfield, Gary and Franklin Monfort. 1988. "Are American Schools Resegregating in the Reagan Era?" Reported in Harold W. Stanley and Richard G. Niemi, eds., *Vital Statistics on American Politics.* Washington, DC. Congressional Quarterly Press, 326–27.

Ovando, Carlos J. and Virginia P. Collier. 1985. *Bilingual and ESL Classrooms.* New York: McGraw-Hill.

Padilla, Amado M. and Rene A. Ruiz. 1973. *Latino Mental Health.* Rockville, MD: National Institute of Mental Health.

Padilla, Fernando V. and Carlos B. Ramirez. 1974. "Patterns of Chicano Representation in California, Colorado and Nuevo Mexico," *Aztlan* 5 (Spring), 189–233.

Padilla, Raymond V., ed. 1983. *Theory, Technology, and Public Policy on Bilingual Education.* Rosslyn, VA: National Clearinghouse for Bilingual Education.

Patella, Victoria and William P. Kuvlesky. 1973. "Situational Variation in Language Patterns of Mexican American Boys and Girls," *Social Science Quarterly* 53 (March), 855–64.

Pedraza-Bailey, Silvia. 1985a. *Political and Economic Migrants in America: Cubans and Mexicans.* Austin, TX: University of Texas Press.

Pedraza-Bailey, Silvia. 1985b. "Cuba's Exiles: Portrait of a Refugee Migration," *International Migration Review* 19 (Spring), 4–34.

Penley, Larry E., Sam Gould, and Lynda Y. de la Vina. 1984. "The Comparative Salary Position of Mexican American College Graduates in Business," *Social Science Quarterly* 65 (June), 444–54.

Persell, Caroline Hodges. 1977. *Education and Inequality.* New York: The Free Press.

Pettigrew, Thomas F. 1971. *Racially Separate or Together?* New York: McGraw-Hill.

Pettigrew, Thomas F. 1976. "Black Mayoral Campaigns." In Herrington J. Bryce, ed., *Urban Governance and Minorities.* New York: Praeger, 14–29.

Pettigrew, Thomas F. and Robert L. Green. 1976. "School Desegregation in Large Cities: A Critique of the Coleman 'White Flight' Thesis," *Harvard Education Review* 46 (February), 1–53.

Pifer, Alan. 1984. "Bilingual Education and the Hispanic Challenge." In Marguerite Ross Barnett and Charles C. Harrington, eds., *Readings on Equal Education,* Volume 7. New York: AMS Press, 165–82.

Pitkin, Hannah F. 1967. *The Concept of Representation.* Berkeley, CA: The University of California Press.

Poinsett, Alex. 1970. *Black Power Gary Style.* Chicago: Johnson.

Polinard, J. L. and Robert D. Wrinkle. 1988. "The Impact of District Elections on the Mexican American Community: The Electoral Perspective." Paper presented at the annual meeting of the Midwest Political Science Association, Chicago.

Polinard, J. L., Robert D. Wrinkle, and Thomas Longoria. 1988. "Mexican Americans and Educational Policy: The Impact of Change to District Elections." Paper presented at the annual meeting of the American Political Science Association, Washington, DC.

Polloway, Edward A. 1984. "The Integration of Mildly Retarded Students in the Schools: A Historical Review," *Remedial and Special Education* 5 (July/August), 18–28.

Portes, Alejandro and Robert L. Bach. 1985. *Latin Journey: Cuban and Mexican Immigrants in the United States.* Berkeley, CA: University of California Press.

Portes, Alejandro and Rafael Mozo. 1985. "The Political Adaptation Process of Cubans and Other Ethnic Minorities in the United States," *International Migration Review* 19 (Spring), 35–64.

Prasse, David P. 1988. "Legal Influence and Educational Policy in Special Education," *Exceptional Children* 54 (January), 302–08.

Pressman, Jeffrey L. and Aaron B. Wildavsky. 1973. *Implementation.* Berkeley, CA: University of California Press.

Prewitt, Kenneth. 1970. "Political Ambitions, Volunteerism, and Electoral Accountability," *American Political Science Review* 64 (March), 5–17.

Prohias, Rafael and Lourdes Casal. 1980. *The Cuban Minority in the U.S.* New York: Arno Press.

Radin, Norma. 1988. "Alternatives to Suspension and Corporal Punishment," *Urban Education* 22 (January), 476–95.

Ramirez, J. David. 1986. "Comparing Structured English Immersion and Bilingual Education," *American Journal of Education* 95 (November), 122–48.

Ramírez, Manuel and Alfredo Castañeda. 1974. *Cultural Democracy, Bicognitive Development, and Education.* New York: Academic Press.

Rangel, Jorge C. and Carlos M. Alcala. 1972. "Project Report: De Jure Segregation of Chicanos in Texas Schools," *Harvard Civil Rights-Civil Liberties Law Review* 7 (March), 307–92.

Ravitch, Diane. 1978. "The White Flight Controversy," *The Public Interest* 51 (Spring), 135–49.

Redford, Emmette S. 1969. *Democracy in the Administrative State.* New York: Oxford University Press.

Reschly, Daniel J. 1988a. "Minority MMR Overrepresentation and Special Education Reform," *Exceptional Children* 54 (January), 316–23.

Reschly, Daniel J. 1988b. "*Larry P.! Larry P.!* Why the California Sky Fell on IQ Testing," *Journal of School Psychology* 26 (Summer), 199–205.

Reschly, Daniel J. and Frank M. Gresham. 1988. "Adaptive Behavior and the Mildly Handicapped." In Thomas R. Kratochwill, ed., *Advances in School Psychology,* Volume VI. Hillsdale, NJ: Lawrence Erlbaum Associates, 249–82.

Rist, Ray C. 1970. "Student Social Class and Teacher Expectations: The Self-Fulfilling Prophecy in Ghetto Education," *Harvard Educational Review* 40 (August), 411–50.

Rist, Ray C. 1973. *The Urban School: A Factory for Failure.* Cambridge, MA: MIT Press.

Rist, Ray C. 1978. *The Invisible Children: School Integration in American Society.* Cambridge, MA: Harvard University Press.

Rivera, George, Jr. 1974. "Nostros Venceremos: Chicano Consciousness and Change Strategies." In F. Chris Garcia, ed., *La Causa Politica.* Notre Dame, IN: University of Notre Dame Press, 217–25.

Robinson, Theodore P. and Thomas R. Dye. 1978. "Reformism and Black Representation on City Councils," *Social Science Quarterly* 59 (June), 133–41.

Robinson, Theodore P. and Robert E. England. 1981. "Black Representation on Central City School Boards Revisited," *Social Science Quarterly* 62 (September), 495–502.

Robinson, Theodore P., Robert E. England, and Kenneth J. Meier. 1985. "Black Resources and Black School Board Representation: Does Political Structure Matter?" *Social Science Quarterly* 66 (December), 976–82.

Robinson, William W. 1948. *Land in California.* Berkeley, CA: University of California Press.

Rodgers, Harrell R. and Charles S. Bullock, III. 1972. *Law and Social Change.* New York: McGraw-Hill.

Rodgers, Harrell R. and Charles S. Bullock, III. 1976a. *Coercion to Compliance.* Lexington, MA: D.C. Heath.

Rodgers, Harrell R. and Charles S. Bullock, III. 1976b. "School Desegregation: A Multivariate Test of the Role of Law in Effectuating Social Change," *American Politics Quarterly* 4 (April), 153–76.

Rodriguez, Alfredo and Roy Christman. 1988. "Spanish Language Voters and English Language Ballots in Santa Clara County." Paper presented at the annual meeting of the Western Political Science Association, San Francisco.

Romzek, Barbara S. and J. Stephan Hendricks. 1982. "Organizational Involvement and Representative Bureaucracy: Can We Have It Both Ways?" *American Political Science Review* 76 (March), 75–82.

Roos, Peter D. 1978. "Bilingual Education: The Hispanic Response to

Unequal Educational Opportunity,"*Law and Contemporary Problems* 42 (Autumn), 111–40.

Rosenbaum, James E. 1976. *Making Inequality: The Hidden Curriculum of High School Tracking.* New York: John Wiley & Sons.

Rosenbaum, James E. 1980. "Track Misperceptions and Frustrated College Plans," *Sociology of Education* 53 (April), 74–88.

Rosenthal, Robert and Lenore Jacobson. 1968. *Pygmalion in the Classroom: Teacher Expectation and Pupils Intellectual Development.* New York: Holt, Reinhart and Winston.

Rourke, Francis E. 1984. *Bureaucracy, Politics and Public Policy,* 3rd ed. Boston: Little Brown.

Rowan, Brian and Andrew W. Miracle. 1983. "Systems of Ability Grouping and the Stratification of Achievement in Elementary Schools," *Sociology of Education* 56 (July), 133–44.

Rubin, Donald B. 1983. "Iteratively Reweighted Least Squares." In Samuel Kotz and Norman L. Johnson, eds., *Encyclopedia of Statistical Sciences,* Volume 4. New York: John Wiley and Sons, 272–75.

Rubovits, Pamela C. and Martin L. Maehr. 1973. "Pygmalion Black and White," *Journal of Personality and Social Psychology* 25 (February), 210–18.

St. John, Nancy. 1971. "Thirty-Six Teachers, Their Characteristics, and Outcomes for Black and White Pupils," *American Educational Research Journal* 8 (November), 635–48.

St. John, Nancy. 1975. *School Desegregation: Outcomes for Children.* New York: John Wiley & Sons.

Salinas, Guadalupe. 1973. "Mexican-Americans and the Desegregation of Schools in the Southwest." In Erwin Flaxman, ed., *Educating the Disadvantaged.* New York: AMS Press, 445–78.

Saltzstein, Grace Hall. 1979. "Representative Bureaucracy and Bureaucratic Responsibility," *Administration and Society* 10 (February), 465–75.

Saltzstein, Grace Hall. 1983. "Personnel Directors and Female Employment Representation," *Social Science Quarterly* 64 (December), 734–46.

Saltzstein, Grace Hall. 1989. "Black Mayors and Police Policies," *Journal of Politics* 51 (August), 525–44.

Samora, Julian. 1971. *Los Mojados: The Wetback Story.* Notre Dame, IN: University of Notre Dame Press.

Samora, Julian and Patricia Vandel Simon. 1977. *A History of the Mexican American People.* Notre Dame, IN: University of Notre Dame Press.

Samuda, Ronald J. and Sandra L. Woods, eds. 1983. *Perspectives in Immigrant and Minority Education.* New York: University Press of America.

Sánchez, George I. 1940. *Forgotten People: A Study of New Mexicans.* Albuquerque: University of New Mexico Press.

Sánchez, George I. 1951. *Concerning Segregation of Spanish Speaking Children in the Public Schools.* Austin, TX: University of Texas Press.

San Miguel, Guadalupe, Jr. 1982. "Mexican American Organizations and the Changing Politics of School Desegregation in Texas, 1945–1980," *Social Science Quarterly* 63 (December), 701–15.

San Miguel, Guadalupe, Jr. 1984. "Conflict and Controversy in the Evolution of Bilingual Education in the United States—An Interpretation," *Social Science Quarterly* 65 (June), 505–18.

San Miguel, Guadalupe, Jr. 1987. *"Let All of Them Take Heed": Mexican Americans and the Campaign for Educational Equality in Texas, 1910–1981.* Austin, TX: University of Texas Press.

Santiago Santiago, Isaura. 1986. "The Education of Hispanics in the United States." In Dietmar Rothermund and John Simon, eds., *Education and the Integration of Ethnic Minorities.* New York: St. Martin's Press, 150–84.

Santillan, Richard. 1988a. "Latino Politics in the Midwestern United States: 1915–1986." In F. Chris Garcia, ed., *Latinos and the Political System.* Notre Dame, IN: University of Notre Dame Press, 99–118.

Santillan, Richard. 1988b. "The Latino Community in State and Congressional Redistricting, 1961–1985." In F. Chris Garcia, ed., *Latinos and the Political System.* Notre Dame, IN: University of Notre Dame Press, 328–48.

Schermerhorn, R.A. 1956. "Power as a Primary Concept in the Study of Minorities," *Social Forces* 35 (October), 53–56.

Schultz, Theodore W. 1961. "Investment in Human Capital," *American Economic Review* 51 (March), 1–17.

Scritchfield, Shirley A. and J. Steven Picou. 1982. "The Structural Signifi-cance of Other Influence for Status Attainment Processes: Black-White Variations," *Sociology of Education* 55 (March), 22–30.

Semmel, Melvyn I., Jay Gottlieb, and Nancy M. Robinson. 1979. "Main-streaming: Perspectives on Educating Handicapped Children in the Public School." In David C. Berliner, ed., *Review of Research in Education* 7. Washington, DC: American Educational Research Association, 223–81.

Sexton, Patricia Cayo. 1972. "Schools: Broken Ladder to Success." In Francesco Cordasco and Eugene Bucchiono, eds., *The Puerto Rican Community and Its Children on the Mainland.* Metuchen, NJ: Scare-crow Press, 386–402.

Sheffield, James F., Jr. and Lawrence K. Goering. 1978. "Winning and Losing: Candidate Advantage in Local Elections," *American Politics Quarterly* 6 (October), 453–68.

Shepard, Lorrie A. 1987. "The New Push for Excellence: Widening the Schism Between Regular and Special Education," *Exceptional Children* 53 (January), 327–29.

Shockley, John Staples. 1974. *Chicano Revolt in a Texas Town.* Notre Dame, IN: Notre Dame University Press.

Shonkoff, Jack P. 1982. "Biological and Social Factors Contributing to Mild Mental Retardation." In Kirby A. Heller, Wayne H. Holtzman, and Samuel Messick, eds., *Placing Children in Special Education.* Washington, DC: National Academy Press, 133–81.

Sigelman, Lee and Albert K. Karnig. 1976. "Black Representation in American States—Comparison of Bureaucracies and Legislatures," *American Politics Quarterly* 4 (April), 237–46.

Sigelman, Lee and Albert K. Karnig. 1977. "Black Education and Bureau-cratic Employment," *Social Science Quarterly* 57 (March), 858–63.

Silva, Helga. 1985. *The Children of Mariel: Cuban Refugee Children in South Florida Schools.* Miami: The Cuban American National Foun-dation.

Silver, Catherine Bodard. 1973. *Black Teachers in Urban Schools.* New York: Praeger.

Simmons, Cassandra A. and Nelvia M. Brady. 1981. "The Impact of Abili-ty Group Placement Decisions on the Equality of Educational Oppor-tunity in Desegregated Elementary Schools," *Urban Review* 13 (Summer), 129–33.

Simon, Herbert A. 1969. *Sciences of the Artificial.* Boston: MIT Press.

Singer, Judith D., John A. Butler, Judith S. Palfrey, and Deborah K. Walker. 1986. "Characteristics of Special Education Placements: Findings for Probability Samples in Five Metropolitan School Districts," *Journal of Special Education* 20 (Fall), 319–37.

Slavin, Robert E. 1982. *Cooperative Learning.* New York: Longman.

Sleeter, Christine E. and Carl A. Grant. 1985. "Race, Class, and Gender in an Urban School," *Urban Education* 20 (April), 37–60.

Smith, Elsie J. and Lee N. June. 1982. "The Role of the Counselor in Desegregated Schools," *Journal of Black Studies* 13 (December), 227–40.

Smith, James P. and Finis R. Welch. 1986. *Closing the Gap: Forty Years of Economic Progress for Blacks.* Santa Monica, CA: Rand Corporation.

Smith, Marzell and Charles D. Dziuban. 1977. "The Gap Between Desegregation Research and Remedy," *Integrated Education* 15 (November/December), 51–55.

So, Alvin Y. 1987a. "Hispanic Teachers and the Labeling of Hispanic Students," *The High School Journal* 71 (October/November), 5–8.

So, Alvin Y. 1987b. "High-Achieving Disadvantaged Students: A Study of Low SES Hispanic Language Minority Youth," *Urban Education* 22 (April), 19–35.

Sonenshein, Raphael J. 1989. "The Dynamics of Biracial Coalitions: Crossover Politics in Los Angeles," *Western Political Quarterly* 42 (June), 333–54.

Southern Regional Council. 1973. *The Student Pushout: Victim of Continued Resistance to Desegregation.* Atlanta: Southern Regional Council.

Stein, Colman Brez, Jr. 1986. *Sink or Swim: The Politics of Bilingual Education.* Westport, CT: Praeger.

Stewart, Joseph, Jr. and Charles S. Bullock, III. 1981. "Implementing Equal Education Opportunity Policy," *Administration and Society* 12 (February), 427–46.

Stewart, Joseph, Jr. and James F. Sheffield, Jr. 1987. "Does Interest Group Litigation Matter? The Case of Black Political Mobilization in Mississippi," *Journal of Politics* 49 (August), 780–800.

Stewart, Kenneth L. and Arnoldo De León. 1985. "Education is the Gateway: Comparative Patterns of School Attendance and Literacy

Between Anglos and Tejanos in Three Texas Regions, 1850–1900," *Aztlan* 16 (Spring), 177–95.

Stoddard, Ellwyn R. 1973. *Mexican Americans.* New York: Random House.

Stodolsky, Susan and Gerald Lesser. 1971. "Learning Patterns in the Disadvantaged," *Harvard Educational Review,* Reprint Series, No. 5, 22–69.

Stone, Chuck. 1971. *Black Political Power in America.* New York: Dell.

Stowers, Genie N. L. 1987a. "Ethnic Political Development: The Cuban Transition to Power in Miami, 1955–1985." Paper presented at the annual meeting of the Urban Affairs Association, Akron, OH.

Stowers, Genie N. L. 1987b. "Ethnic Group Impact Upon Urban Policy: The Crucial Case of Cubans in Miami." Paper presented at the annual meeting of the American Political Science Association, Chicago.

Stowers, Genie N. L. 1988. "Cuban Political Participation and Class Status." Paper presented at the annual meeting of the Southwestern Social Science Association, Houston, TX.

Subramaniam, V. 1967. "Representative Bureaucracy: A Reassessment," *American Political Science Review* 61 (December), 1010–19.

Taebel, Delbert A. 1977. "Politics of School Board Elections," *Urban Education* 12 (July), 153–66.

Taebel, Delbert. 1978. "Minority Representation on City Councils," *Social Science Quarterly* 59 (June), 142–52.

Taeuber, Karl E. and David R. James. 1982. "Racial Segregation Among Public and Private Schools," *Sociology of Education* 55 (April/July), 133–43.

Taeuber, Karl E. and Anna F. Taeuber. 1965. *Negroes in Cities.* Chicago: Aldine.

Taylor, Patricia A. and Susan Walker Shields. 1984. "Mexican Americans and Employment Inequality in the Federal Civil Service," *Social Science Quarterly* 65 (June), 381–91.

Teitelbaum, Herbert and Richard J. Hiller. 1977. "Bilingual Education: The Legal Mandate," *Harvard Educational Review* 47 (May), 138–70.

Thomas, Gail E. and Frank Brown. 1982. "What Does Educational Research Tell Us About School Desegregation Effects?" *Journal of Black Studies* 13 (December), 155–74.

Thompson, Frank J. 1978. "Civil Servants and the Deprived: Socio-Political and Occupational Explanations of Attitudes Toward Minority Hiring," *American Journal of Political Science* 22 (May), 325–47.

Tirado, Miguel David. 1970. "Mexican American Community Political Organization," *Aztlan* 1 (Spring), 53–78.

Tobias, Sigmund, Carryl Cole, Mara Zibrin, and Vera Bodlakova. 1982. "Teacher-Student Ethnicity and Recommendations for Special Education Referrals," *Journal of Educational Psychology* 74 (February), 72–76.

Tobias, Sigmund, Mara Zibrin, and Cindy Menell. 1983. "Special Education Referrals: Failure to Replicate Student-Teacher Ethnicity Interaction," *Journal of Educational Psychology* 75 (October), 705–07.

Travis, Toni-Michelle C. 1986. "Boston: The Unfinished Agenda," *PS* 19 (Summer), 610–17.

Trejo, Arnulfo D., ed. 1979. *The Chicanos: As We See Ourselves*. Tucson, AZ: University of Arizona Press.

Trent, William T. 1981. "Expert Opinion on School Desegregation Issues." In Willis D. Hawley, ed., *Assessment of Current Knowledge About the Effectiveness of School Desegregation Strategies*. Nashville, TN: Vanderbilt University Institute for Public Policy Studies.

Troike, Rudolph C. 1984. "Research Evidence for the Effectiveness of Bilingual Education." In Marguerite Ross Barnett and Charles C. Harrington, eds., *Readings on Equal Education,* Volume 7. New York: AMS Press, 183–93.

Tropea, Joseph L. 1987a. "Bureaucratic Order and Special Children: Urban Schools, 1890s–1940s," *History of Education Quarterly* 27 (Spring), 29–53.

Tropea, Joseph L. 1987b. "Bureaucratic Order and Special Children: Urban Schools, 1950s–1960s," *History of Education Quarterly* 27 (Fall), 339–61.

Tuck, R. 1946. *Not With the Fist*. New York: Harcourt, Brace & World.

Tucker, Harvey and Harmon Zeigler. 1980. *Professionals Versus the Public*. New York: Longman.

Tucker, James A. 1980. "Ethnic Proportions in Classes for the Learning Disabled: Issues in Nonbiased Assessment," *Journal of Special Education* 14 (Spring), 93–105.

Tufte, Edward R. 1974. *Data Analysis for Politics and Policy.* Englewood Cliffs, NJ: Prentice-Hall.

Turner, Paul R., ed. 1982. *Bilingualism in the Southwest.* Tucson, AZ: The University of Arizona Press.

Tyack, David B. 1974. *The One Best System: A History of American Urban Education.* Cambridge, MA: Harvard University Press.

U.S. Bureau of the Census. 1980. "Persons of Spanish Origin in the United States: March 1979," *Current Population Reports* Series P–20, No. 354. Washington, DC: U.S. Government Printing Office.

U.S. Bureau of the Census. 1986. *Statistical Abstract of the United States, 1987.* Washington, DC: U.S. Government Printing Office.

U.S. Bureau of the Census. 1987. *The Hispanic Population in the United States: March 1986 and 1987 (Advance Report).* Washington, DC: U. S. Government Printing Office.

U.S. Bureau of the Cencus. 1989. *Statistical Abstract of the United States, 1989.* Washington, DC: U.S. Government Printing Office.

U.S. Commission on Civil Rights. 1971. *The Unfinished Education: Outcomes for Minorities in Five Southwestern States,* (Report II: Mexican-American Educational Series). Washington, DC: U.S. Government Printing Office.

U.S. Commission on Civil Rights. 1974. *Toward Quality Education for Mexican Americans,* (Report VI: Mexican-American Education Study). Washington, DC: U.S. Government Printing Office.

U.S. Commission on Civil Rights. 1976. *Fulfilling the Letter and Spirit of the Law: Desegregation of the Nation's Schools.* Washington, DC: U.S. Government Printing Office.

U.S. Senate. 1967. *Bilingual Education, Hearings,* Hearings. 90th Cong., 1st Sess., Special Subcommittee on Bilingual Education, Committee on Labor and Public Welfare. Washington, DC: U.S. Government Printing Office.

U.S. Senate. 1970. *Equal Educational Opportunity,* Hearings . . . Part 8—Equal Educational Opportunity for Puerto Rican Children. 91st Cong., 2nd Sess., Select Committee on Equal Educational Opportunity. Washington, DC: U.S. Government Printing Office.

Uslaner, Eric M. and Ronald E. Weber. 1983. "Policy Congruence and American State Elites," *Journal of Politics* 45 (February), 183–96.

Valverde, Sylvia A. 1987. "A Comparative Study of Hispanic High School Dropouts and Graduates," *Education and Urban Society* 19 (May), 320–29.

Velez, William. 1989. "High School Attrition Among Hispanic and Non-Hispanic White Youths," *Sociology of Education* 62 (April), 119–33.

Verba, Sidney and Norman Nie. 1972. *Participation in America.* New York: Harper and Row.

Verdugo, Naomi Turner and Richard R. Verdugo. 1984. "Earnings Differentials Among Mexican American, Black, and White Male Workers," *Social Science Quarterly* 65 (June), 417–25.

Vigil, Maurilio E. 1988. "Hispanics Gain Seats in the 98th Congress after Reapportionment." In F. Chris Garcia, ed., *Latinos and the Political System.* Notre Dame, IN: University of Notre Dame Press, 275–290.

von Maltitz, Frances Willard. 1975. *Living and Learning in Two Languages.* New York: McGraw-Hill.

Wainscott, Stephen H. and J. David Woodard. 1988. "Second Thoughts About Second-Generation Discrimination," *American Politics Quarterly* 16 (April), 171–92.

Wakefield, Howard E. 1971. "Rural School Boards." In Lee C. Deighton, ed., *Encyclopedia of Education,* Vol. 8. New York: MacMillian, 70–73.

Walker, Deborah K., Judith D. Singer, Judith S. Palfrey, Michele Orza, Marta Wenger, and John A. Butler. 1988. "Who Leaves and Who Stays in Special Education: A 2-Year Follow-up Study," *Exceptional Children* 54 (February), 393–402.

Wang, Margaret C. and Jack W. Birch. 1984. "Comparison of a Full-Time Mainstreaming Program and a Resource Room Approach," *Exceptional Children* 51 (September), 33–40.

Ward, Fred. 1978. *Inside Cuba Today.* New York: Crown Publishers.

Warren, Christopher L., John F. Stack, Jr., and John G. Corbett. 1986. "Minority Mobilization in an International City: Rivalry and Conflict in Miami," *PS* 19 (Summer), 626–34.

Weber, Max. 1946. From Max Weber: *Essays in Sociology.* H.H. Gerth and C. Wright Mills, trans. New York: Oxford University Press.

Weinberg, Meyer. 1977a. *Minority Students: A Research Appraisal.* Washington, DC: National Institute of Education, U.S. Government Printing Office.

Weinberg, Meyer. 1977b. *A Chance to Learn: The History of Race and Education in the United States.* London: Cambridge University Press.

Weinberg, Meyer. 1983. *The Search for Quality Integrated Education.* Westport, CT: Greenwood Press.

Weisberg, Robert. 1978. "Collective vs. Dyadic Representation in Congress," *American Political Science Review* 72 (June), 535–47.

Welch, Finis. 1987. "A Reconsideration of the Impact of School Desegregation Programs on White Public School Enrollment, 1968–1976," *Sociology of Education* 58 (July), 215–21.

Welch, Susan, John Cromer, and Michael Steinman. 1975. "Differences in Social and Political Participation: A Comparison of Some Anglo and Mexican Americans," *Pacific Sociological Review* 18 (July), 361–84.

Welch, Susan and John R. Hibbing. 1984. "Hispanic Representation in the U.S. Congress," *Social Science Quarterly* 65 (June), 328–35.

Welch, Susan, Albert K. Karnig, and Richard Eribes. 1983. "Changes in Hispanic Local Public Employment in the Southwest," *Social Science Quarterly* 36 (December), 660–73.

Wiley, Tom. 1965. *Public School Education in New Mexico.* Albuquerque: University of New Mexico, Division of Government Research.

Willie, Charles V. and Michael Fultz. 1984. "Do Mandatory School Desegregation Plans Foster White Flight?" In Charles V. Willie, ed., *School Desegregation Plans that Work.* Westport, CT: Greenwood Press, 163–72.

Willig, Ann C. 1985. "A Meta-Analysis of Selected Studies on the Effectiveness of Bilingual Education," *Review of Educational Research* 55 (Fall), 269–317.

Wilson, Barry J. and Donald W. Schmits. 1978. "What's New in Ability Grouping?" *Phi Delta Kappan* 59 (March), 535–36.

Wilson, Franklin D. 1985. "The Impact of School Desegregation Programs on White Public-School Enrollment, 1968–1976," *Sociology of Education* 58 (July), 137–53.

Wilson, Kenneth and Alejandro Portes. 1980. "Immigrant Enclaves: An Analysis of the Labor Market Experiences of Cubans in Miami," *American Journal of Sociology* 86 (September), 295–319.

Wilson, William J. 1973. *Power, Racism and Privilege.* New York: The Free Press.

Wolfinger, Raymond. 1965. "The Development and Persistence of Ethnic Voting," *American Political Science Review* 59 (December), 896–908.

Wolfinger, Raymond E. and Steven J. Rosenstone. 1980. *Who Votes?* New Haven, CT: Yale University Press.

Wollenberg, Charles M. 1978. *All Deliberate Speed: Segregation and Exclusion in California Schools: 1855–1975.* Berkeley, CA: University of California Press.

Wrinkle, Robert D. ed. 1971. *Politics in the Urban Southwest.* Albuquerque: University of New Mexico, Division of Government Research.

Wrinkle, Robert D. and Lawrence W. Miller. 1984. "A Note on Mexican American Voter Registration and Turnout," *Social Science Quarterly* 65 (June), 308–14.

Ysseldyke, James E., Martha Thurlow, Janet Graden, Caren Wesson, Bob Algozzine, and Stanley Deno. 1983. "Generalizations From Five Years Research on Assessment and Decision Making: The University of Minnesota Institute," *Exceptional Education Quarterly* 4 (Spring), 75–93.

Yudof, Mark G. 1975. "Suspensions and Expulsions of Black Students from the Public Schools," *Law and Contemporary Problems* 39 (Spring), 374–411.

Zirkel, Perry A. 1973. "Puerto Rican Parents: An Educational Survey," *Integrated Education* 11 (November/December), 20–26.

Court Cases Cited

Bradley v. Milligan, 402 F.Supp. 1096 (E.D. Mich. 1975).

Brown v. Board of Education, 347 U.S. 483 (1954).

Cisneros v. Corpus Christi Independent School District, 324 F.Supp. 599 (S.D. Tex. 1970), appeal docketed, No. 71-2397 (5th Cir. July 16, 1971).

Delgado et al. v. Bastrop Independent School District of Bastrop County, et al., Docket No. 388 (W.D. Tex. June 15, 1948).

Diana v. State Board of Education, C.A. No. C-70-37 (N.D. Calif. 1973).

Diana v. State Board of Education, C.A. No. C-70-37 (N.D. Calif. 1970).

Edgewood Independent School District v. Kirby, Texas SupCt, No. C-8353, 1989.

Evans v. Buchanan, 393 F. Supp. 428 (D. Del. 1975).

Gonzales v. Sheely, 96 F. Supp. 1004 (D. Ariz. 1951).

Hart v. Community School Board of Brooklyn District #2, 383 F. Supp. 699 (E.D.N.Y., 1974), aff'd 512 F.2d 37 (2d Cir., 1975).

Hernandez v. Driscoll Consolidated Independent School District District, 2 Race Rel. L. Rep. 329 (S.D. Tex. January 1, 1957).

Independent School District v. Salvatierra, 33 S.W.2d 790 (Tex. Civ. App.—San Antonio, 1930), cert. denied, 284 U.S. 580 (1931).

Keyes v. School District Number One, Denver, Colorado, 380 F.Supp. 673 (D. Colo. 1973).

Keyes v. School District Number One, Denver, Colorado, 521 F.2d 465 (10th Cir. 1975).

Larry P. v. Riles, 495 F.Supp. 926 (N.D. Cal. 1979).

Lau v. Nichols, 414 U.S. 563 (1974).

Mendez v. Westminster School District, 64 F. Supp. 544 (S.D.Cal. 1946), aff'd, 161 F.2d 774 (9th Cir. 1947).

Morgan v. Hennigan, 379 F. Supp. 410 (D. Mass. 1974).

Romero v. Weakley, 131 F. Supp. 818 (S.D. Calif. 1955).

Ross v. Eckels, 434 F.2d 1140 (5th Cir. 1970).

Ross v. Eckels, 486 F.2d 649 (5th Cir. 1972).

San Antonio v. Rodríguez, 411 U.S. 1 (1973).

Serna v. Portales Municipal Schools, 499 F.2d 1147 (10th Cir. 1974).

Serrano v. Priest, 96 Cal.Rptr 601, 487 P2d 1241 (1971).

Tasby v. Estes, 412 F.Supp. 1192 (N.D. Tex. 1976).

U.S. v. Texas Education Agency, 467 F.2d 848 (5th Cir. 1972).

Index

Ability grouping. *See* academic grouping

Academic achievement, of Hispanic students, 81-82

Academic grouping: benefits of, 21-3, 36n26; conflicts with integration, 20, 202; and Cuban-American students, 137-8; definition of, 34n17; and discrimination, 16-7, 20-23; based on language, 79-80; and Mexican-American students, 137-8; as permanent, 19; policy recommendations, 218-9; prevalence of, 18; and Puerto Rican students, 137-8; relationship to discipline, 140-4; relationship to educational attainment, 140-4; and social class, 20-21; impact on self-esteem, 21

Access to education, role of political power, 5

Achievement: lack of data on, 126; of Puerto Rican students, 64, 65. *See also* educational achievement

Active representation, 87-90

Administrative representation (Hispanic): impact of Anglo poverty on, 107; access to, 11-13; impact on changes in teachers, 112; of Cuban Americans, 98; impact of Hispanic education on, 107; impact of immigration on, 116; of Mexican Americans, 98; of Puerto Ricans, 98;

representation ratios, 103-7; impact of school board members on, 107; impact on teacher representation 13, 109-110

Administrators, as policymakers, 6. *See also* discretion

Affirmative action, 12

Americanization, as goal of schools, 61

Anglo, definition of, 32n2

Anglo poverty: impact on administrative representation, 107; impact on bilingual classes, 151; impact on graduation rates, 156; impact on school board representation, 10, 95, 97; and second-generation discrimination, 209; impact on teacher representation, 109-110;

Appointed school boards: impact on Hispanic representation, 94-5, 97; politics of, 8

At-large elections: as detrimental to minority candidates, 8; and Hispanic representation, 92; and Mexican-American politics, 52; and Puerto Ricans, 48; proposal to abolish, 216; impact on school board representation, 94-5, 97;

Badillo, Herman, 47

Bay of Pigs, 39, 44

Bicultural education, 220; as goal, 75; prized by Puerto Ricans, 73

DATE DUE